FLEEING
THE UNIVERSAL

SUNY Series, Intersections: Philosophy and Critical Theory
Rodolphe Gashé, Editor

FLEEING
THE UNIVERSAL

The Critique of Post-Rational Criticism

CARL RAPP

State University
of New York Press

Published by
State University of New York Press

© 1998 State University of New York

FORDHAM
UNIVERSITY
LIBRARY
NEW YORK, NY
LINCOLN
CENTER

Printed in the United States of America

For information, address the State University of New York Press,
State University Plaza, Albany, NY 12246

Production by Bernadine Dawes • Marketing by Patrick Durocher

Library of Congress Cataloging-in-Publication Data

Rapp, Carl, 1946–
    Fleeing the universal : the critique of post-rational criticism /
Carl Rapp.
        p.   cm. — (SUNY series, Intersections : philosophy and
critical theory)
    Some chapters are revisions of articles previously published in
various sources from 1987 to 1991.
    Includes bibliographical references and index.
    ISBN 0-7914-3625-X (hc : alk. paper). — ISBN 0-7914-3626-8 (pbk.
: alk. paper)
    1. Critical theory—Controversial literature. I. Title.
II. Series: Intersections (Albany, N.Y.)
B809.3.R37   1998
142—dc21   97-47021
                                                                CIP

1 2 3 4 5 6 7 8 9 10

Consciousness . . . is explicitly the *Notion* of itself. Hence it is something that goes beyond limits, and since these limits are its own, it is something that goes beyond itself. . . . thus consciousness suffers this violence at its own hands: it spoils its own limited satisfaction. When consciousness feels this violence, its anxiety may well make it retreat from the truth, and strive to hold on to what it is in danger of losing. . . . its fear of the truth may lead consciousness to hide, from itself and others, behind the pretension that its burning zeal for truth makes it difficult or even impossible to find any other truth but the unique truth of vanity—that of being at any rate cleverer than any thoughts that one gets by oneself or from others. This conceit which understands how to belittle every truth, in order to turn back into itself and gloat over its own understanding, which knows how to dissolve every thought and always find the same barren Ego instead of any content—this is a satisfaction which we must leave to itself, for it flees from the universal, and seeks only to be for itself.

—G. W. F. Hegel, *Phenomenology of Spirit*

Contents

Preface

This book is meant to be taken as a rejoinder to the assault against philosophy or, more precisely, against speculative knowing, that in recent years has been one of the hallmarks of literary and cultural theory. My thesis is a simple one, namely, that the chief varieties of "critical" theory with which I am here concerned are themselves unable to pass muster and that, consequently, speculative knowing may still be seen as a viable project.

As the ideas expressed in this book were forming in my mind, I was encouraged by many people, whose own ideas on the matters I discuss were often quite different from mine and who therefore must not be supposed necessarily to agree with the conclusions I have reached. Nevertheless, without their encouragement I would certainly have been the poorer. I am particularly grateful to James M. Edie and to Donald G. Marshall for their interest in my earliest efforts to develop a critical appraisal of deconstruction. Numerous colleagues at the University of Georgia have also shown a helpful interest by reading and discussing with me various portions of my manuscript. Among former colleagues, I must thank Marion Montgomery and James Colvert, who always expressed their faith in me, as well as the late Edward Krickel and the late E. C. Bufkin, whose companionship cannot be forgotten or replaced. Among my present colleagues, I especially appreciate the interest and support of Jonathan Evans, John Boyd, Anne Williams, Walter Gordon, and James Kibler. To Richard Dien Winfield, of the Department of Philosophy, I owe the largest debt of thanks. Without the stimulus of his conversation and without his persistent encouragement, this book would not have been brought to completion.

It remains only to say that this book is for my wife Kay, who patiently endured its production and who provided the necessary interruptions.

Acknowledgments

A portion of chapter 1 originally appeared as an essay in *Literature as Philosophy / Philosophy as Literature,* edited by Donald G. Marshall (Iowa City: University of Iowa Press, 1987), and is reprinted here with permission.

Chapter 5 originally appeared in a slightly different form in the Spring 1987 issue of *Modern Age: A Quarterly Review* (P.O. Box AB, College Park, Md. 20740), and is reprinted here with permission.

Chapter 7 originally appeared in a slightly different form in the Fall 1987 issue of *The Georgia Review,* and is reprinted here with permission.

Chapter 8 originally appeared in a slightly different form in the Spring 1991 issue of *Critical Review,* and is reprinted here with permission.

WHAT IS POST-RATIONAL CRITICISM?

In the pages that follow, I propose to examine critically the phenomenon of post-rational criticism. Under this rubric, I would include not only the literary or textual analyses inspired by poststructuralist thinkers like Jacques Derrida and Michel Foucault, but also most of the cultural criticism that has been devoted to the exegesis of what Lyotard and others have called "the postmodern condition." All of this criticism may be considered post-rational to the extent that it is based on the belief that we have recently become the benefactors of "a formidable indictment of physical and moral science"[1] and that, as a consequence, we are now living in the aftermath of reason, looking back in one mood or another at the failure of reason's projects. On the basis of this belief, it has been assumed by many scholars that philosophy in the traditional sense ("Philosophy" with a capital "P," as Rorty terms it) has run its course or played itself out. Indeed, the handwriting was already on the wall, it seems, when Kant offered to trace the boundaries or the limits of reason, but the great blows came later from the likes of Marx and Nietzsche, who made it their business to expose the social and psychological origins of apparently rational thinking. By the end of the nineteenth century, the most exciting philosophers had become, in fact, antiphilosophical, like William James in the United States or like Bergson in France. Antiphilosophers conveyed the impression that they had discovered how small a thing philosophy really is in the overall life of the mind, being a sort of rigid mental posture affecting to exclude other, more flexible postures. In our own century, we have had not only anthropological and psychoanalytic "histories" of consciousness, but also a rich array of language philosophers who have sought to explain philosophical ideas as the epiphenomena of semiotics or deep grammar. To the post-rational critic, it is clear that philosophy has been all but obliterated by the assaults made against it by a variety of different thinkers working in a variety of different fields (including that of philosophy itself) over the last one hundred and fifty years. That being the case, we are now presumably in an excellent position to lay bare the last vestiges of philosophic error in the expressions and institutions of the West and, at the same time, to contemplate with confidence the newer forms of life and thought that will characterize the post-Western, postphilosophical culture of the future.

Post-rational criticism, as it is now being practiced, imagines itself to be coming toward the end of a transition process. In part, it seeks to extend or to refine upon those earlier critiques of reason that constitute its heritage. In part, it seeks to give a positive content to the prospect of living and thinking post-rationally. As a particular branch of post-rational criticism, deconstruction has tended to focus more specifically on the critical task of dismantling reason's fictions, whereas the new pragmatism, as some have termed it, has concerned itself with the constructive task of trying to imagine the content of postphilosophical culture. Somewhere between these two is a third branch of post-rational criticism, the so-called new historicism, which shuttles back and forth between the complementary projects of criticism and construction, seeking to combine analytical disillusionment with visionary zeal. In fact, all three of these branches or schools of post-rationalism are keenly aware of each other, and their respective endeavors tend to overlap considerably. To a large extent, the differences between them are simply differences in emphasis. Nevertheless, since they do present us with differences, I have thought it best to discuss them as distinctive versions of the contemporary effort to get past philosophy.

What, finally, is wrong with this effort? To what extent does post-rational criticism itself succumb to criticism? By way of answering these questions, I intend in this book to show that all three of the post-rational schools I discuss—deconstruction, the new pragmatism, and the new historicism—are guilty of a radical misunderstanding of themselves, which prevents them from grasping the extent to which they are involved in, and therefore expressive of, the intellectual traditions they affect to criticize. Oddly enough, each school prides itself on having achieved an intense form of self-consciousness, an almost Lutheran feeling of penitence, regarding its own regrettable complicity with the traditions or conventions of discourse, and thus each school might well retort that what it has to offer is precisely *an understanding* of the extent to which it is involved in and expressive of that which it seeks to criticize. The deconstructionist openly acknowledges, and by so doing implicitly detaches himself from, the traces of logocentrism that must linger in his own demonstrations of the insidiousness of logocentrism. Similarly, the new pragmatist, ever mindful that philosophical canons must come into play whenever one's own discourse lapses into argument or proof, studiously avoids direct confrontation with past positions and instead calls attention to the rhetorical character of all positions, including his own. Finally, the new historicist almost always comes forward to confess, at one point or another in his exposition, that his own thinking cannot help but be affected by the very same factors—gender, ethnicity, social position—that have hitherto impaired the thinking of other people, making objectivity in thought impossible. Thus, in each instance, an exposé of the prerational or subrational mechanisms governing all possible organizations of ideas is imagined to be enhanced, rather than weakened, by an admission that the critic's own presentations must themselves be skewed by these same mechanisms. To the objection, "Doesn't this mean that your own account of things has something wrong with it?" the critic simply replies, "Yes, of course. There is always something wrong with every account of things, and I'm glad to admit that the inadequacy of my own view of this matter helps to confirm my thesis concerning it." But surely such a palinode as this depends entirely on the doctrine it ostensibly qualifies, and, in each case, the doctrine in question is the problem. In its key insights, the doctrine itself cannot properly be maintained, and consequently the elucidations it has to offer with respect to the factors that supposedly limit or impair a doctrine cannot be maintained, either.

How, then, is deconstruction, for instance, related to philosophy—not in the ways it claims to understand (in having to use a language that necessarily incorporates logocentric biases) but in ways it has no grasp of, ways that elude its own kind of self-consciousness? One thing to notice about it is that, like most other forms of post-rationalism, it represents a continuation of transcendentalism, that is to say, it proposes to extend the eighteenth- and nineteenth-century inquiries into the transcendental conditions of knowledge or experience. In the wake of Hume and Kant, it became an exciting thing to investigate the extent to which consciousness or thinking does not simply *reflect* the world of experience but rather *determines* that world by virtue of its own particular constitution or by virtue of the categories employed in the act of having an experience. In the twentieth century, it became similarly exciting to investigate the extent to which language does not simply *reflect* the thought it appears to convey but rather *determines* that thought by means of its own inherent structures or grammatical possibilities. Eventually, the old version of the transcendental inquiry into what was required in order for there to be an experience of anything was replaced by the new, linguistic version of the same inquiry. Accordingly, language replaced mind as the focus of the inquiry, as the ultimate explanation of what earlier thinkers had regarded as the work of consciousness. Subjectivity evolved into textuality. Likewise, intersubjectivity evolved into intertextuality or the openness of texts, one to another. In the end, language became what earth, or air, or fire, or water had been to the pre-Socratics: a metaphysical first principle, in relation to which other things could only be seen as appearances or temporary manifestations. From Wittgenstein and Heidegger to Benjamin Lee Whorf, the race was on to show that language was the truth or the reality of whatever it was that the vulgar had previously regarded as true or real. Immensely helpful in this effort was the fact that a student of language, Ferdinand de Saussure, appeared to have shown that language itself was autonomous or self-constituting, being entirely a matter of inward coherence or internal relations rather than depending on external relations with ulterior facts or meanings to which it might be supposed to correspond. Indeed, in order for language to have the character of that which is transcendental, it seemed necessary not only that it be determinative with respect to all possible objects of thought or experience, but also that it *not* be determined, or dictated to, by anything outside itself, demanding representation or correspondence. If language were not free from such external allegiances or pressures, the very essence of its transcendental character would be jeopardized.

Curiously, the linguistic form of transcendentalism seemed to many intellectuals less metaphysical than the old mentalistic version, language having a materialistic or phenomenalistic appearance which allowed it to become the object of a host of empirical sciences. For this reason, language did not seem to have an occult character. Clearly, an immense body of detailed knowledge had been acquired concerning it, to which those who seek to explain the influence of language on thought have easy access. Or so it would appear. In fact, all the knowledge we have of language according to the *sciences* of language carries with it assumptions about the world, about historical processes and events, about persons and objects, which are similar to those made and acted upon by the other empirical sciences. Such knowledge is neither more reliable nor less conditioned than the knowledge that comes to us from any empirical inquiry. Thus, the knowledge of language cannot be the basis of an inquiry that seeks consistently to demonstrate that knowledge as such is nullified or rendered problematic by its own linguistic constitution. One of the problems with deconstruction is, accordingly, that the knowledge that necessarily informs its own characteristic notions and strategies is precisely the same kind of knowledge that it seeks to criticize in the texts it examines. If knowledge in general is taken to be unreliable, owing to the conditions and biases that govern its constitution, what are we to make of the knowledge that informs us of this very fact? What is the status of our inquiries into the nature of these very conditions and biases? To what extent can we be said to have a right knowledge or an accurate knowledge of them? If we pose these questions at all, we have entered the domain of philosophy. If we proceed without posing them and simply assume that our knowledge of the conditions of knowledge is correct, we shall, in effect, be begging the very questions we think we are raising. Instead of eluding philosophy, we shall have lapsed into dogmatism.

The new pragmatism tries to avoid this problem by refusing to regard language as the ultimate substance of things or as the basis of a new form of transcendentalism. Pragmatists like Richard Rorty are keenly aware of the drawbacks involved in giving the appearance that one has found a deep explanation of the thought-patterns and behaviors that have characterized Western culture. Deep explanations are, by their very nature, philosophical explanations. Whenever the deconstructionist makes an appeal to the reality of linguistic structures as opposed to the virtual realities suggested by these structures, the Truth About Meaning rises up to displace mere meanings, and we get a creepy feeling that something metaphysical is happening. The right way to be post-rational is, therefore, to avoid aping the projects of rationality (e.g., attempting to distinguish reality and appearances). According to the pragmatist point of view, theories and speculations of almost every kind give us the false impression that we can transcend ourselves and make profound, objective judgments concerning the truth of what is going on around us or within us, whereas the history of philosophy shows us clearly that attempts to do this have never been successful, except in producing fruitless controversies. The only remedy is to immerse oneself in the exigencies of praxis, in the full realization that there is no alternative to praxis and that even speculation or contemplation can be considered a form of praxis. Pragmatists just want people to be themselves, to do what comes naturally, without trying to justify themselves in terms of large-scale conceptions concerning what is true or real or good or beautiful. Nobody ought to have to feel that his experience is inadequate or worthy of reproof simply because it cannot be squared with some theory about the way things really are, or the way things really happened, or the way things really ought to be. Such theories are merely the fantasies of intellectuals, spin-offs from the praxis of intellectuals. Thinking about things in such a way as to produce a theory of them may have a function or an effect in the context of praxis, in the sense that it is associated with a measurable behavior, but such thinking can never be in a position to justify or account for praxis, because it is always, first of all, an expression of it.

But if reflective thinking is no longer to be thought of as capable of *producing* effects, being itself only an effect, what mechanisms can be adduced to explain how it is that life succeeds in getting on? Different pragmatists give slightly different answers to this question. In *The Postmodern Condition,* Lyotard suggests that we look at language game activity. Thus, he explains, by virtue of their having created for us the all-absorbing operations of cybernetics and high technology, the language games of science have simply squeezed out, in Darwinian fashion, the language games of narrative knowledge. As a result, large-scale views concerning who we are, where we have been, and where we are going have all but disappeared or have become incredible, because they have no role to play, no work to do, in the self-adjusting, self-rationalizing processes that now absorb our attention and determine our behaviors. Nobody has to be exhorted anymore to stop thinking in terms of grand interpretations or (as Lyotard calls them) master narratives. It may be recognized as a simple fact that people don't think in such terms. Recommendations about what to do or how to live or what to make of it all are clearly beside the point, since thinking already knows what to do or how to behave within the context of the language games that are now being played. These games are what they are, they change or evolve as they do, and they fall into oblivion whether we will or no. A part of wisdom is to accept the fact that this is precisely what has happened to the language games of philosophy. They have become extinct.

In *Consequences of Pragmatism,* Rorty also propounds the view that philosophy has become obsolete or phased-out, but he takes the extra step of exhorting his readers not to look back. To do so, he claims, would be to risk being seduced by philosophical concepts and questions. The urge to situate what we are already doing inside the framework of a philosophical explanation or justification is still strong enough, in his view, to require deliberate suppression, whereas the immanent logic already at work in the socially situated projects of our various lives still requires to be embraced with a good will. Rorty's writing is deliberately rhetorical rather than analytical, although specimens of analysis are sometimes exhibited to us so that we can admire their futility. The object of this strategy is to induce in the reader a wariness with regard to older thought-forms and an enthusiasm for new ones, without creating the impression that any particular form is truer or better than another according to specifiable criteria. To *demonstrate* anything would be to lapse back into a philosophical frame of mind; to *induce a change of mind* through artful rhetoric is to be genuinely postphilosophical. From this point of view, it might be said that Lyotard's presentation of pragmatism is a little too close to being a demonstration that something is the case concerning the history of language game activity in Western culture.

In fact, both Lyotard and Rorty are guilty of promulgating a master narrative, since they both subscribe to a large-scale view which pretends to know what the whole of philosophy is like, including how it rose up and became dominant and why it is now petering out. They know, and can explain, what its relations are to prephilosophical, nonphilosophical, and postphilosophical thought-forms, which, in fact, is too big a thing to know by their own standards. Rorty knows that all the philosophers from Plato to Hegel were failures and consequently the Western philosophical tradition has come to grief. Such a summary overview would have to be supported by countless historical and philosophical judgments in order not to be utterly arbitrary or merely personal. Indeed, in order to justify any final judgment concerning the Western tradition as a whole, one would have to have synthesized a massive amount of knowledge in just the sort of way that pragmatism claims to disallow. Thus, a global view concerning the history and validity of a large number of thought-forms is offered up as the basis for asserting that global views are impossible and that there can be no such thing as the knowledge of knowledge. Thus, in an impressive retelling of both the emancipation narrative and the speculative narrative, Lyotard launches his thesis that intellectuals have stopped thinking in terms of precisely these two narratives, an idea that, if taken seriously, would make his own account of the matter of no account.

The new historicists are no less critical of traditional notions than the deconstructors or the new pragmatists. Like the deconstructors, they seek out the underlying factors or conditions that have conspired to produce the views people form concerning the nature of things or the meaning of events. The biases and orientations that are built into language, and hence formative with regard to rhetoric, are among those things which they try to take into consideration. Like the new pragmatists, they view with suspicion the various rationalizations that lurk in interpretations of cultural phenomena, ever noting the interestedness, the nonneutral character, of those who aspire to give accounts of things. Up to a point, the criticism spawned by this kind of suspicion is both reasonable and useful. Anything that adds to our knowledge of the historical circumstances associated with the interpretation or the production of cultural phenomena must necessarily increase the power of our own subsequent notions. Trouble comes only when the new historicist tries to be hugely skeptical concerning the validity of all accounts of things based on any notions whatsoever. The factors that work so insidiously to skew our judgments may, when he broods upon them, cause him to despair of ever attaining even a modest amount of truth. Sometimes this despair takes the form of an apology to the effect that nobody (not even the apologist himself) can be adequately free from gender bias, ethnic bias, class bias, and so on. Sometimes it takes the paradoxical form of an insistence on the value, as well as the necessity, of being socially situated and therefore, at least potentially, politically engaged. As a result, one's criticism may be regarded as having the power of vector. On the level of praxis, as opposed to the level of disinterested speculation, one can dispense quickly with the idea of getting at the truth of anything (truth being, after all, a vain thing to a post-rationalist) and then get down to one's real business, which is to make a political gesture—a gesture either of solidarity or of opposition—as regards other persons or groups.

Here again, however, a hugely skeptical position is simply an impossibility. The discovery that knowledge has been skewed by a variety of factors or circumstances that one has come to know of cannot be used as evidence that knowledge per se is unachievable. To do so would be to rely on the knowledge one has acquired concerning the factors or circumstances.

And how is *this* knowledge to be explained? Surely we find ourselves in a curious predicament if we think that we can't know the world around us or the history that has come before us, because of impairments inherent in the knowing process itself, but at the same time we *can* know that this is the case and even, in some detail, how it is the case. As Hegel observes in the *Science of Logic,* there is something absurd about imagining that we cannot think about things as they are in themselves but that, when we think about the transcendental conditions or empirical circumstances of such thinking as we are capable of, our ideas about *these* things are perfectly satisfactory, "as if, so to speak, only the *kind of objects* were different, and one kind, namely things-in-themselves, did not fall within the scope of our knowledge but the other kind, phenomena, did."[2] Indeed, the more extensive our knowledge becomes concerning that which shapes or deflects our knowledge, the more glaring this paradox becomes. We may, for example, be advised to suspend our judgment concerning the interpretations of things contained *in* books until after we have examined the social processes involved in the production *of* books, so as to avoid being imposed upon by the points of view determining the interpretations. This would be a good idea, were it not for the fact that our principal access to these processes is through the knowledge contained in books. In order to put any single book on trial, with the promise to render a verdict on it after we have examined the economic, social, and cultural contexts that have called it into being or at least shaped its appearance, we should have to be taking for granted already the manifest content of countless other books. This is the case because the knowledge we have of all these contexts and processes depends on the arguments and demonstrations of previous authors. The illusion seems to be that if every book could be historicized or contextualized, then a right understanding of the factors that *shape* books would everywhere be triumphant over the bemused contents *of* books. In fact, of course, a particular kind of argument would be driving the whole mammoth analysis, and that argument, put forward as the content of a certain number of books, would itself be only the apex of a pyramid of supporting arguments, all of them taken for granted to the extent that they would be accepted as constitutive of the view that arguments per se are suspicious and ought to be regarded with profound skepticism. When the whole work was accomplished and the factors involved in the production of all books were revealed, history and nature would not be exposed as ideological fictions fabricated by certain kinds of socially situated intellectuals, as has sometimes been suggested. Rather, they would remain intact, as both the assumed ground and the unintended consequence of the entire critical effort.

As I have already stated, post-rational critics have not been unaware that their own projects are contaminated with the virus of rational thinking. By openly acknowledging this fact, they seem to imagine that what is essential in post-rational wisdom can be preserved from infection. Thus, they often appear to be saying, "We are the only ones who are willing to admit that all knowledge is contaminated, including even our own." But it is precisely this last little insight that cannot be maintained without making an effort to obliterate the knowledge constituting its own foundation. Thus, the final gesture of post-rational wisdom must be to abandon knowledge by effecting a strategic collapse (i.e., a rational collapse) into what it takes to be the prerationalized, preorganized materials and processes from which knowledge has sprung so outrageously. For the deconstructionist, this means that particular notions or outlooks, such as those that appear to be promulgated in works of philosophy and literature, must be regarded as having arisen improperly from the infinity of notions or outlooks that happen to be implicit in the linguistic medium. Wisdom would be, not to propound anything, but to savor the medium. For the pragmatist, it means that theory-building must be regarded as an impractical (indeed impossible) effort to suspend or control praxis, so that wisdom must be to accept one's placement in praxis. And, finally, for the historicist, it means that the effort to get at the truth of history or politics must be regarded as mistaken, the wise thing being to recognize the primacy of ethical or political action. Everywhere the implication is pretty much the same: a return must be effected from concepts to percepts. The alienation we have suffered at the hands of philosophy must be undone by a descent into the pure immanence of aesthetic and/or political experience. The substance of this experience, apart from whatever it can be made into, is pleasure or pain, delight or aversion, empowerment or impediment. The value of literature has little to do with the inferences that might be drawn by readers or writers concerning the import of experience. Its real value has to do with the fact that it presents surd-like conglomerates of experience which, properly apprehended, are resistant to analysis or inference. In a postphilosophical culture, thought would remain permanently infatuated with these conglomerates, refusing to go beyond them. Until such time as this culture is fully in place, the duty of the post-rational critic is to reinstate the conglomerates by deconstructing whatever it is they have been made into.

The trouble with the recommendation that we plunge into praxis, or hover close to aesthetic or political experience, or simply accept the surd-like character of language games, being able only to play them but not to think about them, is that each of these options is motivated by a *judgment* that has been made against philosophy in favor of some other thing that has been *judged* to be an alternative to philosophy. These judgments are themselves speculative or philosophical in character. If a rich perceptual life is deliberately embraced as an alternative to thinking with concepts, it is only because a conceptual distinction has already been made between percepts and concepts. Thus, philosophy continues to call the shots for post-rational behaviors or practices whenever they receive any kind of encouragement or preferment. In the same way, whenever reason is said to be limited or opposed by that which is incorrigible to reason or beyond the purview of reason, the judgment that this is the case is itself an exercise of reason, which is evidently *not* to be identified either with the "limited" reason it is looking at or with the unsurveyable "other than reason" it is also looking at. As Hegel points out in his review of G. E. Schulze's *Critique of Theoretical Philosophy,* "It cannot be proved about the rational . . . that it only exists within the relationship, that it stands in a necessary relation to another; for it is itself nothing but the relationship." Since "the rational is relation itself," it "has no opposed counterpart; it includes both of the finite opposites, which are mutual counterparts, within itself."[3]

A case in point is modern art, which frequently sought to express modalities of sensibility or aspects of experience impervious to reason and therefore beyond the reach of the categories associated with philosophy. Indeed, much of this art, at the time of its first appearance, seemed devoid of conceptual content, as though it had no desire to represent anything other than its own concrete forms and textures. Gradually, it became clear that this art *could* be explained thematically, if only by pointing to the fact that its practitioners imagined themselves to be liberating art from its traditional moral and intellectual obligations. The new art was, in truth, full of theories concerning the autonomy of art, theories that had the effect of dictating a wide array of aesthetic gestures and practices thought to be conducive to the exhibition of just this autonomy. Telling the story of *why* modern art was doing what it was doing, in relation to the various theories that had been developed having to do with the materials of art or the processes of art, became a growth industry in the twentieth century, spawning the age of criticism and providing an indispensable commentary to works of art that were considered to be, curiously enough, absolutely unconditioned and perfectly concrete. As an allegory of the consequences of post-rational criticisms of philosophy, modern art in its various permutations had to be explained over and over again until the concepts behind it were at last reasonably clear. In effect, instead of representing the triumph of art over philosophy, as was sometimes claimed, it more nearly represented the triumph of philosophy over art, being the result of much theorizing concerning the nontheoretic character of art.[4] (Tom Wolfe shows this wittily in *The Painted Word.*)

The paradoxical persistence of philosophy in post-rational theories and practices is, very largely, the theme of this book. In my first chapter, "The Transcendentalist Impulse in the Projects of Contemporary Criticism," I have tried to show that the Romantic (and post-Romantic) effort to bypass philosophy has been prompted from the beginning by philosophical considerations which have culminated, in our own time, in the emergence of various schools of transcendentalist criticism, all committed to the task of excavating the hidden foundations of knowledge and all committed, in one way or another, to metaphysics. This consequence, I think, has much to do with the fact that the Romantic ambition of reinstating the autonomy of poetry (reversing Aristotle's subordination of poetry to philosophy) was itself incorrigibly philosophical. By renouncing the Aristotelian subordination, the Romantics hoped that poetry might regain its original mythopoeic function of providing us with a consciousness of ourselves-in-the-world without recourse to the sophistications and distinctions of reflective thinking. But the aim of going back to an original, pre-philosophical form of consciousness was in its own way a piece of late sophistication, which remained ever conscious of the distinction between prereflective and reflective thinking. It was, therefore, despite its own good intentions, a reflective yearning for prereflection. Looking down from the height of its own sophistication, Romantic and post-Romantic reflection began to devise the various strategies of modern art, according to which poetry or art or literature might purify itself by expelling from itself all philosophical agendas or else, alternatively, enlarge itself by incorporating within itself the cognitive functions usurped by science and philosophy. No matter which way it went, the renovation of aesthetic sensibility was the brain-child of a certain kind of critical thinking, in relation to which it remained thoroughly, though often covertly, dependent. The standpoint from which the renovation was contemplated was that of the figure Hegel describes in his lectures on aesthetics under the rubric of "the romantic artist," a figure who, in his sophistication and self-consciousness, more nearly resembled Wallace Stevens than the pre-Homeric bard. Precisely because he had come to regard the fiction-making process itself as a deeper thing than the fictions it produced, this figure could not, in fact, be associated with the unself-consciousness of prereflective art.

But if modern art was spawned by reflections on the limits and dangers of reflective thinking, twentieth-century criticism was replete with its own reflections on just these limits and dangers. A particular concern of the critics was to show that the intentions of artists and authors could be disregarded to advantage, being either unreachable or unreal and therefore, in a manner of speaking, red herrings in the path of critical interpretation. In this way, literary and artistic works could be taken as expressions of phenomena or situations much more interesting than the designs of their designers. These designs smacked too much of reflective thinking to be taken as anything more than froth or debris floating on the surface of deeper realities. When they were not totally disregarded as irrelevant or unavailable, they were treated as the superficial effects or virtual images of the actual forces (whether psychological, political, or linguistic) that had given rise to them. Thus were launched the various transcendental inquiries into the factors or conditions responsible for shaping cultural phenomena, whether by means or in spite of the conscious deliberations associated with their production. The less amenable these factors or conditions were to rational consideration or rational manipulation, the more transcendentally powerful they appeared to the critics who inquired after them. After all, it was the underpinnings, not the products, of reflective thinking that most intrigued them. The goal was to get at what was *before* or *behind* thinking, and anything that could be said to have been produced *by* thinking, or as a *result* of thinking, could not very well be said to be the explanation of the thinking that, in fact, explained *it*. Eventually, the critics succeeded in identifying a variety of structures or processes, which they hoped might be regarded as absolutely constitutive of all writing, all thinking, all cultural expression, and so on. In my first chapter, I discuss in sequence both the structuralist and the poststructuralist versions of psychological transcendentalism, political (or sociological) transcendentalism, and linguistic transcendentalism, which I take to be the chief varieties that have flourished in the second half of this century. Metaphysical speculation was rife in every one of these projects, despite the good intentions of the projectors themselves, who were trying their best to explain philosophy (and numerous other matters) without actually being philosophical. Deconstruction, as the poststructuralist version of linguistic transcendentalism, and the new historicism, as a poststructuralist version of political (or sociological) transcendentalism, may thus be understood in relation to each other and in relation to the emergence of post-rational criticism in general. At the end of this chapter, the new pragmatism is discussed in terms of the effort it made to disclose the fact that even poststructuralist theorizing must be deeply problematic, transcendentalism being essentially a philosophical project. Thus, pragmatism affected to provide a postscript to transcendentalism, a sort of palinode wherein all explanatory ambitions might be renounced or retracted. But it too was a form of transcendentalism, reducing theory itself to the unanalyzable, incorrigible mechanisms of its own constitution, as seen in the behaviors or whims of sovereign persons or sovereign groups of persons, i.e., virtuoso geniuses or interpretive communities. In reducing ethics and politics to the actual behaviors of individuals and communities, the pragmatists arrived at their own set of "first principles," without realizing, or at least without admitting, that anything metaphysical had happened.

The virtuoso genius, except that he was an individual, was not all that different from the interpretive community, in that both might be regarded as having an absolute authority over the theories and interpretations that they themselves either produced or confronted. They themselves were the terminus of explanation, being the source of theories and interpretations. Persons were the engines driving theory, and theories concerning the constitution of personal positions (like those invented by the psychological, political, and linguistic transcendentalists) could not be the explanation *of* persons, since they, like all the other theories, were being driven *by* persons. As soon as anybody appeared with an account of what it was that persons or groups of persons were actually doing and why they were doing it, an account that might appear to have genuine explanatory power with respect to the matters it dealt with, the thought would occur that such an account must, of course, be only an *expression*—an intransitive expression—of the person or group of persons who sponsored it. The egoism of the interpretive community was hardly less than that of the virtuoso genius. The existence of such communities could be used strategically in several different ways. Instead of grappling with the content of a theory or a claim not to one's liking, one could dismiss it as merely the articulation of a particular group's inherently unjustifiable ethos or ideology. On the other hand, if one's own claims were attacked, one could disavow all personal responsibility and simply claim kin with the others constituting one's own interpretive community, falling back on the indefeasibility of the communal mind-set. Thus, the egoism of a particular community was either indefensible (if one wished to attack it) or unassailable (if one wished to defend it), it being the bedrock of all possible justifications or authorizations naïvely offered in its behalf.

The egoism of the virtuoso genius was merely a concentrated form of the same arbitrariness. Hegel describes it as the consequence of that first wave of transcendental speculation culminating in Fichte's philosophy, especially as interpreted by Romantic literary theorists such as Friedrich von Schlegel. In Hegel's analysis, the egoism of the virtuoso genius is based on the attainment of, or an identification with, an infinite spirituality that knows itself to be other than or prior to all "determinate forms of vision and presentation." This is the position (already referred to) of what Hegel calls "the romantic artist," the position that makes possible the famous "irony" theorized by Schlegel and denounced by Hegel, particularly as described in the latter's lectures on aesthetics but also in his lectures on the history of philosophy. Having transcended "determinate forms of vision and presentation," the virtuoso genius looks down "ironically" at the spectacle of science, religion, and philosophy, knowing these things to have been constituted by the creative power of the Ego, and therefore regarding them as rightly subordinate to the creative power of the artist, who may posit them or cancel them freely, without recourse to external authorizations, having claimed as his own the standpoint of infinite spirituality. The exhibition or proof of the artist's creative power is his ability to "make every determinacy waver and dissolve." In my second and third chapters, I discuss the pertinence of Hegel's assessment of Romantic "irony" and Romantic "humor" to a right understanding of our own transcenders and manipulators of theory, including poets such as Wallace Stevens and William Carlos Williams (Williams being discussed at some length in chapter 3) and critics such as Harold Bloom, Richard Rorty, Jacques Derrida, and Michel Foucault. The object of these two chapters is not only to expose the theoretical foundations of contemporary "antitheory" or "post-philosophy," but also to indicate Hegel's familiarity with positions that imagine themselves to have gone beyond the purview of philosophy, to which the simplest possible rejoinder would be to say: they haven't.

The failure of post-rational criticism to jump free and clear of the philosophy governing its own gestures and practices sends us back, in the middle chapters of this book, to a consideration of certain specific arguments that have been offered in behalf of deconstruction, the new pragmatism, and the new historicism, respectively. In chapters 4 through 9, I have sought to ground my objections to these arguments by focusing on a selection of books and essays wherein the arguments have been advanced by some of their leading proponents. In chapter 4, for example, I focus on J. Hillis Miller's presentation of deconstruction in two important essays, composed when deconstruction was still in vigorous ascendency, mounting toward its apogee. My object in doing so is to make certain that my conclusions concerning deconstruction are rooted in an analysis of specific claims. Similarly, in chapters 5 and 6, I have focused at length on the pragmatism described by Richard Rorty and Stanley Fish, and in chapter 7 I consider the face-off between pragmatism and deconstruction as construed by Christopher Norris in his book *The Contest of Faculties.* In chapter 8 the main emphasis is placed on Jean-François Lyotard's highly influential book *The Postmodern Condition,* although there is also a discussion of another book, *Literature and the Question of Philosophy,* which, like Lyotard's book, attempts to envision how life will proceed after the disappearance of philosophy. Finally, in chapter 9, the new historicism is considered on the basis of claims made in two collections of essays elucidating its various permutations.[5]

In all of these chapters, I have endeavored to reveal the difficulties that present themselves in significant texts by major spokespersons for the doctrines under consideration. The burden of these chapters is, consequently, the criticisms that must be made with respect to these doctrines. At the same time, it will be seen that Hegel's name keeps coming back again and again, like a leitmotif, throughout all the discussions. The reason for this is that Hegel simply anticipated, and refuted in advance, the chief contentions of late twentieth-century post-rationalism. This will seem incredible to those who believe that each age is necessarily superior to that which precedes it, a doctrine notably espoused by Rorty and just as notably repudiated by Hegel (although it is often attributed to him erroneously). Yet it is so. Anyone who peruses the introduction to the *Phenomenology,* or the preface to the *Philosophy of Right,* or (most helpful of all, perhaps) the opening parts of the *Encyclopedia Logic* (i.e., Paragraphs 1–83, with the Remarks and Additions, dealing with the various positions of thought with respect to objectivity), will see at once that Hegel was familiar with the numerous objections raised against philosophy by practitioners of empirical science, who could proceed without it and investigate forever without arriving at it, by religious fundamentalists and virtuoso geniuses, who likewise could proceed without it on the basis of an immediate, unanalyzable contact or identification with the Absolute, and by philosophical skeptics, convinced of either the inadequacy or the smallish range of reason. Hegel's philosophy arises, not in ignorance of these objections, but in answer to them. And the objections themselves are not essentially different from those made familiar to us by the post-rationalists (or postphilosophers) of our own time.[6] The idea that Hegel's system was scrapped by later thinkers, because they could think of objections to it that he never thought of, is simply impossible to entertain after reading collectively the crank-up portions of Hegel's own texts, full as they are of his awareness of the embattled stance of philosophy in relation to the intellectual currents of the day.

Of particular importance in refuting the claims of those who imagine that reason is shackled by gender, by politics, by the immediate circumstances of finite reasoners, by "historically contingent final vocabularies," or by "interpretive communities," is Hegel's contention that essentially different points of view cannot be contemplated or known to exist, except by a thinking that has already transcended the limitations that characterize the points of view it is contemplating, or indeed the limitations that characterize point of view per se, which is to say, by a thinking that is not itself a point of view. Thus, in response to the claim that knowledge is restricted to appearances (which *we* might translate into the claim that each interpretive community can only have its own biased view of other interpret communities, knowing them only according to its own biases but not as they are in themselves), Hegel observes simply that to know that knowledge is only of appearances one would have to know the difference between appearances and reality, which one could *not* know if one had *only* impressions of appearances, as opposed to genuine knowledge. Thus, he contends,

> [I]t is the supreme inconsistency to admit, on the one hand, that the understanding is cognizant only of appearances, and to assert, on the other, that this *cognition* is something absolute—by saying: cognition *cannot* go any further, this is the *natural,* absolute *restriction* of human knowing. Natural things are restricted and they are just natural things inasmuch as they *know nothing* of their universal *restriction,* inasmuch as their determinacy is a restriction only *for us,* not *for them.* Something is only known, or even felt, to be a restriction, or a defect, if one is at the same time *beyond* it. . . . In cognition . . . restriction and defect are only determined as restriction and defect by *comparison* with the Idea that is *present*—the idea of the universal, of something-whole and perfect. It is only lack of consciousness, therefore, if we do not see that it is precisely the designation of something as finite or restricted that contains the proof of the *actual presence* of the Infinite, or Unrestricted, and that there can be no knowledge of limit unless the Unlimited is *on this side* within consciousness.[7]

Here, in a nutshell, is the reason why it is impossible to accede to the view that there can be a knowledge of the integrity of parts but not a knowledge of the integrity of the whole; a knowledge of the divisions and separations that keep things apart and distinguishable, one from another, but not a knowledge of the common frame of reference whereby distinctions become intelligible in the first place; a knowledge of the Many that yet manages to exclude knowledge of the One; or a knowledge of Becoming that does not simultaneously imply, or depend upon, a knowledge of Being. Here too is the reason why it is impossible to accept the new theories of noncommunication (the various "you can't get there from here" theories), according to which different groups of persons cannot know each other's notions because all they could ever possibly know would be *their own notions* of each other's notions—a situation that could not be predicated at all if it were true that each group's knowledge must be confined to its own particular notions, since somebody somewhere—some group or another— would have to be in a position to cognize the disparity between notions, would have to make contact with the variety of notion-sets. And the determination of the constraints pertaining to mere subjectivity could not itself be merely subjective, without losing immediately its own validity. With insights like these, Hegel explicitly rejects the wisdom we tend to regard as a late-breaking development. The continual appeal to Hegel in the critique of post-rationalism has, I think, two important implications. The first is, as I have been suggesting, that the content of post-rational criticism is not exclusively the product of recent intellectual fashions, as though, prior to their appearance, it had not already been conceived. The second is that speculative philosophy may still be regarded as that which lies beyond post-rationalism, being the always possible consequence of recognizing the latter's errors.[8] To believe otherwise would be to suppose that logical sequences are determined by historical happenstance, rather than that historical sequences are intelligible only to logical inquiry. Fashion may be whatever it will without being dictated to by philosophy, and even in the absence of philosophical comprehension, but philosophy *would* be required if one were trying to understand what fashion is and what it portends, though it could not be a philosophy that had learned to regard comprehension itself as a fashion.

In my tenth chapter, I have sought the aid of yet another speculative philosopher, George Santayana, who stands midway between us and Hegel and who performed the excellent service, throughout his long career, of observing and commenting on the transformation of nineteenth-century post-rationalism into twentieth-century forms of the same. Although he did not live to see the schools or movements focused on in this book, Santayana was well aware that philosophy after Kant remained preoccupied with the problem of refining its awareness of the transcendental conditions of thought. He knew that philosophy was constantly reorienting itself in the light of what it took to be awareness breakthroughs, as, for example, in the pragmatisms of James and Dewey or in the various philosophies of language wherein discourse or rhetoric is taken to be constitutive of the objects of knowledge. Much of Santayana's own writing is critical of these "critical" attempts to reestablish the foundations of knowledge by appealing to new sets of props. To anyone who reads him, it will be clear that the substance of his criticisms, like that of Hegel's, remains pertinent to our own forms of transcendentalism, just as he himself remains the most important twentieth-century American thinker to bear in mind in assessing the intellectual situation in which we now find ourselves.

In my last chapter, I have brought Santayana and Hegel together in order to consider the positive contributions that might be made by speculative philosophy to the problems left unsolved by post-rationalism. Despite their differences, these two thinkers broadly agree that the ambition of philosophy is, properly, to provide a speculative comprehension of the essential rationality of all knowledge, indeed of all experience, in direct opposition to the claim (itself comprehensible) that comprehension is impossible. Each gives an account of knowledge that accepts, rather than undermines, the work of knowing, and each account thus given seeks to accommodate the various phases or parts of which knowledge as a whole is composed. The ambition of both Santayana and Hegel is to show that no particular part of knowledge can be regarded as absolute but that the only thing that can or must be so regarded is the spectacle presented by all the parts seen in their free development and coordination. This means, of course, that it is impossible to imagine that knowledge as a whole can be adequately explained in terms of the particular categories employed by a particular science, such as economics or linguistics or psychology. The idea that thinking or knowing per se can be rightly grasped as a thing hedged in or overshadowed by realities that can themselves be detected only through recourse to a partial science seems, to Hegel and Santayana both, an absurdity. As an alternative, Hegel proposes that the whole gamut of categorical concepts be examined, according to the dialectic or the logic that determines their relations and differences. A test of the completeness of such a survey would be that all the kinds of knowing, including those manifested by the various sciences, might be shown to be informed by particular concepts spread across this gamut. The various shapes and postures of knowing could thus be coordinated according to the logical relations of their informing concepts, thereby offsetting the tendency of particular sciences to absolutize their own points of view. As Hegel observes, the concepts that inform all thinking are not independent of one another. They pass into and out of each other by virtue of the fact that they imply each other dialectically or contain each other implicitly. To arrest this passage of concepts into and out of each other by sequestering particular concepts and building upon them, as though they were absolute in themselves or independently real apart from one another, would be to adopt a position grounded in abstraction, since it is only the whole array of concepts, grasped according to their connections, that is truly concrete. Speculative philosophy is, by definition, nothing other than this grasp.

With Santayana, the goal is essentially the same as it is for Hegel, though the method seems different. In *The Life of Reason* (originally conceived as a revisionist reworking of Hegel's *Phenomenology*),[9] Santayana attempts a comprehensive "history of the human mind," focusing on the development whereby unreflective sensibility is transformed into social consciousness and religious consciousness and ultimately arrives at the kinds of self-consciousness required by the arts and sciences. In fact, Santayana's account is more nearly concerned with the logic of this development than with the history of it, since it works by showing what developments make possible what other developments and by showing which developments were retrograde and which were not, progress not being equated with purely temporal sequences. Unlike Hegel, Santayana hesitates to think of philosophy as a science, because he imagines that science itself must be envisioned as a form of knowing (alongside other forms) if it is to be grasped speculatively, and the speculative grasp of science cannot be scientific in the way that the sciences thus grasped are scientific. Of course, Santayana had already begun to think of the empirical sciences or the positive sciences as the typical import of the term "science." Hegel, on the other hand, took the term to mean, in the highest sense, nothing other than genuine knowledge, as opposed to mere opinion or knowledge only of appearances or probabilities. Thus, Hegel, like Santayana, also distinguishes between philosophy construed as a science and the other sciences, so-called, by pointing out that the other sciences begin with already established presuppositions concerning the objects they intend to investigate and the methods to be employed during the course of their investigations, whereas philosophy cannot rightly begin with a method of inquiry already worked out or any presuppositions concerning what deserves to be called "real" or "true" or "actual." If philosophy *did* have any preconceived notions concerning its particular scope or provenance, then it *would* be merely a particular science occupying a place beside all the others, requiring to be coordinated with them rather than being the coordinator of them. Whenever Santayana speaks of the specific doctrines urged by philosophers, it is clear that he considers them to be characterized by particular orientations or predispositions which render them objects of cultural curiosity rather than exercises in speculative comprehension, the goal of the latter being knowledge not bound by predispositions.

Characteristically, Santayana himself begins, not with an expression of confidence in any particular kind or degree of knowledge, but with knowledge claims under suspension in view of the inconsistencies and contradictions that tempt us to muse on what he calls (in *Interpretations of Poetry and Religion*) the "incoherence and instability in human systems of ideas." After all, science and religion seem already incompatible in many respects, the arts have their own ideas of things to impart, and competing philosophies are already on the books, as much in conflict with each other as with common sense. It is precisely because it has assumed such a variety of incompatible shapes that knowledge has become problematic. In remaining focused on these shapes, Santayana makes it his business to understand the connections that make possible a perception of their differences. Each shape tends to be totalizing to the extent that it offers a point of view from which the whole field of experience may be construed according to its own set of categories. But since there are numerous points of view, the true totality can only be established by envisioning the array of viewpoints. Arguments for and against the possibility of attaining such a speculative view of things are themselves easily situated among the materials being envisioned, and, in fact, there is nothing to which speculative philosophy can be related or contrasted that is not itself contained within it or circumscribed by it. Because it already embraces or includes the evidences or proofs that might be supposed to support it, and because no consideration can be brought against it that is not a matter for consideration rather than an obstacle to consideration, Santayana is reluctant to think of it as a definite or particular set of doctrines or as a specific chain of arguments, to which other doctrines or other arguments might be opposed. Being absolute and unconditioned, it cannot be understood rightly as one particular philosophy competing with other philosophies, and thus, he thinks, it cannot be presented, without gross misrepresentation, as a circumscribable system irresolvably opposed by other systems. The right apprehension of it presumably emerges when the thought-forms (art, religion, science, common sense) are reviewed in such a way as to reveal the nonabsolute character of each form, just as, for Hegel, the true philosophy emerges in connection with a perception of the nonabsolute character of the conceptual elements contained in all the particular forms of thinking.

The most curious thing (and the most hopeful thing) about post-rationalism is that it clearly knows more than it believes itself to be capable of knowing. In fixed opposition to itself, it can neither get rid of nor develop the elements of reason which, in fact, it contains. In one way or another, the various forms of post-rational criticism try to speak objectively, universally, or philosophically about the necessity of living subjectively or subphilosophically on the level of mere particulars. Catching itself in this mistake, post-rationalism pleads its case again with new urgency, adding self-recriminations and nontheoretical gestures to bolster its original arguments but always, in effect, repeating the mistake. Speculative philosophy, on the other hand, explicitly begins by focusing directly on the paradoxes that this self-renunciation of reason has engendered, taking the perception of them to be, as Hegel calls it, "the great negative step towards the true Notion of reason."[10] In this way, the critique of post-rational criticism becomes the springboard for a thinking that "will not give up" its ambition to "accomplish in thinking itself the resolution of its own contradictions."[11]

CHAPTER 1

THE TRANSCENDENTALIST IMPULSE IN THE PROJECTS OF CONTEMPORARY CRITICISM

But deep enough, alas! none ever mines.
                    —Matthew Arnold, "The Buried Life"

In recent years, post-rational criticism has been developing the view that there is more wisdom to be found in the structures of poetry than in the arguments of philosophers. According to this view, poetry is not only more philosophical (in a broad sense) than history; it is more philosophical than philosophy itself. And yet anyone who tries to maintain this view must grapple with the opposite view that, in fact, "poetry" and "philosophy" are the names of essentially different enterprises which ought not to be confused with each other. Nothing used to be more common than to hear, from poets and critics alike, that poetry is corrupted when it is forced to carry the burden of ideas or when it is milked for its philosophical implications. Poetry, according to modernists like Eliot and Pound, is a way of registering one's sensibility or a way of doing things with words, not a statement about reality. The content of a poem, interpreted as whatever it may be that it appears to be saying about things, ought to be regarded almost as a necessary evil. When it is obtrusive, as the modernists and the New Critics sometimes feared it might be, it could be argued either that the poem in question is therefore inferior as poetry or else that its content is really a smoke screen (or, as William Carlos Williams called it, "a mere pretext")[1] for something else more intrinsically poetical, having to do with the verbal medium itself. By the same token, philosophers have often insisted that philosophy's search for truth and the aesthetic goals of poetry are fundamentally different. From Plato onward, the complaint against poetry, whenever it has arisen, has been more or less the same: poetry, when it claims to be more than a sensuous diversion, amounts to nothing but mythmaking; and myth, however appealing to the imagination, is ultimately an obstacle to the development of sound thinking based on clear ideas. From the very beginning, so it is argued, poets have attributed an undue importance to their own activities by preferring them to the search for truth or, in most instances, by claiming for themselves a higher wisdom made available to them through deep insight or the power of vision, whereas, in fact, genuine wisdom is available only to those who practice critical thinking. Thus, one way to characterize the history of Western culture would be to say that in the course of that history philosophy has sought, by and large, to purify itself by divesting itself as much as possible of the trappings of poetry, while poetry, especially in modern times, has likewise sought to maintain its own identity by becoming increasingly independent of philosophy.

Although there would certainly be a large grain of truth in such a characterization, in the sense that philosophers and poets often have felt themselves to be in opposition to each other, nevertheless it is equally certain that a rapprochement between poetry and philosophy was effected relatively early in the history of their mutual relations, a rapprochement that has persisted and, indeed, continues to persist, despite the claim, made by post-rational critics, that philosophy has been eclipsed. Formerly, the main condition of this rapprochement was that poetry should play the rather conspicuous role of junior partner, accepting the tasks assigned to it by philosophy. Now, however, this condition has changed. Poetry in the modern period has produced its own credentials, and in general has given the impression of being quite autonomous, although, as I intend to argue, philosophy remains as vigorous as ever behind the scenes, covertly active in its original capacity as senior partner. The new rapprochement, in fact, depends on the impression, which I take to be a false impression, that philosophy has retired altogether from the firm.

The history of the development of our current situation may be sketched briefly. Poetry, as everyone knows, came first, before the appearance of what we now think of as philosophy. In its golden period, as Peacock says, "the whole field of intellect [was] its own. It [had] no rivals, in history, nor in philosophy, nor in science. It [was] cultivated by the greatest intellects of the age, and listened to by all the rest." In Greece, Homer and Hesiod produced poems that serve a philosophical function by purporting to give true knowledge of how things have come to be as they are, that is to say, by showing how history and nature constitute a revelation of the divine will. Nevertheless, even before Plato, the wisdom of the first poets was stark]y opposed by the first philosophers, the Ionian cosmologists, so that in the Republic Plato can speak of "an ancient enmity," "an ancient quarrel between philosophy and poetry."[2] Interestingly enough, in the *Laws*

Plato implies that the old poets had come closer to the truth than the philosophers, since the philosophers were mistaken in assigning the causes of all things to lifeless material substances. In doing this, says Plato, they "gave rise to much atheism and perplexity" so that "the poets took occasion to be abusive—comparing the philosophers to she-dogs uttering vain howlings."[3] But if the Ionians were wrong to deny the priority of mind or soul in the universe and, to some extent, deserved the contempt hurled at them by the poets, now, says Plato, the case is reversed. It is the philosopher—the Platonic philosopher—who now emerges as "a true worshipper of the Gods," in opposition to the ignorant, superstitious poets. Not only do these poets fail to understand properly the things they imitate or describe in their verses, they cannot even understand their own poetic products, as Socrates discovers when he asks some poets to explain to him the meaning of a few difficult passages. Their inability to account for their own poetic activity leads Socrates to conclude, as we learn from the *Apology,* that they in fact possess no wisdom. "Then I knew," he says, "that not by wisdom do poets write poetry, but by a sort of genius and inspiration; they are like diviners or soothsayers who also say many fine things, but do not understand the meaning of them."[4]

Plato's description of poetry as a sort of crude approximation of the genuine insight attainable by philosophy established the latter's superiority so firmly that philosophy's preeminence has never been seriously shaken, despite recent appearances to the contrary. More than two thousand years after Plato, Hegel echoes the Platonic judgment when he observes that "for us art counts no longer as the highest mode in which truth fashions an existence for itself,"[5] the highest mode being for Hegel, as for Plato, the mode of philosophical reflection. Nevertheless, a rapprochement between philosophy and poetry, beyond Plato's conceiving, *did* turn out to be possible after all, so long as poetry was willing to accept a subordinate role in the relationship. Plato himself conceded that certain kinds of poetry might be useful in the life of reason; hymns to the gods, for example, or praises of famous men might conceivably foster the piety and patriotism necessary to the security of the state. It was Aristotle, however, who rescued poetry from the almost total banishment Plato had in mind for it, by suggesting that poetry *is* capable of representing truths that have been determined for it in advance by philosophy. Although it may be the case that poetry cannot determine the truth from scratch, it does have the capacity to present for contemplation certain general truths concerning human nature and the patterns of human experience. In this respect, Aristotle argues, poetry may justly be regarded as "a more philosophical and a higher thing than history."[6] In other words, Aristotle conceives of poetry, not as a blind groping toward truths that are otherwise inaccessible, but rather as a vehicle for conveying such truths as have already been grasped and appropriated. Poetry, according to this view of the matter, is not the product of hysterical or inspired soothsayers; it is the product of intelligent makers who know what they mean to say and who design their poems deliberately, in accordance with their knowledge.

It is impossible to exaggerate the importance of this maneuver, for it constitutes a justification of poetry's claim to intellectual respectability that has remained valid almost until the present time. It permits us to regard the great poems of the Western tradition as deliberate, conscious reflections of ideas, sentiments, and beliefs already grounded in the established institutions or notions of religion and philosophy. This is true not only of explicitly "philosophical" poems like the *Divine Comedy* or the *Essay on Man,* but also of works less overtly didactic, like the plays of Shakespeare. Indeed, prior to the Romantics, poetry was almost always rationalized, whenever it required to be defended or explained, as a re-presentation of thoughts and feelings already known to exist independently of poetry. As Sidney puts it in his *Apology for Poetry,* "any understanding knoweth the skill of the artificer standeth in that idea or foreconceit of the work, and not in the work itself."[7] Sidney, in fact, goes so far as to defend the poets Plato attacks, on the ground that they themselves did not invent their inadequate opinions of the gods, but instead received these opinions from "the very religion of the time." These poets, says Sidney, "did not induce such opinions, but did imitate those opinions already induced."[8] Finally, of course, Sidney bestows the highest honors on poetry rather than philosophy, but he does so only because it seems to him that poems communicate more effectively than philosophical treatises what philosophy itself has to teach us. As "the right popular philosopher," the poet, according to Sidney, "yieldeth to the powers of the mind an image of that whereof the philosopher bestoweth but a wordish description: which doth neither strike, pierce, nor possess the sight of the soul so much as that other doth."[9]

This conception of poetry as a sort of splendid vehicle for ideas originating elsewhere in belief systems or thought systems that are determinative *of* poems rather than determined *by* poems has been under attack for about two hundred years now. Ever since the time of Blake and Wordsworth, a sort of poetic reformation has been under way whose principal aim is to liberate the Muse from her Babylonian Captivity to philosophy. We can see this reformation at work in Blake's angry reaction to the empiricism of Bacon and Locke, to the enlightened skepticism of the *philosophes,* to the materialism of the new physical theories of nature. Indeed, much of the time Blake sounds like those "abusive" poets Plato speaks of who dared. to describe the materialist philosophers of the pre-Socratic period as "she-dogs uttering vain howlings." Blake makes essentially the same gesture, because he refuses to take orders from the dominant philosophers of his own day. He also refuses to take orders from orthodox religious authorities and mainstream theologians, preferring to create his own personal vision of the truth on the basis of what he takes to be his own autonomous imagination. And, in this respect at least, he is hardly more radical than Wordsworth. After all, it is Wordsworth who claims to find in his own mind, in his own experience, and without benefit of traditional mythology, the substance of the profoundest, most philosophical poetry. It is Wordsworth who claims access, through "life's everyday appearances," to "worlds / To which the heaven of heavens is but a veil." This is still, I think, the most extraordinary claim in the whole of modern poetry: the claim that we can have it all—"Paradise, and groves Elysian, Fortunate Fields"—not as a fiction, not as a fantasy or a wish fulfillment, but as "a simple produce of the common day." Poetry, says Wordsworth, is "the first and last of all knowledge," which means that poets *can* start from scratch and they *can* arrive at final truths, not by accepting conclusions already propounded, but by ransacking the materials of their own personal experience and impressions.

At almost the same moment in Germany, the young Schelling (or possibly the young Hegel) was writing these words: "Poetry thereby obtains a higher dignity; it becomes again in the end what it was in the beginning— *teacher* of *(history) the human race* because there is no longer any philosophy, any history; poetic art alone will outlive all the rest of the sciences and arts."[10] In fact, both the Romantic poets and the philosophers of German idealism (in its earlier phase) were developing at the same time a theory of the autonomy or self-sufficiency of the self-conscious imagination. According to this theory, the ultimate goal of wisdom is not to acquire correct notions having to do with Paradise and groves Elysian and Fortunate Fields. It is to experience these things directly or immediately in the world all around us, and, further, to experience this experience itself in acts of artistic self-consciousness. The production of poetry wherein one can endlessly experience and reexperience one's experiences becomes the highest thing of all. In such poetry, one encounters the self (the mind as "lord and master," to use Wordsworth's phrase) constructing itself objectively to itself; one encounters self-thinking thought. After that, who needs philosophy? After that, philosophy itself would be mean descent.

We are still working out the implications of this Romantic reversal of Aristotle's maneuver. And it makes no difference whether one is considering the "art for art's sake" or "pure poetry" school at one end of the spectrum or the "myth-making" school at the other end of the spectrum. Poets who cultivate aesthetic experience as an alternative to truth are as much affected by the Romantic reversal as the poets who cultivate it as the means to truth. Both groups believe that poetry must be permitted to develop according to its own laws and interests, whether it comes, as Pater says, "proposing frankly to give nothing but the highest quality to your moments as they pass, and simply for those moments' sakes,"[11] or whether it comes, in Eliot's phrase, as "a way of controlling, of ordering, of giving a shape and a significance to the immense panorama of futility and anarchy which is contemporary history."[12] The claims for poetry in our day, whether they be pitched high or low, whether they be based on the assumption that poetry can absorb the whole of philosophy into itself or on the contrary assumption that it can expel philosophy out of itself, have at least this much in common: the belief that poetry cannot properly regard itself as the handmaiden of philosophy.

This belief, I would argue, is mistaken, for it is certainly untrue to say that modern poetry has succeeded either in absorbing philosophy or else in detaching itself from it altogether. In spite of the illusion that it has gained its independence, poetry remains, in a curious way, just as subordinate as it ever as. It could hardly be otherwise, since the *theory* of the autonomy of the poetic imagination is itself a philosophical creature, and all *judgments* concerning the scope and value of poetry are themselves philosophical in character. The fact that modern art has become intensely self-conscious regarding the superiority of its own modes of cognition and expression is precisely what enables us to say that it is propelled by theory or by theoretical considerations. The less mimetic, the less discursive, the less representational this art has been, the more obvious it has also been that this is the case. Imagism, abstractionism, surrealism, and minimalism all have theoretical foundations that justify or legitimate their productions. In fact, the more unsophisticated, or postsophisticated, a poem appears to be, the more sophisticated the theory generally is that dictates its demeanor. The disappearance of overt attitudinizing in art must not be taken to signify art's independence from philosophy, as Paul Valéry makes clear in the following passage, which describes how the late nineteenth-century poets liberated their poems from carrying a philosophical burden:

> It was a time of theories, curiosities, commentaries, and passionate explanations. A young and somewhat stern generation rejected the scientific dogma which was beginning to be unfashionable, without adopting the religious dogma which was not yet so. In the profound and scrupulous worship of the arts as a whole, it thought it had found an unequivocal discipline or even a truth. A sort of religion was very nearly established. . . . But the works of that period did not themselves positively disclose these preoccupations. Quite to the contrary, one must note carefully what they prohibit and what ceased to appear in poems during the time of which I am speaking. It would seem that abstract thought, formerly admitted even into verse, having now become almost impossible to combine with the immediate emotions that it was desired continually to arouse, being banished from a poetry that was endeavoring to reduce itself to its own essence, and dismayed by the multiple effects of surprise and of music demanded by modern taste, had betaken itself to the preparatory phase and to the theory of poetry. Philosophy, and even ethics, tended to shun the actual works and take their place among the reflections preceding them. This was a very real *progress*.[13]

The kind of "progress" Valéry is referring to in this passage continued to be a preoccupation with the modernist poets, such as Pound and Williams. For example, in a letter to the editor of *View*, Williams remarks with his usual bluntness: "Brilliant articles cry out to be written. Why bother? No one would read them. The thing is, make the things that such world shaking deductions would imply and OMIT the deductions."[14] On another occasion, and at greater length, Williams explained to his published James Laughlin that poetry works much better when the thought with which it is associated is not put "into" it but instead is made "the spring-board for what the setup it indicates induces objectively in things." In other words, says Williams, "if you think this way, then it should induce you to see a hog or a wife or a fifty cent piece *that* way—whatever that way would be. That would be poetic creation."[15]

It fell to the critics of modern poetry to reverse this procedure. By taking poems about hogs or wives or fifty-cent pieces and working backward, the critic eventually arrived at the "spring-board" of thought that explained the poems. If it was difficult to extricate the thought contained in a poem by Eliot or Pound, it was relatively easy to see how the .strategy of the poem had been dictated by a nexus of theories concerning the history of culture and the psychology of perception. A complex philosophy of human experience was contained in these theories, and it was this philosophy that explained the substance and manner of poems like *The Waste Land* or "In a Station of the Metro," poems designed to present little globules of experience rather than thoughts about it. Such poems, no matter how surd-like in character, no matter how concrete or recalcitrant to the understanding, were in fact subordinate to the theories that set them up and accounted for their workings. But, if in this way philosophy was calling the shots for literature by designing its production, it was also busy at the other end of things in the minds of those who offered to be the interpreters and explainers of literature. These interpreters and explainers were not necessarily satisfied with what the authors themselves had said about the guiding principles of their own works. Indeed, it was partly an effect of modernist theory that the conscious intentions or deliberate designs of authors came to be seen as trivial by comparison with the intellectual-and-emotional complexes attested to by images or by comparison to the intricate patterns made by the mind of Europe over the course of its long, transindividual life. In any case, throughout most of the twentieth century, the authority of authors, conceived in terms of intentions or purposes governing the production of works of conscious art, came to be regarded by almost every school of literary criticism as a metaphysical illusion best dispensed with. Authors were like things-in-themselves, inferred realities imagined to explain textual phenomena in the same way that the gods (or God) had been imagined to explain natural phenomena. Authorial intention was in truth a mirage or a hypostasis; if such a thing as intention did exist, it was certainly unknowable, and even if it could be known, as something distinct from textual phenomena it would be irrelevant or beside the point. Marxists, Freudians, myth critics, New Critics, structuralists, post-structuralists—all had some strategy for conceiving the author as a metaphysical embarrassment or, at best, as an epiphenomenon in relation to more important things. Curiously, the effect was to reinstate the old Socratic judgment that poets really don't know what they are talking about. Just when it seemed that poets were about to be regarded, as they had been in ancient times, as seers or sages purveying the deepest or the highest of all wisdom, they were swept aside by other intellectuals as an irrelevant nuisance to the project of attaining a right understanding of the meaning of poetry. In this way, philosophy once again rose up over poetry.

The critics who formed the various schools of literary criticism did not, by and large, see themselves as philosophers. When they had an academic affiliation, they were associated with departments of language and literature rather than departments of philosophy. Moreover, they had heard that philosophy *as metaphysics* was a thing of the past, which had been crushed by the philosophers themselves in the second half of the nineteenth century and the first half of the twentieth. Contemporary philosophers seemed to spend their time tidying up truth tables or refereeing language games, thus helping other intellectuals to avoid logical or verbal confusions. Meanwhile, these other intellectuals, particularly the ones working in the human sciences such as psychology, sociology, anthropology, economics, and linguistics, had developed the "right" categories for understanding all forms of human behavior and human consciousness, including those that manifested themselves as literature. These categories were not philosophical, because they had not been developed in philosophy departments by persons calling themselves philosophers. They were scientific, and because they had originated in departments of science, the critics who employed them could do so without having to feel responsible for them. To apply them to literature was to be "interdisciplinary," not speculative. And yet the results seemed strangely metaphysical. In almost every one of its shapes or forms, literary criticism became a kind of transcendentalism. The ideas that authors themselves seemed to have had, as conscious makers or deliberate designers of their own works, were, of course, suspended or bracketed as problematical fictions. The real issue was to determine *how* such ideas, or the semblance of such ideas, had ever arisen in the first place. Could they be explained, for example, as the consequence of psychic formation dramas, whereby consciousness as we now know it has come to be constituted? Could our present thinking turn out to be a sort of false consciousness in relation to the deeper structures and processes hypothesized by psychoanalysts and anthropologists? Myth critics like Joseph Campbell and Northrop Frye answered in the affirmative, in response to the pioneering work of Frazer, Freud, and Jung. Feminist critics, more recently, responding in part to suggestions made by Lacan and Foucault concerning the rationalizations at work in self-identification, developed their own theories having to do with the factors involved in the gendering of consciousness. All these inquiries into the constitution of consciousness, whether based on theories of the unconscious persistence of primordial thought patterns, or on theories of the engendering of ego or the engendering of gender, were (and are) transcendental in character, because they focus not on the ideas that consciousness itself has produced but on the factors or conditions that constrain consciousness, impelling it from within to arrive at just these ideas. The ideas appear as the manifest content of literary works and other cultural products, the factors or conditions that unconsciously determine them as the latent content of the same works. The producers of works need not be aware (in fact, they are usually totally unaware) of what is transcendental in their own activity. Thus, it is the transcendental inquirer—the critic—who can best explain how it is that the works are as they are.

Along with the psychological explainers of consciousness, there went another group of political or sociological explainers, including Marxists, Marxist revisionists, Frankfurt School disciples, and "power" archeologists (after the fashion of Foucault). This group specialized in explaining how various kinds of consciousness are shaped or constrained by social, political, and economic pressures, with the result that the ideas formed by consciousness can mostly be dismissed as the bits and pieces of an ideology, always improperly conceived by its own advocates because their own thinking is always informed by it transcendentally. Here again, the manifest content of literary work was more or less identified with the conscious intentions of the writers who produced them, whereas the latent content, visible only to the transcendental inquirer, was the ideological position implied by those intentions. A third group of transcendental critics rose up on the basis of structural linguistics and the science of semiology or semiotics. This last group explained consciousness (and, consequently, literature) in terms of the ways in which language imposes on thinking its own characteristic features and possibilities. For these critics, language was the key to everything discoverable or intelligible. Awareness of its transcendental functions with respect to all forms of intellectual inquiry constituted, for them, a "linguistic turn," and language study came to be regarded as the new organon of thought. In some ways, linguistic transcendentalism did indeed become the most powerful and the most influential form of transcendentalism in the twentieth century. It was hard to explain linguistic phenomena in terms of psychological or sociological *events*. It was much easier to explain psychological and sociological *explanations* of events in terms of their own necessary inscription of linguistic phenomena. Nevertheless, as the poststructuralist critics made clear, it was not impossible for the chief forms of transcendentalism (the psychological, the sociological, and the linguistic) to overlap or coalesce. Revisionist structuralists (who called themselves deconstructionists) began to talk about the political implications of unmasking "bad" ideologies through their own special form of hyper-close reading. Feminist critics began to discuss the manner in which seemingly neutral conceptions of things were rooted in psychological processes whereby consciousness had been gendered according to the "deep" politics of male/female relations. Cultural critics, like the New Historicists, began to incorporate the notions developed by linguistic and psychological transcendentalists into their own analyses of the dynamics of cultural formations. Thus, the feeling sometimes arose that the various forms of transcendentalism might be reconciled with each other or at least work collaboratively toward the common goal of explaining the constitution of consciousness.

It was sincerely hoped that the structures and processes the transcendentalists themselves had adduced would be regarded not as metaphysical entities but only as the legitimate products of scientific discovery and rigorous reasoning. After all, the original home of their key concepts was simply one or another of the social sciences, such as linguistics or psychology in their more ordinary forms. If pressed very hard for credentials, the transcendentalists could always fall back on these sciences for support. Most of the time, however, what they in fact produced did look suspiciously like metaphysics. Like the original transcendentalists—like Kant himself—they knew that the seemingly real world of space and time, although it appeared to have a nature and a history, was in fact a construction of consciousness and could be reduced in a twinkling to the ideas that

consciousness had had of it. Ideas were fictions. The idea of consciousness itself as an actually existing entity was a fiction. It was impossible to
explain ideas by referring to the objects to which they appeared to correspond, because these objects themselves were compacted of ideas. They
stood inside the ideas they appeared to have instigated. It was similarly
impossible to explain ideas by referring to an object or an entity from
which they might be supposed to emanate (an entity such as mind or consciousness), because this entity was available to us only through our ideas
of it. Somehow the mechanisms of ideation had to be imagined without
reference to anything independent of ideation. A more suitable term than
"ideation" was the term "interpretation." Everything could be reduced (or
infinitely expanded) by taking it to be the product of interpretation. To
focus on the activity of interpretation itself was to interpret it. Since the
objects of interpretation were constituted by interpretation, it was impossible to derive knowledge by studying the objects themselves empirically.
The right thing to do was presumably to expose the transcendental character of the activity of interpretation in relation to the constituted objects. To
do this, one had to investigate the nature or character of the interpretive
process without making the mistake of grounding it on its own productions,
on the objects that it itself had invented. A netherworld of hypothetical
actions and entities had to be summoned up in order to explain interpretation, once it was clear that the world constructed by interpretation could
not be adduced as the cause of the process by means of which it had been
constructed. Perversely, it seemed, the result of transcendentalism was metaphysics.

Santayana had called attention to this result in his analysis of Kantian
transcendentalism in *The Life of Reason.* In Kant's "mythology," says
Santayana, "the whole skeleton and dialectical mould of experience came
to figure . . . as machinery behind the scenes, as a system of non-natural
efficient forces." Indeed, Santayana continues, Kant's "fundamental over-
sight and contradiction lay in not seeing that the concept of a set of conditions was the precise and exact concept of nature, which he consequently
reduplicated, having one nature before experience and another after. The
first thus became mythical and the second illusory; for the first, said to
condition experience, was a set of verbal ghosts, while the second, which
alone could be observed or discovered scientifically, was declared ficti-

tious."[16] The concept of a nature *before* experience, which is the condition *of* experience, achieves truly metaphysical proportions in the depth psychology of Jung and in the structural anthropology of Lévi-Strauss, which have both been strongly influential on critics who lean toward the psychological form of transcendentalism. The nature *after* experience, which the vulgar think of as reality, is for these critics a construction of consciousness, and therefore, strictly speaking, fictitious. The true reality, the one that is much more important than that which consciousness constructs, is the universal human mind, the primordial or archaic mind that persists into the present through the agency of what Jung calls the collective unconscious. It is this mind, invisible to the uninitiated, that expresses itself, latently or symbolically, in the productions of consciousness, and it is this mind which is the ultimate focus of the psychological transcendentalists.

Jung's metaphysics can he seen clearly in the Tavistock Lectures of 1935. There Jung proclaims:

> The deepest we can reach in our exploration of the unconscious mind is the layer where man is no longer a distinct individual, but where his mind widens out and merges into the mind of mankind—not the conscious mind, but the unconscious mind of mankind, where we are all the same. As the body has its anatomical conformity in its two eyes and two ears and one heart and so on, with only slight individual differences, so has the mind its basic conformity. On this collective level we are no longer separate individuals, we are all one. You can understand this when you study the psychology of primitives. . . . Primitive mentality expresses the basic structure of the mind, that psychological layer which with us is the collective unconscious, that underlying level which is the same in all.[17]

In assuming that primitive mentality is more expressive of the basic structure of mind than sophisticated consciousness because it is less given to distinctions between individuals or between subject and object, Jung flirts with the idea that it might be possible to return, in some sense, to the original wholeness of the universal mind, in relation to which consciousness itself is a "fall." Thus he muses:

> The outstanding fact about the primitive mentality is this lack of distinction between individuals, this oneness of the subject with the object, this *participation mystique,* as Lévy-Bruhl terms it. . . . Because the basic

structure of the mind is the same in everybody, we cannot make distinctions when we experience on that level. . . . In the underlying collective level there is a wholeness which cannot be dissected.[18]

Indeed, Jung concludes, "if you begin to think about participation as a fact which means that fundamentally we are identical with everybody and everything, you are led to very peculiar theoretical conclusions." Although Jung advises his auditors not to "go further than those conclusions because these things get dangerous," it is clear that Jung has already gone so far as to hypothesize a metaphysical entity ("the unconscious mind of mankind") and to speculate mythically on the fall into individuality and the recovery of original wholeness. Jung's description of the inferential status of the one mind is powerfully reminiscent of the traditional argument for the existence of God from the evidences of design in nature. He admits:

> We cannot deal with the unconscious processes directly because they are not reachable. They are not directly apprehended; they appear only in their products, and we postulate from the peculiar quality of those products that there must be something behind them from which they originate. We call that dark sphere the unconscious psyche.[19]

It was, of course, precisely the point of natural theology that it was similarly reasonable to postulate from the peculiar quality of natural phenomena that there must be something behind *them* from which *they* originate. In this respect, Jung's work shows how the type of thinking that once expressed itself as natural theology eventually found a new home for itself in modern "depth" psychology. That the one mind is conceived as a producer of effects and therefore as a metaphysical agent or power is clear from this remark (again from the Tavistock Lectures):

> [O]ur personal psychology is just a thin skin, a ripple upon the ocean of collective psychology. The powerful factor, the factor which changes our whole life, which changes the surface of our known world, which makes history, is collective psychology, and collective psychology moves according to laws entirely different from those of our consciousness. The archetypes are the great decisive forces, they bring about the real events, and not our personal reasoning and practical intellect. . . . Sure enough, the archetypal images decide the fate of man. Man's unconscious psy-

chology decides, and not what we think and talk in the brain-chamber up in the attic.[20]

When T. S. Eliot invoked "the mind of Europe" in his essay "Tradition and the Individual Talent," declaring it to be "much more important" than the individual minds of particular persons, it must have been clear to at least some of his readers that he was revealing his affinity with the metaphysics of idealism. For some reason, the affinity of Jung's thinking with this same metaphysics has seemed less clear to those critics who assume that "depth" psychology is essentially a postphilosophical development.

Lévi-Strauss, despite his criticism of Jung's theory of archetypes, shares with Jung a belief in the universal mind, which is the transcendental condition of all social and cultural phenomena. In his essay "Language and the Analysis of Social Laws," he speculates on the power of linguistics to disclose the "universal laws" of the mind:

> Among all social phenomena, language alone has thus far been studied in a manner which permits it to serve as the object of truly scientific analysis, allowing us to understand its formative process and to predict its mode of change. This results from modern researches into the problems of phonemics, which have reached beyond the superficial conscious and historical expression of linguistic phenomena to attain fundamental and objective realities consisting of systems of relations which are the products of unconscious thought processes. The question which now arises is this: Is it possible to effect a similar reduction in the analysis of other forms of social phenomena? If so, would this analysis lead to the same result? And if the answer to this last question is in the affirmative, can we conclude that all forms of social life are substantially of the same nature—that is, do they consist of systems of behavior that represent the projection, on the level of conscious and socialized thought of universal laws which regulate the unconscious activities of the mind?[21]

As is well known, Lévi-Strauss answered these questions in the affirmative, reaching the conclusion toward the end of his career (in the Massey Lectures) that, "notwithstanding the cultural differences between the several parts of mankind, the human mind is everywhere one and the same and that it has the same capacities."[22] On this level of universality, however, the constructions of "the human mind" are not to be confused with the conscious intentions of individuals or groups. Because the universal mind thinks deeply or structurally, it produces "fundamental and objective realities consisting of systems of relations" that are quite beyond the thoughts of those whom these systems define. Thus, "we are led to conceive of social structures as entities independent of men's consciousness of them (although they in fact govern men's existence), and thus as different from the image which men form of them as physical reality is different from our sensory perceptions of it and our hypotheses about it."[23] The universal mind, as Lévi-Strauss conceives it, is in fact constructing an expression of itself that completely transcends the purposes of those who are collectively its instruments. Because this is the case, it is possible to say that "myths get thought in man unbeknownst to him." Of his own work, Lévi-Strauss can say:

> I don't have the feeling that I write my books. I have the feeling that my books get written through me and that once they have got across me I feel empty and nothing is left. . . . That is, my work gets thought in me unbeknown to me.
>
> I never had, and still do not have, the perception of feeling my personal identity. I appear to myself as the place where something is going on, but there is no 'I', no 'me.' Each of us is a kind of crossroads where things happen. The crossroads is purely passive; something happens there. A different thing, equally valid, happens elsewhere. There is no choice, it is just a matter of chance.[24]

Indeed, as the colossal supersubject emerges from behind the smoke screen of apparently disparate cultural materials, Lévi-Strauss's thought verges toward the mythology of the original unity of this subject, which has collapsed into the differentiated cultures spread out in time and space but can still be recognized as the underlying reality of their difference. This mythology is implied when Lévi-Strauss asserts that, although it cannot be supposed "that cultures have tried systematically or methodically to differentiate themselves from each other," nevertheless it is true "that they *developed* characteristics of their own and *became* different from each other."[25] By using linguistics as the key to all mythologies, we can (in thought) reverse this development and contemplate the primordial supersubject. However, since the cultures themselves did not will their differentiation but in fact cultural differentiation is simply the mechanism whereby the super-subject articulates itself or extrapolates itself, it is both necessary and good that on a certain level differences should remain and not be sublated though "over-communication":

> In order for a culture to be really itself and to produce something, the culture and its members must be convinced of their originality and even, to some extent, of their superiority over the others; it is only under conditions of under-communication that it can produce anything.[26]

The fall into difference is really a fortunate fall, and the total mystery that offers itself to contemplation is the mystery whereby the one eternally pours itself out into the many and, simultaneously, reconstitutes itself as the one. Ordinary consciousness being unaware of this mystery, it is available only to the transcendental inquirer who, through awareness of it, "shall have the hope of overcoming the opposition between the collective nature of culture and its manifestations in the individual."[27] Like Jung, Lévi-Strauss presses toward the overcoming of all oppositions mysteriously and necessarily introduced by consciousness or culture:

> If we are led to believe that what takes place in our mind is something not substantially or fundamentally different from the basic phenomenon of life itself, and if we are led then to the feeling that there is not this kind of gap which is impossible to overcome between mankind on the one hand and all the other living beings—not only animals, but also plants—on the other, then perhaps we shall reach more wisdom, let us say, than we think we are capable of.[28]

Thus, by recognizing the unity of the supersubject, we can come to participate in the unity of all living things, cancelling the false consciousness that takes differences to be absolute or final. Indeed, what makes this consciousness false is its inability to arrive, when left to its own devices, at the metaphysical hypostasis of the supersubject or at the hypostasized identity of all living things. Transcendentalism establishes these hypostases in the minds of the adept.

Another group of psychological transcendentalists, eschewing the supersubject so dear to the myth critics and the structural anthropologists, were the neo-Freudians who followed in the wake of Lacan. Like the Freudians before them, these critics were interested in psychogenesis. Their ambition was to construct, as it were, a *psychogony,* a sort of interior,

microcosmic version of Hesiod's *theogony.* Consequently, they explored
the dramatic, constitutive processes which might be imagined as the background history of the ego or the self in individual persons. That is to say,
they attempted to track the evolution of the self by observing speculatively the sequential stages whereby the preself or the not-yet-formed self
is gradually transformed into a mature consciousness capable of knowing
both itself and the world in which it finds itself. These transcendentalists
shared with their Jungian and structuralist counterparts a sort of contempt
for the notions that the mature consciousness itself was capable of arriving at. The world developed by consciousness was a mere construction, a
fiction, whose substance was a set of verbal ghosts imposed on consciousness as the reward, or penalty, of maturation through the acquisition of
language. The true reality was the metaphysical realm of the pre-self, a
realm wherein consciousness was forged, as upon an anvil. A sound grasp
of the metaphysics of this realm would serve the adept as an antidote to
the judgments later passed off as "knowledge" by a consciousness forget-
ful of its own formation process.

A formidable practitioner of psychological transcendentalism in the
above sense is the critic Julia Kristeva, who, in her "search for that which
produces, shapes, and exceeds the operating consciousness,"[29] has found
it useful to posit a distinction between what she terms the *semiotic* component of language and the *symbolic* component. The pre-self or proto-self
makes its appearance in the semiotic component, whereas the fully-formed
self, the ego, is operative in the symbolic. The implications of psychogenesis
as a whole are displayed to the adept in the subsisting relations between
these two components, which are mutually necessary or correlative in virtually every instance of language but at the same time opposing or antithetical in their tendencies, like Love and Strife in Empedocles, or like the
Indeterminate and the Determined in Anaximander (who, of all the ancient
cosmologists, comes closest to prefiguring Kristeva's microcosmology).
The semiotic component is the preverbal disposition *toward* language,
which has no access to signs, no means to predicate, no way of focusing
on a signified object, and "therefore no operating consciousness." It is
best regarded, says Kristeva, as "an uncertain and indeterminate articulation because it does not yet refer (for young children) or no longer refers
(in psychotic discourse) to a signified object for a thetic consciousness."
The semiotic remains, however, the permanent substratum of all discourse,

waxing larger in the multiplicity or indeterminacy of poetry, almost disappearing in the seemingly clear determinations of science. The semiotic is associated with the rhythms and pulsations of the infantile body, being "detected genetically in the first echolalias of infants as rhythms and intonations anterior to the first phonemes, morphemes, lexemes, and sentences." Indeed, semiotic activity is "a mark of the workings of drives" stemming from "the archaisms of the semiotic body," a body "dependent vis-à-vis the mother." It is, in essence, the aboriginal expression of "instinctual drive and continuous relation to the mother." Unfortunately, in the process of maturation, the ego comes to realize the symbolizing powers of language and immerses itself in meanings or significations at the expense of the old semiotic activity, which is consequently repressed. The symbolic function of language becomes operative in terms of "the thetic and predicative constraints of the ego's judging consciousness." Everywhere the semiotic threatens to bubble up and reclaim its ancient rights, but the symbolic is always there, imposing law and order by means of its clear, univocal significations. Thus, the warm blandishments of the somatic and the maternal are ever at war with the cold dictates of the intellectual and the paternal. Never finally subdued, the semiotic disposition persists in language (maximally in poetry) in order "to signify what is untenable in the symbolic, nominal, paternal function" which seeks to master it.

In Kristeva's description of it, the whole thing is a sort of morality play in which the imprudently exiled energy of the body—"the nonsemanticized instinctual drive that precedes and exceeds meaning"—appropriately disrupts (always minimally, in modern literature maximally) the usurping power of rational consciousness. In fact, the ordinary selfhood of the actual, individual person, in this gigantic contest of powers, or dispositions, or functions, is swallowed up. At best, it is only one of many sites where the contest is going on, "a kind of crossroads where things happen," as Lévi-Strauss would say. At worst, it functions as one of the artificially stabilized "signifieds," testifying to a fixation with identity and permanence. This is true not only of personal identity but also with respect to "man as signified phenomenon." Instead of soaring upward into the unity of the super-subject, Kristeva drops into "the gap opened up between signifier and signified" in order to pursue "a questionable subject-in-process" which may be supposed to exist "in an economy of discourse other than that of thetic consciousness." Discourse is here conceived as the substance of all appearances, the first principle of everything that is or can be determined through the reciprocal waxing and waning of the semiotic and the symbolic (viewed mythically as countervailing tendencies or forces). In effect, Kristeva accomplishes a sophisticated return to the metaphysics of the pre-Socratics, whose Titanic thoughts are deliberately recuperated in renewed opposition to the Olympian "ascendence of theoretical reason."

The political or sociological version of transcendentalism was just as various in its options as the psychological version. Here too there was a structuralist option, made venerable through a tradition going back to Marx himself, but not limited only to Marxists. According to this option, thoughts and opinions emanating from particular persons were to be regarded as expressions of the socio-economic position of those persons in the all-inclusive political structure that made them possible. Thoughts and opinions were always ideological in nature, that is to say, they were always explicable in terms of the point of view that organized them, and this point of view was itself accounted for by referring to the structural position of the thinkers who had it, as defined by their class, race, or gender. The transcendental conditions of thinking were thus the conditions imposed by the position of particular thinkers in the overall structure of society. If one pressed forward with considerations based on the interests and conclusions of consciousness, one found oneself in a world of fictions, full of wish-fulfillments and rationalizations. The right way was to work backward from the fictional signifieds to the home-base ideologies that had spawned them, and from thence to the structural position that accounted for the ideologies. At the end of the line was the structure itself—Society—the ultimate author of the notions appearing in the heads of thinkers. This was the political version of the supersubject sought after by Jung and Lévi-Strauss. To many, it seemed less metaphysical in political terms or in terms of sociology, but it was still, for all that, a matter of metaphysics. Indeed, the social supersubject was practically invisible to thinkers who restricted themselves to the manifest content of consciousness, riddled as that was with ideological mystifications. It required, in order to be seen, the presence of a transcendental philosopher, who, like Dr. Pangloss, could translate seemingly unrelated or miscellaneous phenomena back into the structural coherence of politics, conceived as the metaphysical substrate of everything else. Thales had worked pretty much the same way with water, establishing what was later to become a familiar pattern. According to Thales, there was water (which everybody could see) and then there was everything else that was seemingly not water but was, in fact, a modification of water, despite appearances to the contrary. Thus, there was *ordinary* water alongside other things, and there was *metaphysical* water, the underlying substance or principle of every appearance, making it possible to say that all things have the deep structure of water, that deep down things are really watery or water-like. Similarly, the transcendental philosopher, pursuing the supersubject of Society, found it convenient to distinguish between politics as a particular form of human activity, alongside other forms or other interests, and politics conceived as the underlying substance or principle of every activity. Thus, after the fashion of Thales, it seemed possible to say that politics (in the metaphysical sense) was really at the bottom of everything, that all notions, all occurrences, all situations, were in fact deeply political, when rightly understood.

Just as the pre-Socratic cosmologists had trouble fixing on which substance or principle was to be regarded as truly ultimate, going sometimes with water, sometimes with air, sometimes with fire or earth (and sometimes with dynamic combinations of such elements), so the transcendentalists focused sometimes on the politics of class, sometimes on the politics of gender or race, and sometimes on the dynamic interaction of these fundamental elements. Usually, it was necessary to invoke at some point a philosophy of history in order to explain social transformations, not in terms of the opinions or decisions of individual persons, but in terms of the underlying, dialectical development of the social supersubject, unfolding according to its own necessary laws. Particular societies in particular periods of history had imagined themselves (or their various constitutive institutions) to be based on the natural order of things, or on the dictates of the Divine Will, or on concepts of what is fitting or just. In reality, all manner of thinking about such matters was itself socially constructed and thus could not be appealed to as the cause of its own concoction. The actually existing structure of society was, on the other hand, precisely the cause of all those dreams of justification or legitimation that society had had about itself prior to the advent of the new transcendentalists. It seemed relatively simple, after all, to engage in historical studies that would bypass the self-deceived consciousness of previous social formations and go directly to the underlying metaphysical substance of that consciousness, which is to say, to the absolute, ungrounded reality of class relations, race relations, or gender relations.

The resulting discoveries usually had to do with large-scale patterns. As it turned out, society had been mostly a grim affair, involving class conflict, race conflict, and gender conflict. Despite the complexities of the details of these conflicts, the basic situation was always the same: a dominant group could always be detected in the act of suppressing, through violence, duplicity, or ideological bemusement, a subordinate group composed of "others." If cultural materials were sifted long enough and patiently enough, they could always be shown to be more or less disguised expressions of this basic situation. Again, the transcendental inquirer was obliged to become a sort of natural theologian, postulating from "the peculiar quality" of cultural products that "there must be something behind them from which they originate." Since this something could not be the design of nature or the will of God, it had to be the malevolent energy of the social supersubject. Just as Eliot had hypostasized, as an awesome thing, "the mind of Europe," so the political transcendentalists hypostasized the mind of Western society or Western culture as a vicious or handicapped thing, afflicted with a genius for oppression and exploitation, and characterized by certain inveterate propensities, such as logocentrism, Eurocentrism, phallocentrism, and other centrisms bent on turning away from (or mastering) whatever might be deemed marginal or eccentric. While ordinary intellectuals contented themselves with the themes and issues that comprise the manifest content of Western thought, the political transcendentalists explored the metaphysical underworld of these all-determining centrisms.

Most of the structuralizing transcendentalists felt that the actual structure of society *could* be described or specified at any given moment, provided there was enough information to work with. Instead of musing on the tropisms or centrisms of Western society as a whole from Homer to the present, the Marxists, for example, focused more narrowly on the injustice of capitalist social structures since the Industrial Revolution. The ideology that sustained these structures was their special target, and their ambition was to demonstrate the difference between the true nature of the structures and the false description of them that had been generated by their supporting ideology. A further ambition was to reconstitute society according to a new plan designed to secure justice as a demonstrable feature of new social structures. A different group of transcendentalists—the poststructuralists—noticed that the structuralist project could not be carried out except on the basis of knowledge. Indeed, the whole thing seemed to depend on the assumption that reliable knowledge had been ascertained, or at least was potentially ascertainable, through the human sciences. If this knowledge was itself arbitrarily or problematically constituted, transcendentally conditioned by its own formation processes, skewed or vectored in ways not yet sufficiently noticed, then it was, after all, an insecure foundation. It looked as though perhaps the structuralists hadn't been transcendental enough in basing themselves on the constructed knowledges achieved by the human sciences (history, economics, psychology, and so on). It might be more transcendental to inquire into the conditions that had shaped the consciousness reflected in the canons of these very sciences. An exemplary practitioner of the new inquiry was Michel Foucault, who was openly skeptical of the large-scale patterns adduced by the various "knowers" of society on whom the structuralists depended. Foucault made it his task to show that much of what we take for granted as simply "scientific" or "objective" knowledge is really the byproduct or outcome of social and political forces whose influence on what we take to be true or real has been forgotten.

Foucault's project seemed eminently empirical and practical. His idea was to produce a concrete historical account of the "discursive practices" that had led to the adoption of principles and notions eventually regarded as axiomatic by the sciences they were responsible for creating. In order to criticize the world created and presided over by knowledge, it was necessary to understand how knowledge itself had emerged in the context of actual historical situations and in response to the social and political pressures at work in those situations. From his own researches, Foucault concluded that the theories and practices that tend to guide our conceptions of human nature and human society are, in fact, based on arbitrary or problematic distinctions between what is rational and what is irrational, what is normal and what is abnormal, what is natural and what is unnatural, and so on. The gist of the human sciences has been to establish certain right ways of thinking about the nature of human beings, which, in turn, have had the effect of making it possible to determine which behaviors may be deemed socially appropriate and which may be deemed inappropriate. If these distinctions could be shown to be arbitrary or political at their point of origin, then the intellectual and social institutions that lean upon them and give them currency might themselves be deprived of their own legitimacy. It was a radical idea, and it seemed to go deeper than the structuralists had gone, precisely because it was skeptical of the whole project of organizing knowledge in such a way as to arrive at appropriate or definitive structures capable of producing right accounts of things or right remedies. Foucault's approach was widely influential and eventually inspired such critics as the New Historicists.

Was there anything metaphysical about it? There seemed not to be. It was just a history of certain key moments when fundamental assumptions had been made, when fundamental attitudes and orientations had been established, which would be determinative with respect to subsequent research and transcendental with respect to the knowledge produced by that research. It was a history that brought the transcendental down to earth by exposing its empirical origins and circumstances. Of course, there was no way to avoid at least some reliance on already established knowledge, and so, to a degree, Foucault's own researches might be accused of employing, or reinscribing, notions and assumptions as political or arbitrary in their own origins as the ones they were being used to investigate. As Foucault himself explained in an interview with Duccio Trombadori: "In the course of my works, I utilize methods that are part of the classic repertory: demonstration, proof by means of historical documentation, quoting other texts, referral to authoritative comments, the relationship between ideas and facts, the proposal of explanatory patterns, etc. . . . From this point of view, whatever I assert in my writing can be verified or refuted as in any other history book."[30] A serious questioning of the reliability of knowledge that was itself dependent on knowledge even as it engaged in the act of producing knowledge seemed peculiar to some. It might just be that some knowledge was problematic whereas other knowledge was not, but Foucault appeared to be suggesting that it was not the content but rather the rules and mechanisms governing knowledge production per se that were the problem. Self-consciousness about the problematic status of truth in general seemed to require that the "truth" of one's own work be acknowledged as similarly or equally problematic. Said Foucault: "The problem of the truth of what I say is very difficult for me, and it's also the central problem. It's essentially the question which up to now [1970] I have never answered." One way to approach the problem was simply to admit that *no* scholarship could escape the condition of being conditioned, the condition of being a fabrication. "People who read me," said Foucault to Trombadori, "even those who appreciate what I do, often say to me, laughing, 'but in the end you realize that the things you say are nothing but fictions!' I always reply: who ever thought he was writing anything but fiction?" This reply in fact suggested something of great importance. If the content of all knowledge (including that contained in the criticism of knowledge) was fiction, the important thing would not be to replace a "wrong" content with a "right" content. The important thing would be to resist the canonization or institutionalization of certain privileged fictions at the expense of whatever it was the privileged fictions arbitrarily ruled out or excluded. The manifest content of knowledge—anybody's knowledge—was, in a way, beside the point. The essential thing was to determine who was using knowledge to exercise power, or maintain control, over whom. How were they doing it, and at what human cost? Knowledge was a smoke screen for power, and power was the metaphysical substratum.

What made power metaphysical for Foucault was that it was finally so nebulous, so difficult to pin down. The development of schemes for placing it in the right places, even for distributing it equally all around, was precisely the problem. Politicians—even Marxists—were always trying to help people out by thinking up programs or policies or systems that would solve the problem, but programs, policies, and systems *were* the problem. The type of coercion that Foucault wished to examine was intrinsic, it seemed, to all kinds of structure, all kinds of authority, all kinds of institution. Resistance to power could not be organized or programmed without becoming the opposite of itself. Foucault's critique of knowledge was finally a criticism of the human sciences for defining "man" and for producing categories that restrict human possibility. When Foucault spoke of "the death of man," he did not mean, as was sometimes supposed, that there was no such thing as man or human nature. He meant that man became a ridiculous caricature of himself when reduced to being an object of study by the human sciences or when produced as a known phenomenon in connection with scientific research. The genuine nature of man simply eluded the clumsiness, the fixity, of categorical description.

At the heart of the human sciences was not to be found the "human essence." If the promise of the human sciences had been to allow us to discover man, they certainly hadn't maintained it. But as a general cultural

experience, it was a matter rather of the constitution of a new "subjectivity" through the operation of a "reduction" of the human subject into an
object of knowledge *(connaissance).* (123)

In one sense, man died or disappeared when the analytical probings of
science failed to turn up anything that could be identified as man's nature
or man's essence. In another sense, however, "man" as the residuum produced by just these probings is also scheduled to disappear as soon as the
silly categories employed therein are exposed as the pernicious fabrica-
tions they really are. Man as conceived by psychology, sociology, anthropology, and so on, will die as soon as the authority of these sciences is
recognized as arbitrary. The "death of man" in this sense of the term, the
death of man as a reduced object with an ascertainable content, was wel-
comed by Foucault because it meant that the real man, who eludes categories and descriptions, will be back again. Man as the knowable phenomenon
will have given way to man as an infinite, never-to-be-pinned-down, absolute spirit, for whom Western science itself can only be a passing phase, a
strictly temporary incarnation of itself. Foucault took man in the latter
sense of the term very seriously indeed; it is not this man who is destined
to die, but rather the stick-figure of pretentious science.

Foucault was not an essentialist because he did not believe that man
has a content with specific qualities. Rather, he believed, it is man's glory
and agony to be an infinite spirit, never to be fixed but always in the process of becoming "other" than itself, "different" from itself, "more" or
"less" than itself. The content of Foucault's metaphysics (for the most
part, implicit in his satires on sham objectivity) comes through clearly in
this passage:

> [I]n the course of their history, men had never ceased constructing them-
> selves, that is, to shift continuously the level of their subjectivity, to consti-
> tute themselves in an infinite and multiple series of different subjectivities
> that would never place us in the presence of something that would be "man."
> Man is an animal of experience, he is involved *ad infinitum* within a pro-
> cess that, by defining a field of objects, at the same time changes him,
> deforms him, transforms him and transfigures him as a subject.[31]

Ordinary humanism had to be rejected because it came too close to saying
that man was something in particular that ought to be perpetuated just as it
is. Foucault thus had trouble with Marx's phrase "man produces man":

> For me, what must be produced is not man identical to himself, exactly as nature would have designed him or according to his essence; on the contrary, we must produce something that doesn't yet exist and about which we cannot know how it will be. (121)

The idea that "researchers" might build up piles of information-bits, like giant sand-heaps, without being touched or transformed in the process, seemed ridiculous to Foucault. Of course, such persons were constructing for themselves the identity of sand-heap collectors. The routinization of both science and society was the true death of the spirit, although at the same time it was also one of the forms that the spirit had chosen for itself in the course of its ceaseless transmogrifications. Resistance to that form was really a pressing onward of the process through what might be described as a closer identification *with* the process. The truth was not to *be,* but to be always *becoming.* Following the example of Nietzsche, Blanchot, and Bataille (and, in fact, aligning himself with a tradition that includes Emerson and reaches back ultimately to the German Romantics), Foucault tried hard to elude objectification and to be instead truly spiritual by being always in a state of process or transition. Of his own books he wrote:

> [T]he books I write constitute an experience for me that I'd like to be as rich as possible. . . . I write precisely because I don't know yet what to think about a subject that attracts my interest. In so doing, the book transforms me, changes what I think. As a consequence, each new work profoundly changes the terms of thinking which I had reached with the previous work. . . . When I write, I do it above all to change myself and not to think the same thing as before. . . . Thus I don't construct a general method of definitive value for myself or others. What I write does not prescribe anything, neither to myself nor to others. At most, its character is instrumental and visionary or dream-like.[32]

Experience was sought after, not so that knowledge could be built up, but so that the subject or the self could be obliterated in its current shape and thus acquire a new shape. The subject, Foucault thought, must be torn away from itself

> in such a way that it is no longer the subject as such, or that it is completely "other" than itself so that it may arrive at its annihilation, its dissociation.
>   It is this de-subjectifying undertaking, the idea of a "limit-experience"

that tears the subject from itself, which is the fundamental lesson that I've learned from these authors [Nietzsche, Blanchot, and Bataille]. And no matter how boring and erudite my resulting books have been, this lesson has always allowed me to conceive them as direct experiences to "tear" me from myself, to prevent me from always being the same.[33]

In short, the metaphysics of Foucault is the metaphysics of infinite subjectivity, which is opposed, not only to finite subjectivity in the form of the various roles imposed on us by society, but also to finite subjectivity in the form of the various definitions of "man" imposed on us by science. The function of a transcendental inquiry is to show that cultural materials are inevitably saturated with the traces of these impositions, which have had (and continue to have) the effect of impeding or obscuring the exercise of our own infinite subjectivity. The subtext of all literary works, including even those composed by the adept, would be the implied drama wherein the author has succumbed to current conceptual limitations or in some way been affected by the politics that has produced them. But in the compositions of the adept, there would be more evidence of resistance and, eventually, the singular presence of a confession testifying to the virtual necessity of authorial bemusement, despite the intransigence of resistance to the same. There was, it would seem, a striking resemblance between Foucault's metaphysics of infinite subjectivity and Kristeva's metaphysics of "the questionable subject-in-process," and twenty-five or thirty years earlier the term "existentialism" would have been used without hesitation to denote both positions. But the time for that had passed, and a new set of terminologies had come into fashion.

Concomitant with psychological and sociological transcendentalism was linguistic transcendentalism. This transcendentalism also swept past the ostensible notions or manifest content of consciousness in order to find a deeper reality that was shaping consciousness and determining its productions. This deeper reality proved to be language itself. The world around us was reducible to our ideas about it, because the only access to that world was through ideas. Similarly, ideas were reducible to the expressions that were made of them, because the only access to consciousness was through the articulation of its contents. Just as there were no things apart from ideas, so there were no ideas apart from expressions. Whereas the original transcendentalists, following Kant, had surmised that the things we know must be conformed to the knowledge we have of them, the linguistic transcendentalists surmised that knowledge itself must be conformed to the expressions wherein it resides. Thus, through yet another extension of the Copernican Revolution, language, as the matrix of thought, became the transcendental condition of thought. As far as literary criticism was concerned, the option might still be exercised of remaining on the level of the ideas or notions that a work of art appeared to be expressing, which is to say, on the level of the representations it contained of the world or of its author's view of the world. But to do this would be to remain fascinated by the manifest content of the work, by the fictions or virtual realities associated with this content. The true content was to be found only in the verbal mechanisms that were actually responsible for producing the work's appearances. The difference between the manifest content and these mechanisms was precisely the difference between appearance and reality. Serious critics accordingly turned their attention to the task of explaining how the language of a work was responsible for creating the apparent meanings that the work seemed to be projecting.

Saussure's distinction between the signified and the signifier was regarded by many as decisive. The signified was what a signifier meant or imported. It was, quite simply, the significance of a sign. The signifier was the sign itself. Objects could appear only to the extent that they could be signified, which meant they were dependent on the vehicle of the sign. But the sign, as it turned out, was not reciprocally dependent on the content of its signification. To account for a sign, one could not appeal to what it signified. The sign was what it was because of the way it was differentiated from other signs. It had differential relations *only with other signs* in the same sign system. The parts of a language referred to other parts of the same language, not to external realities. The supposition that the operations of language were determined or constrained by the necessity to conform to anything outside of language was dismissed as a pre-Copernican superstition. In departments of language and literature, the separation of the signifier from the signified was seen as the last blow to the correspondence theory of truth. Language had become the self-communing absolute ground of whatever could be signified. Its long, misconceived vassalage to reality was at last known to have been based on an illusion. Because of the dependence of all signified entities on language, and because of the independence and autonomy of language in relation to the significations produced by language, it was finally clear that language was the ultimate principle of all things, or the metaphysical substance of things. Here again, the essential paradigm had been established by Thales with regard to the metaphysics of water. Just as there had been, for Thales, ordinary water (alongside other things) and metaphysical water (the underlying principle of all things), so, for the linguistic transcendentalists, there was ordinary language (such as French or Russian) and there was metaphysical language (conceived as the underlying explanatory principle of all things whatsoever). As we have seen, Lévi-Strauss was among those who surmised that "all forms of social life" might best be studied using the model of structural linguistics, which is to say, by regarding them as sign-systems composed of phoneme-like elements having internal structural relations with each other according to the principle of binary opposition, combination, or correlation. A chain of signifiers might be composed of ordinary words (in the case of languages like French or Russian), but it might also be composed of aunts and uncles, if one were thinking of a kinship-system as a kind of language or as a linguistic phenomenon consisting of arrangements of signifying elements. It might be composed of hemlines and waistlines if one were thinking of clothes-fashion as an expressive or communicative language. In this way, the study of sign-systems could be detached from the study of merely verbal phenomena and applied in a much broader way to virtually any phenomena that might be conceived as intelligible or comprehensible. There might be a semiotics of economic transactions or a semiotics of deceit or desire. Nature itself was organized, and behaved, like a language in the totemizing, myth-making consciousness of primitive peoples, but no more so than in the taxonomies and conceptual systems of modern scientists. The unconscious mind, which had hitherto guarded its secrets so jealously, became an open book as soon as Freud and Lacan noticed that it was structured like a language.

Berkeley had claimed that "to be is to be perceived," but the linguistic transcendentalists knew a deeper truth: to be is to be signified. To be signified is to be dependent on a signifier. A signifier cannot exist outside a system of signifiers in which the elements are mutually or reciprocally constitutive of each other. Thus, to be is to be enclosed within language. Language alone (in the metaphysical sense) is truly the Absolute, whether hypostasized as substance or as mind. And yet, somehow, neither hypostasis seemed quite adequate. It *could* be said (and in fact it was said)[34] that "language" . . . thinks man and his world," but to say this one had to reach into the world for a process or an entity (thinking, mind) and then adduce that process or entity as the underlying explanation of the world as a whole. It was the very genius of metaphysics to do this, as was clear from Thales' treatment of water, but it was rather like saying that tortoises, together with everything else in the world, were to be explained by their dependence on a supertortoise. It seemed wrong to take part of a whole, which was itself (like the other parts) in need of explanation, and make it the explanation of the whole from which it was taken. The concept of substance was equally fraught with difficulties, since it too seemed to be based on an analogy with particular known substances. Furthermore, a substance was something signified, just as mind was something signified. No signified phenomenon, no designated entity, could be imagined as the cause of the interacting signifiers upon which its own existence depended. If language (in the metaphysical sense) was indeed absolute, if language could be said to determine or characterize every effort that might be made to determine *it* or characterize *it,* then it was always necessarily in the position of transcending every possible determination or characterization that might be made of it. It was, strictly speaking, impossible to pin down. It could not be supposed to present for contemplation either a definite structure or a specifiable system of its own infinite operations. Strictly speaking, it was indeterminate and nonrectifiable. On the basis of this insight, deconstruction was born.

There was a certain amount of irony in the situation. After it had been decided that all forms of social life were structured like a language, indeed that everything thinkable by consciousness and unconsciousness alike was structured like a language, it seemed odd that language itself should be the one thing that was not structured like a language. But if language was truly infinite or indeterminate, it was hard to see how it could exhibit anything that could be called a structure. A structure required a point of orientation, a center or a focus of operations, some material that it might be said to define, and some way to be seen as a whole so that it might be determined as a structure. But there was nothing outside of language (in the metaphysical sense) to which it might he applied, or which it might be said to organize, or in relation to which it might be defined, or from which it might be distinguished. Being indeterminate, it could not have, it could not be, a structure. Since there was no way to get outside of language, there was no way to view it as a whole or describe it objectively. Its center was simply everywhere and its circumference was nowhere.

The structuralists had hoped that by adducing linguistic or semiotic structures they could call attention to what was transcendental in human awareness of reality, conscious or unconscious. From the point of view of deconstruction, the adducing of such structures required that certain key terms, certain privileged signifiers, be regarded as pointing to something important in reality, some signified phenomenon (like God or the fashion industry) that could be imagined as having relations with other signified phenomena. The structured awareness or behavior of human beings, as they oriented themselves in one way or another to the world around them, was an effort to give all things a stable, determinate meaning. It was an effort to focus on the signified and to make *that* determinative or funda-mental by conforming to its requirements. This penchant for giving an order to things, for thinking and behaving according to systematic pat-terns, was indeed something transcendental with respect to human aware-ness, and it was clearly built into cultural materials and was an aspect of their condition. But deeper still than this penchant was the underlying vola-tility of the signifiers themselves, churning and seething on a level far below all mere arrangements or organizations of them. On this, the lowest of all levels, the relations subsisting within the infinite networks of the signifier took no notice of the requirements laid down by consciousness (or unconsciousness) for a right apprehension of the signified. Language (in the metaphysical sense) as the interminable welter of words, as the structureless sea of signifiers, cared not a straw for the virtual realities summoned up by "key" terms and "privileged" signifiers. Readers and writers were constantly making the mistake of supposing that language might be compelled to elucidate the interests and themes that conscious-ness regarded as important. To a large degree, consciousness might focus its attention exclusively on its favorite notions while engaging in the act of reading or writing. But whether it did so or not, the verbal substratum would go on being itself, providing instance after instance of the multi-plicity or indeterminacy inherent in the implicitly infinite network of sig-nifying signs. The necessity of giving inadvertent testimony to that which both explains and minimalizes virtual reality for consciousness is, for the deconstructionist, the inescapable, built-in condition—a truly transcendental condition—of reading or writing. The sublime power or force that is here ascribed to language (in the metaphysical sense) is, once again, suggestive of Anaximander's account of the Unlimited or the Boundless or the Indeterminate as the eternal beginning and final destination of all that is clear and definite but also unstable and impermanent. All explanations, all determinations, all virtual realities that appear to consciousness, are to be imagined as welling up inexplicably and then subsiding back, like ocean waves, into something (a force, a material) that simply cannot be adequately conceived. Thus, deconstruction hoped to elude metaphysics by hypostasizing the Indeterminate as that which eludes hypostasis.

Taken all together, the transcendentalist critics, in the various forms and schools we have been considering, were among the most powerful intellectuals of the twentieth century. A few of them deigned to call themselves philosophers, but most did not. Instead, they tended to think of themselves, or were thought of by others, as theorists. Theory was apparently capable of giving a deep explanation of the materials and products of culture. Both literature and philosophy were products of culture. Therefore, they were amenable or susceptible to theory-based analysis. On the strength of such reasoning as this, it became possible for literary critics who were theoretically informed to see themselves as the true custodians of literature who had safely bypassed philosophy, leaving it behind as an extinct literary genre or as a relic fit for museum display in the philosophy departments of universities. Meanwhile, throughout the precincts of theory, metaphysical speculation was raging almost uncontrollably, as we have just seen. Precisely because it was not recognized as such, metaphysics, in the form of theory, had a field day. To the degree that it continued to manifest itself in the metaphysical speculations of theory, philosophy continued to maintain its influence on those who asserted the independence of poetry (and other forms of literature) from philosophy.

Despite the fact that their own views of what they were doing could not be considered authoritative, the poets themselves, as I have already suggested, were clearly working in terms of theories—theories, moreover, that were consonant with, or dependent upon, the theories of transcendentalist criticism. Pound and Eliot wrote poems that were allusions to the social or psychological supersubject, conceived as the *Weltgeist* or "the mind of Europe." In this respect, they were comparable to transcendentalists like Jung and Lévi-Strauss, who sought to establish, with respect to knowledge, the priority of large, inclusive patterns. Other poets, such as Frost or Williams or Stevens, worked as the poststructuralists worked, to undermine the validity of patterns and to question the permanence of results. These poets alluded to the fragility, the instability, of truth. Truth, to them, was immediate or temporary, always a fictional construct and therefore always vulnerable to the next wave of experience with its new set of possibilities. This was the other side of the transcendentalist critique of knowledge, which dissolved knowledge into the deeper reality of its own constitutive processes. It was clear, then, whichever way one looked at it, that poetry was in the grip of theory: theory had either spawned it in the heads of poets or else received it in the heads of literary critics. The question of whose theory had priority could be sidestepped by simply declaring the author's intention (what Sidney had referred to as the "idea or foreconceit of the work") a fiction. As a result, poetry fell entirely under the sway of such theory as was at the disposal of the critics, who might use it freely in order to illustrate the metaphysics of the social or psychological super-subject, or the metaphysics of the "questionable subject-in-process," or the metaphysics of infinite subjectivity, or the metaphysics of the signifier. To the extent that the poets themselves were not imagined to be excluded from the wisdom contained in such metaphysics, they enjoyed the co-partnership with philosophy that Aristotle had envisioned for them two thousand years earlier. To the extent that they *were* imagined to be so excluded, they were back where Socrates and Plato had left them, gripped helplessly by forces they knew not of.

The transcendentalist critics had no intention whatsoever of subverting poetry. All they wanted was to subvert the pretensions to knowledge associated with thetic consciousness. Their dismissal of authorial intention was not primarily a judgment against authors; it was a judgment against the view that thetic consciousness ought to be considered authoritative with respect to the cultural products that appeared to emanate from it. Gradually, it became clear that their own analyses might be subjected to the same negative judgment, if they were taken to be a form of knowledge concerning the matters with which they dealt. Their own theories ought to be nothing more than a further exhibition of the conditions and processes they affected to examine. Otherwise, the critique of knowledge would itself be guilty of having pretensions to knowledge no less insupportable than any other such pretensions.

There were essentially two ways of responding to the charge that transcendentalism had inadvertently produced a valid knowledge concerning the processes and conditions of knowledge. One way was to accept the charge as a compliment and then to return the compliment by permitting one's own arguments to be subjected to a transcendental analysis. Cheerfully, the transcendentalists offered up their own productions, not as an embarrassing (because supposedly impossible) exercise in rational thinking, but as a further illustration of the underlying metaphysical realities they themselves had adduced. Thus, Lévi-Strauss did not lord it over others because he had managed to uncover the organizational patterns of the psychological supersubject. Instead, he acknowledged openly that, as much as anyone else, he too was captured and held by just these patterns. His own books had not been produced deliberately through an egotistical act of consciousness; rather, they had "gotten thought" in him through a process "unbeknown" to him. Like everyone else he had studied, he was only a "place where something is going on," a "crossroads where things happen," and the crossroads was "purely passive." Similarly, Kristeva acknowledged, in her essay "From One Identity to an Other," that her own distinction between the semiotic and the symbolic looked suspiciously like a production of thetic consciousness ("one should begin by positing," etc.).[35] But, by virtue of this acknowledgment, she called attention to her own effort to bear witness to, *not* master, a literary experience that "remains nevertheless something other than this analytical theory, which it never stops challenging." As she put it, "It is probably necessary to be a woman . . . not to renounce theoretical reason but to compel it to increase its power by giving it an object beyond its limits." Thus, instead of *being* reasonable, one was really putting reason to the test by showing its limitations, or at least speaking of its limitations, in relation to something incorrigibly "other" than reason. Foucault, for his part, admitted that the character of his own writing was "instrumental and visionary or dream-like." It was, he declared, an exercise in preventing himself from being always "the same" (and besides, "who ever thought he was writing anything but fiction?").

In essence, these transcendentalists managed to have their cake and eat it too. By offering up their own productions as further evidence of the metaphysical processes and substances they themselves had shown to be inherent in all cultural phenomena, they could both affirm and deny their own special authority in relation to the matters they discussed. Their own arguments locked into place and became virtually unassailable the moment they were dissolved into the metaphysical components that transcendentalism itself had called attention to. In this way, any weakness or unsoundness that might be detected in a transcendentalist argument could be explained by referring to the incorrigible properties of the metaphysical substratum, which were always manifesting themselves in ways that exceeded or disrupted the conventions of mere argument. It was a no-lose situation, since the transcendentalists were, in effect, right when they were right and right when they were wrong. A further consequence of allowing their own arguments to be dissolved into the metaphysical realities they themselves discovered was that the transcendentalists could thereby join hands with all the other producers of cultural expressions. In accordance with the fact that one's favorite form of metaphysics had the power to supply a unified field for explaining all cultural materials, distinctions between disciplines and genres collapsed. The opposition between poetry and philosophy could at last be seen as a superficial opposition between different sets of intentions. If authorial intention could be disregarded with respect to poets, it could also be disregarded with respect to philosophers or theorists. If thetic consciousness was relatively trivial, it was so all across the field. The deep metaphysical realities that expressed themselves in poems were essentially no different from those that expressed themselves in bus schedules or philosophical treatises. To the discerning eye, there was a continuity of force or a continuity of substance that absolutely connected all forms of expression, apart from the egotistical designs of their human fabricators. The transcendentalists could claim, on these terms, to be just as "unknowing" as the poets they studied, being unable to control by their own intentions the metaphysical realities that expressed themselves, by necessity, in their works.

The next step was to appropriate the term "poetry" in such a way as to identify it with the latent content of all cultural materials, including the texts produced by transcendentalist criticism. Thus, on one side of a divided line there was thetic consciousness, which concerned itself with "signified" phenomena or "virtual" realities and which consequently produced a "manifest" content of messages on the level of what Kristeva called "the symbolic." On the other side of the line, there was the social or the psychological supersubject, or the questionable subject-in-process, or language conceived as the Absolute, which was itself the "latent" content, or the "actual" reality, of the chain of signifiers, grasped, on the level of what Kristeva called "the semiotic," as medium rather than as message. By using "poetry" as a general term for whatever appeared on the second side of the line and "philosophy" as an equally general term for whatever appeared on the first side, the transcendentalists who were so inclined could claim not only that they were sympathetic to poetry but also, more emphatically, that they themselves were poets. By holding fast to these arguments, one could make any argument disappear into the background and, at the same time, make the poetic substance of argument loom large in the foreground. Through metaphysics, the ancient quarrel between philosophy and poetry could be resolved in favor of poetry, after all.[36]

This, as I have said, was one way of responding to the charge that transcendentalism could not take into account its own seemingly valid knowledge of the limits and conditions of knowledge. Like Wittgenstein at the end of the *Tractatus,* the transcendentalists imagined that it might be possible to renounce ex post facto the very arguments that had led them to conclude that argumentation was illusory or spurious. It was like producing a text that understood that its own propositions about meaningfulness were themselves, by their own authority, meaningless. For the transcendentalists who took this route, the Cretan liar paradox became the moment of "the uncanny" in which self-consciousness attained its highest peak of intensity.

But there was another way to detach oneself from the philosophical or theoretical side of transcendentalism, and it was this second way that was chosen by the more pragmatic transcendentalists, such as Richard Rorty and Stanley Fish. The pragmatists remembered that the goal of transcendentalism was to expose the transcendental character of thinking or interpreting without making the mistake of explaining these processes in terms of their own products or in terms of the objects that thinking and interpreting themselves had invented. But the only way to give an account of these processes was to think about them or to interpret them, and thus all the problems and ambiguities associated with the phenomena one wished to investigate would necessarily be incorporated into the activity of one's own investigation. Thinking about thinking would be like interpreting interpretation. Whatever the foibles or limitations that characterized the nature of thinking, they could only be repeated transcendentally in the thinking that presumed to expose them. The idea that there could be a valid knowledge concerning the conditions of knowledge was therefore a hopeless illusion, forever dependent on the presuppositions as well as the conclusions that it was trying to examine. A skeptical critic might observe that, although the pragmatists were determined to regard the entire transcendentalist project as futile and self-defeating, their own determination of this fact was itself dependent on the transcendentalist insight that the conditions of knowledge cannot be properly explained by an appeal to the objects that knowledge itself has constituted. Thus it happened again that transcendentalism became the basis for a repudiation of the transcendentalist inquiry.

There was, however, a difference between the theorists and the pragmatists with respect to the manner in which they concealed their own philosophizing. The theorists imagined that all projects, behaviors, and expressions (including those associated with philosophy) would simply pale by comparison, or else disappear from view altogether, when placed alongside the metaphysical realms to which they had called attention. By virtue of their awful grandeur, these realms had it in their power to scatter or absorb all mere arguments and notions concerning themselves. The pragmatists rightly feared, however, that these realms would prove embarrassing if they were taken as the ground, rather than the result, of acts of interpretation. There was simply no getting around or getting past interpretation: to focus on interpretation could never be anything more than to interpret it, and there was no sense waxing mystical about the uncanniness of the transcendental regress. The upshot of all this for the pragmatists was that the persons (or groups of persons) who produced interpretations were to be understood as the bedrock explanation of the interpretations they produced. Metaphysics went up in a puff of smoke, and when the air had cleared, there were only people to be seen, engaged in their various interpretive activities in ways that grounded their ideas but that were not grounded by ideas, apart from the ideas formed about them in the heads of other persons engaged in similar interpretive activities. Notions of reality could be explained as a function of the actions of persons, but these actions could not themselves be explained as a function of any real situation without appealing to a notion of that situation that was itself a function of the actions of persons. "Busy day, busy people" was the bottom line of transcendentalism, the terminus of the transcendental regress.

The poststructuralists wavered slightly between attachment to their own theories and the recognition, which they shared with the pragmatists, that even these same theories ought to be regarded as properly belonging to the "philosophy" side of the divided line, the side presided over by thetic consciousness. They expressed misgivings concerning their own demonstrations, they crossed out or put "under erasure" their own concepts, and they acknowledged the constantly mutating character of their own interpretive activity. (As we have seen, Kristeva openly admitted the irony of positing a distinction between "the semiotic" and "the symbolic" that might be supposed to give an accurate account of the character of their mutual relations, while Foucault admitted the priority of eluding all existing conceptions of things, including his own.) But the pragmatists wished to be even more resolute in resisting the blandishments of theory, and, from their point of view, the poststructuralists were themselves liable to be misconstrued because of the Heideggerian mists that still enveloped their rhetoric. From the pragmatist point of view, the right way to proceed was not to vanish into one or another of the metaphysical realms that had been conjured up by theory. The right way was to insist on a full recognition of the subordinate status of theories with respect to persons. The way to be "poetical" was not to identify oneself with the productive power of the supersubject or the infinite volatility of the linguistic medium or the indeterminate articulations of infants and psychotics. It was to make an open display of one's personal independence, or spiritual freedom, in opposition to all mere theories, even the ones spawned by transcendentalism. As pure egotism, intention was reinstated.

To be "poetical" was not to be possessed or inspired or an unknowing crossroads or the site of a contest between mythical forces or tendencies. It was to be self-conscious, willful, and, above all, playful. It was to make deliberate gestures, sometimes in a show of solidarity, sometimes in a show of opposition, with regard to other persons. Very broadly, the world could be divided into those who knew that notions were subordinate to persons and those who still believed that persons ought to be conformed to, or explained by, notions. The task of persons in the first group was not to produce a right account of things or to wax metaphysical; it was to give a display of personal power sufficient to convert or confound persons who insisted on remaining in the second group. As Rorty explained, it would be folly to seek to *demonstrate* that poetical gestures were superior to philosophical arguments or that knowledge was not all it was cracked up to be, because such demonstrations, as the transcendentalists had discovered, were necessarily self-defeating. What was required was a superbly ungrounded exhibition of poetical willfulness or poetical power:

> The *weakest* way to defend the plausible claim that literature has now displaced religion, science, and philosophy as the presiding discipline of our culture is by looking for a philosophical foundation for the practices of contemporary criticism. That would be like defending Galilean science by claiming that it can be found in the scriptures, or defending transcendental idealism as the latest result of physiological research. It would be acknowledging the authority of a deposed monarch in order to buttress the claims of a usurper. The claims of a usurping discipline to preside over the rest of culture can only be defended by an exhibition of its ability to put the other disciplines in their places.[37]

In other words, instead of trying to demonstrate that literature (or poetry, as I have been calling it) is deeper or nearer to the truth of things than philosophy, the shrewd critic will permit his or her criticism to be an open display of poetical techniques or rhetorical manipulations with respect to whatever materials have offered themselves up to be thus shaped or worked. After all, the significance of Derrida's criticism was not that Derrida had discovered the truth about texts (for example, that they are irreducibly poetical in the richness or complexity of their meanings) but that he had exercised his option to play around poetically with the texts he chose to interpret:

> Derrida regards the need to overcome "the book"—the notion of a piece of writing as aimed at accurate treatment of a subject, conveying a message which (in more fortunate circumstances) might have been conveyed by ostensive definition or by injecting knowledge straight into the brain—as justifying his use of any text to interpret any other text. The most shocking thing about his work—even more shocking than, though not as funny as, his sexual interpretations of the history of philosophy—is his use of multilingual puns, joke etymologies, allusions from anywhere to anywhere, and phonic and typographical gimmicks. It is as if he really thought that the fact that, for example, the French pronunciation of "Hegel" sounds like the French word for "eagle" was supposed to be relevant for comprehending Hegel. But Derrida does not want to comprehend Hegel's books; he wants to play with Hegel. He doesn't want to write a book about the nature of language; he wants to play with the texts which other people have thought they were writing about language.[38]

In fact, what Rorty noticed (and approved of) was that Derrida had not subordinated himself to the materials with which he concerned himself but instead had shaped them in such a way as to make them a vehicle for his own self-expression. And he had done this in order to assert the autonomy of his own sensibility in opposition to the apparently objective claims and requirements of so-called reality. It was not a new position, after all, although it seemed such to many of Derrida's readers. It was, at bottom, a return to the position that had been developed by the German Romantics, particularly by Friedrich von Schlegel, and that Hegel had discussed under the rubric of "irony" in his analysis of the dissolution of art. It was a position that Hegel associated with the idealism of Fichte, and thus it had been worked out as a consequence of the first wave of transcendentalist philosophizing initiated by Kant. In the twentieth century, it appeared once again as the logical consequence of the newer forms of transcendentalism that had occupied the century's intellectuals. The fact that Hegel's description of it remains pertinent to its most recent incarnations bears witness not only to the power of his philosophy but also to the continuing presence of Romantic ideas in contemporary thought. It is, therefore, to Hegel's analysis of irony as a consequence of transcendentalist theorizing that we must now turn our attention.

CHAPTER 2

HEGEL'S CONCEPT OF THE DISSOLUTION OF ART

For many contemporary students of art, the most surprising thing in Hegel's lectures on fine art is the judgment that art has come to the end of its development, that "for us art counts no longer as the highest mode in which truth fashions an existence for itself," since, though "we may well hope that art will always rise higher and come to perfection," the truth is that "the form of art has ceased to be the supreme need of the spirit."[1] This judgment often comes as a shock, and, to students of nineteenth- and twentieth-century art especially, it must seem both mistaken and perverse. Could it not be taken as simply another piece of evidence that Hegel was compelled by his system to imagine his own time and place as the culmination of history? Surely art has gone on developing throughout the various periods and movements that have come along since Hegel's time. There have been schools and programs almost without number, and in the modern period particularly the intention of being profoundly experimental or radically new was frequently proclaimed. How then is it possible to take Hegel's judgment seriously? How can it be taken as expressing anything other than narrowness of mind? Heidegger, we know, took it very seriously. Writing in 1935, he says:

> The judgment that Hegel passes in these statements cannot be evaded by pointing out that since Hegel's lectures in aesthetics were given for the last time during the winter of 1828–29 at the University of Berlin, we have seen the rise of many new art works and new art movements. Hegel never meant to deny this possibility. But the question remains: is art still an essential and necessary way in which that truth happens which is decisive for our historical existence, or is art no longer of this character? . . . The truth of Hegel's judgment has not yet been decided; for behind this verdict there stands Western thought since the Greeks, which thought corresponds to a truth of beings that has already happened. Decision upon the judgment will be made, when it is made, from and about this truth of what is. Until then the judgment remains in force."[2]

Heidegger, of course, believed that the judgment would collapse as soon as "Western thought" was discerned to be a sort of wrong turn, or digression, away from the truth of Being. Accordingly, he worked hard to outflank the entire tradition on which, it seemed, Hegel's judgment depended. Despite his implicit hostility to the judgment, he was right, I think, to suspect that there are depths within it that need to be examined, if it is to be rightly understood. In fact, I shall argue in this chapter that Hegel's description of the endstage of art (his description, that is, of the dissolution of the romantic form of art) was uncannily prophetic of future developments. Moreover, it is precisely these developments, many of which seek to get around philosophy or to go beyond it (as did Heidegger), that bear out the judgment and keep it "in force."

To begin with, it is necessary to understand what Hegel means when he says that art is no longer "the highest mode" of truth, no longer "the supreme need" of the spirit. This implies that art can still be *one* mode of truth or *one* need of the spirit, just not the *highest* mode or the *supreme* need. It also implies that there was a time when things were different. There was a time when art was the focal point of spirit and truth. The whole of Hegel's *Aesthetics* is, in fact, an account of the constantly shifting ratios between the requirements of spirit and truth, on the one hand, and the capacities of sensuous configuration, on the other. In terms of this account, with its broad categories of Symbolic, Classical, and Romantic art, art becomes intelligible first as a quest for form, then as the achievement of form, and finally as a repudiation of form. In a sequence of phases or stages, the spirit first seeks its reflection, then attains its reflection, and finally scorns its reflection, in the various configurations of which art is capable. Each configuration attests to, or makes possible, a particular type, or a particular degree, of self-consciousness on the part of spirit. Thus, the development of art bears witness to a corresponding development in spiritual self-consciousness. At the beginning of its development, spirit can express itself only by means of art and in terms of art. There is, as yet, no other form of consciousness, no other medium for thinking. Such thinking as is possible makes its appearance as art. Art waxes as the expressive possibilities of sensuous configuration are more and more realized. Eventually, after it attains a sufficient degree of self-consciousness, thinking begins to detach itself, as it were, from the limitations inherent in such configuration, passing first into the form of religion and ultimately into the form of philosophy. In short, as Hegel sees it, there was a time when thinking struggled to raise itself up to the level of art, a time when it might be said to have achieved all that *can* be achieved on the level of art, and finally a time when it became something more or something other than could be made to appear on that particular level. The crucial thing to notice here is that, according to Hegel, the entire process of these spiritual developments is itself reflected after a certain manner in art. Thus, the inability of the spirit to achieve an adequate reflection of itself in art is precisely that which is reflected, eloquently or pathetically, in Symbolic art. Similarly, the achievement of the spirit's reflection of itself in the representation of natural or physical forms, either of gods or of men, is that which is reflected, beautifully, in Classical art. And finally, in the last stage of the process, the insufficiency of sensuous configuration to the requirements of spirit is exactly that which is reflected, or at least suggested, in the configurations of Romantic art. The paradox, then, of the Romantic form of art is that it strikingly expresses in actual works of art the fact that the spirit can no longer express itself completely or satisfactorily by means of artistic representations. Hence, in Hegel's formula, "romantic art is the self-transcendence of art but within its own sphere and in the form of art itself."[3]

If Hegel's account of these matters is followed closely enough, it becomes clear that art "ceased to be the supreme need of the spirit" when first religion, and then philosophy, appeared on the scene. It ceases to be the supreme need of the spirit, not by passing out of existence, but by becoming subordinate to these later forms of spirit. As soon as art is willing to be didactic or allegorical with respect to religious truth or moral truth, at that very moment it is "no longer the highest mode in which truth fashions an existence for itself." In later antiquity after Aristotle, and throughout the whole of the Christian era, this is the position in which art finds itself. Whatever positive truths it may illustrate or inculcate, it is all the while, simultaneously, reflecting the fact that it has gone into service and that, by virtue of its new function, which is to point "beyond itself,"[4] it exists after all in a state of "self-transcendence." Since it has been exhibiting this fact about itself for more than two thousand years now, there is no reason to infer from Hegel's judgment concerning its limits that art has come at last to the end of its tether. There is indeed no reason to suppose that it might not remain indefinitely in the state Hegel calls the state of "self-transcendence."

But, if that is the case, why does Hegel speak as though the art of his own time were going through the pangs of a culminating dissolution? If even Romantic art is capable of reaching a final moment of disintegration, a sort of climactic conclusion beyond which no further development seems possible, does not this portend that art *is* over and done with? One way to answer this last question would be to say that what Hegel means by the dissolution of Romantic art is something that is still going on and might well go on forever. Virtually all the art movements since Hegel's time have exhibited, in one way or another, tendencies or attitudes which Hegel himself described as belonging to the dissolution of Romantic art. This is just as true in the case of modern experimental art as it is in the case of nineteenth-century realist or symbolist art. It is equally true with respect to the various gestures attributed to postmodern art. And since one of the principal gestures of this last kind of art has been to roam freely over the history of art in search of previous styles that might be recycled into new works of art, there is no reason to assume that the future of art may not consist of an endless series of appropriations of what has gone before, or an endless repetition of previous artistic gestures, undertaken in a spirit of sympathy or even in a spirit of irony. Thus, I would argue, we are still moving *through* the process Hegel refers to as the dissolution of Romantic art.

In order to understand what Hegel means by this dissolution, it is necessary to realize that what he was looking at primarily was the phenomenon of German Romanticism. The breakup of what he called the Romantic form of art was, in fact, occurring through the agency of what later scholars would refer to as the Romantic Movement, with which Hegel was exactly contemporary. The effect of Romanticism (in this sense of the term) was, as Hegel saw it, to intensify the already-existing subordination of art to the higher spiritual interests it could never hope to mirror adequately. But, at the same time, this intensified subordination was associated with a new concept of spirit, which demanded that a new set of artistic gestures be made in proper deference to spirit. The old way of being subordinate was no longer adequate now that a new idea of spirit had evolved.

As we have seen, the Romantic form of art (in Hegel's sense of the term) had begun almost as soon as it was recognized that God could not be apprehended properly as a sensuous appearance or natural form. "In general," says Hegel, "it was early in history that thought passed judgement against art as a mode of illustrating the idea of the Divine; this happened with the Jews and Mohammedans, for example, and indeed even with the

Greeks, for Plato opposed the gods of Homer and Hesiod starkly enough."[5] After the Greeks, it became the business of art to elucidate human nature and human destiny according to the conceptions of these things attained by philosophers and theologians. Particular human experiences became intelligible, and thus fit for study or representation, by virtue of the patterns made possible by such conceptions. By pointing beyond itself in this fashion, art produced wonderful things, among them *The Divine Comedy, The Faerie Queene,* and *Paradise Lost,* to mention only literature. Human subjectivity, it might be said, came home to itself or realized itself in a world that transcended particular perceptions. A right apprehension of this world was not taken to be primarily afforded by purely personal experiences. Thus, art was required to live constantly in a state of "self-transcendence" by pointing to the superior reality of the conceptual patterns that rendered personal experience intelligible.

The background of Romanticism (as we now use the term) was the paramount importance given to the inner life by Protestant theology and the equal importance given by modern philosophy to the mechanisms of concept formation. For the German Romantics, it was the philosophy of Kant, especially as interpreted or completed by Fichte, that seemed to require a new conception of spirit and, correspondingly, a new conception of art. According to the new philosophy, as it was understood by the Romantics, the human mind was itself in a position of spiritual authority with regard to all conceptions whatsoever, since, in fact, the origin or seat of both percepts and concepts *was* the human mind. Instead of explaining subjectivity in terms of realities made accessible by religion and philosophy, subjectivity itself became the explanation of just these realities. As a result, the spiritual life seemed best defined by those who evidenced the deepest grasp, or made the freest exercise, of their own subjective powers. Such persons thought of themselves, or were thought of by others, as the absolute spiritual centers of worlds they themselves made through the agency of their own imaginations. From the point of view of the Romantics, it was not only art but also religion and philosophy (as previously accepted) that ceased to be the supreme need of the spirit. Implicitly claiming the standpoint of the spirit, the Romantics tended to regard all embodiments of spirit, all external manifestations of spirit, as impediments to their own grasp of the true nature of spirit, and it is this standpoint, or the effort to reach this standpoint, that accounts for the dissolution of Romantic art, as Hegel describes it. For once again art is required to bear witness to the fact that the spirit that drives it or produces it cannot be given an adequate external form, only this time what is meant by spirit is "the inwardness of heart and thinking."[6]

Without so naming it, Hegel presents what we call Romanticism (i.e., the art of his own contemporaries) as the culmination of tendencies already present from the beginning in the Romantic form of art, and he connects those tendencies with the realization in Christianity that God had become man. Thus, even in Romantic art, the Divine is still "the absolute subject-matter of art":

> But the Divine had to objectify itself, determine itself, and therefore proceed out of itself into the secular content of subjective personality. At first the infinity of personality lay in honour, love, and fidelity and then later in particular individuality, in the specific character which coalesced with the particular content of human existence. Finally this cohesion with such a specific limitation of subject-matter was cancelled by humour which could make every determinacy waver and dissolve and therefore made it possible for art to transcend itself. Yet in this self-transcendence art is nevertheless a withdrawal of man into himself, a descent into his own breast, whereby art strips away from itself all fixed restriction to a specific range of content and treatment, and makes *Humanus* its new holy of holies: i.e. the depths and heights of the human heart as such, mankind in its joys and sorrows, its strivings, deeds, and fates. Herewith the artist acquires his subject-matter in himself and is the human spirit actually self-determining and considering, meditating and expressing the infinity of its feelings and situations. . . .[7]

In reaching its climax, art dissolves in response to the requirement that it be a continual display of the artist's own infinity, to which all fixities of form and content must be sacrificed. In Hegel's words:

> Bondage to a particular subject-matter and a mode of portrayal suitable for this material alone are for artists today something past, and art therefore has become a free instrument which the artist can wield in proportion to his subjective skill in relation to any material of whatever kind. The artist thus stands above specific consecrated forms and configurations and moves freely on his own account, independent of the subject-matter and mode of conception in which the holy and eternal was previously made visible to human apprehension.[8]

Because of his new self-consciousness, the Romantic artist no longer feels bound by the determinate conceptions of religion and philosophy but instead makes himself superior to them, emerging (at least in his own mind) as the highest form of intellectual. Thus:

> The artist need not be forced first to settle his accounts with his mind or to worry about the salvation of his own soul. From the very beginning, before he embarks on production, his great and free soul must know and possess its own ground, must be sure of itself and confident in itself. The great artist today needs in particular the free development of the spirit; in that development all superstition, and all faith which remains restricted to determinate forms of vision and presentation, is degraded into mere aspects and features. These the free spirit has mastered because he sees in them no absolutely sacrosanct conditions for his exposition and mode of configuration, but ascribes value to them only on the strength of the higher content which in the course of his re-creation he puts into them as adequate to them.[9]

Hegel's description of the Romantic artist is not restricted in its application to the major figures of the Romantic Movement in Germany, nor even to the phenomenon of European Romanticism in general. It applies to numerous later artists as well, and not merely to them but also to all those other intellectuals who arrived at the conclusion that thinking is essentially a process of invention or fiction-making and that truth (or what passes for truth) is always to be understood as an arbitrary construction, grounded only in the imaginations of individuals or groups. Antiphilosophers and literary critics, especially in the twentieth century, became increasingly adept at overcoming "determinate forms of vision and presentation" in all spheres of spiritual activity, including those put forward as definitive with respect to religious and philosophical truth. Instead of restricting themselves faithfully (or superstitiously) to such forms as these, they adopted the standpoint of the Romantic artist and, through the practice of their art, made "every determinacy waver and dissolve." Thus, Hegel's description of the manner in which art was destabilized by the Romantics is also an account of the simultaneous destabilization or dissolution of every other objective spiritual formation.

What did art look like, according to Hegel, as it dissolved? It assumed a variety of shapes, all of them indicative of an unprecedented separation of the spiritual realm from the realm of the external. In previous art, these two realms had been fused into a unity or recognized as an identity, which means that an essentially important subject-matter had been treated in a manner deemed essentially appropriate to it. The subject of art was the truth of things, and this truth was implicitly always distinguishable from erroneous or trivial appearances. The truth of things required to be treated in a particular manner in order to be displayed in its true character. Art had to pay attention to the true structure of reality, which had been imposed on nature and in human experience by the Divine itself. When human subjectivity replaces the Divine, the artist himself becomes the truth of things, and he accordingly enters into a paradoxical relation with respect to both subject-matter and technique, which lose their essential character and acquire instead whatever character he chooses to give them. In Hegel's words,

> [I]f subjective inwardness of heart becomes the essential feature to be represented, the question of which specific material of external actuality and the spiritual world is to be an embodiment of the heart is . . . a matter of accident. For this reason the romantic inwardness can display itself in *all* circumstances, and move relentlessly from one thing to another in innumerable situations, states of affairs, relations, errors, and confusions, conflicts and satisfactions for what is sought and is to count is only its own inner subjective formation, the spirit's expression and mode of receptivity, and not an objective and absolutely valid subject-matter. In the presentations of romantic art, therefore everything has a place, every sphere of life, all phenomena, the greatest and the least, the supreme and the trivial, the moral, immoral, and evil; and, in particular, the more art becomes secular, the more it makes itself at home in the finite things of the world, is satisfied with them, and grants them complete validity, and the artist does well when he portrays them as they are.[10]

Realism, then, is one consequence of the new emphasis on subjective inwardness, surprising as that may seem, since the ability to focus on the actual becomes stronger when the actual stops being regarded as mere packaging for the ideal. As soon as it becomes clear that scope and relevance are not intrinsic to the external world but are dependent rather on subjective interest, the idea that only the true structure of reality deserves representation is replaced by the idea that anything may be foregrounded or emphasized in any degree of detail whatsoever. The actual appearances of things have a validity equal to, or greater than, that which used to be attributed to the eternal verities precisely because they do not contain, locked within them, a core of truth that demands fidelity through resistance to the multiplication of mere instances. At first, it seemed that realism in art might involve the substitution of a new conception of the structure of reality in place of the old one, but by the end of the nineteenth century it was beginning to be understood that realistic representation thrived on the constant addition of new details or new areas of interest and so was fully compatible with a constantly changing focus of attention. Delight in what was odd or out of the way or resistant to previous stereotypes required a perpetual refusal of conventional perspectives rather than adherence to what Hegel calls "an objective and absolutely valid subject-matter." Indeed, an art that makes it its business to do justice to appearances is finally constrained only by the power and range of the artist's sensibility.

But realism was not the only stylistic possibility available to the Romantic artist. It was equally possible to develop an unrealistic or antirealistic style, and in saying so, Hegel anticipates not only what would later be called symbolism but also the various antimimetic tendencies of cubism, surrealism, and abstractionism. Both realism and antirealism are regarded by Hegel as expressions of the new "inwardness": "The aspect of external existence is consigned," says Hegel, "to contingency and abandoned to the adventures devised by an imagination whose caprice can mirror what is present to it, *exactly as it is,* just as readily as it can jumble the shapes of the external world and distort them grotesquely."[11] Realism and antirealism are both thought of by Hegel as deliberate disruptions, even complementary disruptions, of the classical decorum required by "an objective and absolutely valid subject-matter." The disappearance of such a subject-matter has the effect of making style or technique the main focus, so that art becomes self-referential. Thus, "apart from the things depicted, the means of the portrayal also becomes an end in itself, so that the artist's subjective skill and his application of the means of artistic production are raised to the status of an objective matter in works of art."[12] "The application of the means of artistic production raised to the status of an objective matter" is practically the formula for twentieth-century abstract art. But it is no less relevant to the vorticist attitude of Ezra Pound, who was to write, in his memoir of Gaudier-Brzeska: "Our respect is not for the subject-matter, but for the creative power of the artist; for that which he is capable of adding to his subject from himself; or, in fact, his capability to dispense with external subjects altogether, to create from himself or from elements."[13]

For Hegel, the caprice or humor of the Romantic artist alone determines whether the artist shall mirror things exactly or jumble them grotesquely, and so it is humor that provides the key to the instability or volatility of late Romantic art, wherein "every determinacy" is made to "waver and dissolve." If realism allowed for an unprecedented foregrounding of details and aspects hitherto unsuspected, thus altering conventional perspectives, the jumbling of things (as Hegel calls it) also played havoc with conventional notions concerning the relations of things, as established by previous thought. Both styles were calculated to suggest the fragmentary or temporary nature of all notions and perspectives. Hegel's description of the workings of humor in the writings of his own contemporaries (and particularly in the works of Jean Paul) remains pertinent to several twentieth-century masterpieces, such as Pound's *Cantos,* Eliot's *The Waste Land,* or Williams's *Paterson,* not to mention *Finnegans Wake* or *Ulysses:*

> [H]umour is not set the task of developing and shaping a topic objectively and in a way appropriate to the essential nature of the topic, and in this development, using its own means to articulate the topic and round it off artistically; on the contrary, it is the artist himself who enters the material, with the result that his chief activity, by the power of subjective notions, flashes of thought, striking modes of interpretation, consists in destroying and dissolving everything that proposes to make itself objective and win a firm shape for itself in reality, or that seems to have such a shape already in the external world. Therefore every independence of an objective *content* along with the inherently fixed connection of the *form* (given as that is by the subject-matter) is annihilated in itself, and the presentation is only a sporting with the topics, a derangement and perversion of the material, and a rambling to and fro, a criss-cross movement of subjective expressions, views, and attitudes whereby the author sacrifices himself and his topics alike.[14]

Applying his analysis of humor directly to Jean Paul, Hegel continues:

> So with us Jean Paul, e.g., is a favorite humourist, and yet he is astonishing beyond everyone else, precisely in the baroque mustering of things objectively furthest removed from one another and in the most confused disorderly jumbling of topics related only in his own subjective imagination. The story, the subject-matter and course of events in his novels, is

what is of the least interest. The main thing remains the hither and thither course of the humour which uses every topic only to emphasize the subjective wit of the author. In thus drawing together and concatenating material raked up from the four corners of the earth and every sphere of reality, humour turns back, as it were, to symbolism where meaning and shape likewise lie apart from one another, except that now it is the mere subjective activity of the poet which commands material and meaning alike and strings them together in an order alien to them. But such a string of notions soon wearies us, especially if we are expected to acclimatize ourselves and our ideas to the often scarcely guessable combinations which have casually floated before the poet's mind. Especially in the case of Jean Paul one metaphor, one witticism, one joke, one simile, kills the other; we see nothing develop, everything just explodes.[15]

Hegel's dissatisfaction with the workings of humor is clear in these passages. Art, to him, was essentially a matter of achieving definite configurations, of shaping materials into coherent structures or firm patterns. Art, he thought, works by means of sensuous determinations and for the sake of sensuous determinations. But the new art seemed bent on disrupting determinations. It wanted to override them and to produce, instead of them, either fragments that were underdetermined or phantasmagorias that were overdetermined. Art, in the old-fashioned understanding of the term, had indeed ceased to be the supreme need of the artist himself who, in relation to the old conception of art, was deliberately postartistic. In the twentieth century, when the great masterpieces of modern humor appeared, the initial reaction to them was often that of dismay. Eventually, schools of criticism arose that offered to determine how it was that these masterpieces had artfully contrived to produce the *impression* of indeterminacy. These schools produced readings of the works that made them seem artful or determinate after all. But by the end of the century, other schools had appeared, like that of the poststructuralists, who took indetermination seriously and made it once again the fundamental feature of all artistic expression, in the light of which it might be said that all art, properly understood, was in a state of self-transcendence. Thus, Hegel's view that determination itself was coming to be regarded as an obstacle or impediment to the highest form of spiritual life proved to be genuinely prophetic.

The deeper reason for Hegel's dislike of humor (aside from the fact that it was responsible for creating a post-artistic art) is that it turns everything into grist for itself. It rakes up material from the four corners of the earth and every sphere of reality, and it destroys every independence of an objective content. In so doing, it offers itself as the highest form of wisdom, absorbing like an amoeba both religion and philosophy. In Hegel's view, the German Romantics, especially the followers of Fichte, such as Friedrich von Schlegel, had implied that humor or caprice in the self-conscious genius, or in the self-acknowledging spirit of great poets, had absolute authority over the ''thoughts" of theologians and philosophers, so that the exercise of genius or spirit might henceforth be regarded, not as something restricted to the sphere of art alone, but as the ultimate form of thought itself. Art (not in the old-fashioned sense but in the new sense of post-art) would at last emerge as the foundation and substance of every intellectual enterprise. This was not merely implied; it was the explicit aim of the Romantic Movement and, from Hegel's mature point of view, entirely unacceptable. As a young man, Hegel had copied (perhaps even authored) the document that Rosenzweig referred to as "The Oldest Systematic Program of German Idealism," and in that document the hegemony of aesthetics with respect to all other forms of intellectual activity was stirringly proclaimed. Probably Schelling, but possibly Hegel himself or even Hölderlin, had written in this document that "the highest act of reason is an aesthetic act." Thus, "the philosopher must possess just as much aesthetic power as the poet" in order to do justice to the discovery, lately made by Fichte's followers, that "the philosophy of the spirit is an aesthetic philosophy." This discovery had been made in connection with the recognition of "absolute freedom"—"the absolute freedom of all spirits who carry the intellectual world within themselves, and may not seek either God or immortality *outside of themselves*":

> Poetry thereby obtains a higher dignity; it becomes again in the end what it was in the beginning—*teacher* of *(history) the human race* because there is no longer any philosophy, any history; poetic art alone will outlive all the rest of the sciences and arts.[16]

However he may have felt about this matter in the late 1790s, it is certain that Hegel ultimately regarded the aesthetic implications of Fichtean idealism as pretentious and bizarre.

In his lectures on aesthetics, Hegel's contempt for these implications is unmistakable in his account of the famous irony, which he claimed had been theorized by Friedrich von Schlegel as a display of the Fichtean concept of "the ego as the absolute principle of all knowing, reason, and cognition."[17] Hegel's description of the various attitudes and postures associated with this kind of irony is, in effect, a description of what happens when the artist arrogates to himself supreme intellectual authority. In such a case, says Hegel, "nothing is treated *in and for itself* and as valuable in itself, but only as produced by the subjectivity of the *ego*":

> But in that case the *ego* can remain lord and master of everything, and in no sphere of morals, law, things human and divine, profane and sacred, is there anything that would not first have to be laid down by the *ego*, and that therefore could not equally well be destroyed by it. Consequently everything genuinely and independently real becomes only a show, not true and genuine on its own account or through itself, but a mere appearance due to the *ego* in whose power and caprice and at whose free disposal it remains. To admit or cancel it depends wholly on the pleasure of the *ego*, already absolute in itself simply as *ego*.[18]

There is both delight and terror in such self-consciousness on the part of the ego. On the one hand, it is exhilarating for the artist to feel that the world around him is essentially the product of his own imagination, that it is always necessarily a reflection of his own conceptions and interests, and that it can be completely transformed or even annihilated by simply altering these same conceptions and interests, or by performing a new exercise of imagination. On the other hand, it is terrifying to realize that, for this very reason, the ego is essentially isolated in a world without substance or content so that there is nothing essential to which the ego can relate itself or with which it can identify. The result, says Hegel, is that the artist becomes ironical or ambivalent about the worth of the reality he makes for himself and about his own reality-making consciousness.

It is exciting, for example, for "an ironical artistic life" to apprehend itself

> as a divine creative genius for which anything and everything is only an unsubstantial creature, to which the creator, knowing himself to be disengaged and free from everything, is not bound, because he is just as able to destroy it as to create it. In that case, he who has reached this standpoint of divine genius looks down from his high rank on all other men, for they are pronounced dull and limited, inasmuch as law, morals, etc., still count for them as fixed, essential, and obligatory.[19]

At the same time, however, it may also be depressing to contemplate "the vanity of everything factual, moral, and of intrinsic worth, the nullity of everything objective and absolutely valid." In one sense, it appears that the ego "can live only in the bliss of self-enjoyment":

> But, on the other hand, the *ego* may, contrariwise, fail to find satisfaction in this self-enjoyment and instead become inadequate to itself, so that it now feels a craving for the solid and the substantial, for specific and essential interests. Out of this comes misfortune, and the contradiction that, on the one hand, the subject does want to penetrate into truth and longs for objectivity, but, on the other hand, cannot renounce his isolation and withdrawal into himself or tear himself free from this unsatisfied abstract inwardness. Now he is attacked by the yearning which also we have seen proceeding from Fichtean philosophy. The dissatisfaction of this quiescence and impotence—which may not do or touch anything for fear of losing its inner harmony and which, even if pure in itself, is still unreal and empty despite its desire for reality and what is absolute—is the source of yearning and a *morbid* beautiful soul. For a *truly* beautiful soul acts and is actual. That longing, however, is only the empty vain subject's sense of nullity, and he lacks the strength to escape from this vanity and fill himself with a content of substance.[20]

Not here but elsewhere (in his lectures on the history of philosophy), Hegel mentions Novalis as a poet who sets forth the "yearnings of a lofty soul," which desires "a firm and steady basis" but which finds itself enmeshed in "the extravagances of subjectivity": "This subjectivity does not reach substantiality, it dies away within itself, and the standpoint it adopts is one of inward workings and deals with the minutiae of the truth."[21]

In the twentieth century, it was T. S. Eliot who presented this condition as the fate of modern subjectivity, and for years it was not clear to his readers whether he himself shared in the condition or merely analyzed it as the hallmark of twentieth-century *angst*. Nearly all of Eliot's early personae exhibited a hyper-self-consciousness that was capable of ironizing itself by grasping itself immediately as a spectacle of infinitely various possibilities. These personae paralyzed themselves as they viewed themselves, and knew that they were paralyzing themselves, and laughed at themselves for doing what they were doing, and suffered deeply at the same time for doing it. Every contortion in the process was simultaneously experienced and ironized. This condition was superbly defined by Sir Henry

Harcourt-Reilly in *The Cocktail Party* as "the final desolation / Of solitude in a phantasmal world / Of imagination, shuffling memories and desires." The later characters (and Eliot himself) escaped into religion, finding there the "firm and steady basis" sought in vain by the early characters. This was, of course, in keeping with one of the possible outcomes of Romantic irony, as Hegel had indicated when he observed:

> The utter despair in respect of thought, of truth, and absolute objectivity, as also the incapacity to give oneself any settled basis or spontaneity of action, induced the noble soul to abandon itself to feeling and to seek in Religion something fixed and steadfast. . . . This instinct impelling us towards something fixed has forced many into positive forms of religion, into Catholicism, superstition and miracle working, in order that they may find something on which they can rest, because to inward subjectivity everything fluctuates and wavers.[22]

Many of Eliot's readers sympathized deeply with the exquisite sufferings exhibited by the early personae and did not wish to see them resolved by a plunge into religion. Consequently, they refused to follow Eliot's own example after 1927. For these readers, Eliot's display of paralyzed inwardness was their "truth" and indeed the "truth" for modern man. Almost none of them considered that this "truth" had been examined critically by Hegel in the 1820s, and even earlier in the *Phenomenology*.

Although Eliot's version of Romantic irony was immensely popular from about 1920 to about 1960, it appeared thereafter to many critics, such as Harold Bloom, that the truly central, truly indispensable, poet had all along been Wallace Stevens. Eliot had been peerless in his representation of the consciousness that "lives in dread of besmirching the splendour of its inner being by action," and that "flees from contact with the actual world, and persists in its self-willed impotence."[23] Stevens, on the other hand, wavered with a minimum of pain between "the bliss of self-enjoyment" and "a craving for the solid and the substantial." In half of his poetry, he celebrated the Creative Imagination as an absolute, unconditioned power. In the other half, he mused speculatively on what it would be like if one could encounter Reality itself apart from all imaginings, "not ideas about the thing but the thing itself."[24] In a relatively early poem, "The Comedian as the Letter C," Stevens treated both the discovery of subjectivity *and* the quest for "the veritable ding an sich, at last," as an ironical comedy, in which a proliferating series of visions and revisions ended inconclusively as a result of the hero's collapse back into ordinary life. But, in fact, the poem gave memorable expression (at once magnificent and mocking) to the various attitudes and postures that Stevens himself would continue to strike as he fluctuated throughout the rest of his career between allegiance to Imagination and allegiance to Reality. For the most part, Stevens enjoyed his inwardness, and he inspired generations to regard the deliberate act of fiction making as the ultimate exercise of self-awareness. "In the long run," said Stevens, "the truth does not matter,"[25] and "God is a postulate of the ego."[26] "Reality is not what it is," he said. "It consists of the many realities which it can be made into."[27] Similarly, "life is a composite of the propositions about it."[28] Since subjectivity had at last turned out to be the truth of objectivity, a deliberate acceptance of the burden and the glory of subjectivity seemed the ultimate guarantee of authenticity. Thus, "in an age of disbelief, when the gods have come to an end, when we think of them as the aesthetic projections of a time that has passed, men turn to a fundamental glory of their own and from that create a style of bearing themselves in reality. They create a new style of a new bearing in a new reality."[29] In place of objective truth, there was what Stevens called the "supreme fiction": "The final belief is to believe in a fiction, which you know to be a fiction, there being nothing else. The exquisite truth is to know that it is a fiction and that you believe in it willingly."[30] This was the very quintessence of irony. Orwell had called it *doublethink* in *1984,* denouncing it as deliberate self-deception or as the willing suspension of disbelief in what one knows to be false, but, to Stevens's admirers, it was the ultimate act of honesty. "Reality," they agreed, "is an activity of the most august imagination."[31]

But it was ever the privilege of irony to cancel its own constructions, and thus Stevens could say, without impropriety, that "eventually an imaginary world is entirely without interest."[32] This sent the poetry hurtling either toward a new imagination of the world or, alternatively, toward "the world without imagination," "a starker, barer world."[33] In this mood, Stevens could see how small a thing the imagination really was. "Poetry," he would then observe, "has to be something more than a conception of the mind. It has to be a revelation of nature. Conceptions are artificial. Perceptions are essential."[34] Or: "In the presence of extraordinary actuality, consciousness takes the place of imagination."[35] He tried to think of what it would be like to go "beyond the last thought,"[36] and he imagined himself, not imagining, but beholding, "nothing that is not there and the nothing that is."[37] (Unlike Eliot, who had made irony seem infinitely hellish, Stevens made it seem infinitely adventurous, replete with nuances yet to be recorded. There was no longing for escape, only a more and more deliberate pursuit of the various possibilities and implications. The ultimate consistency of Stevens's irony had to do with the fact that he never particularly concerned himself in his poetry with "the solid and the substantial," or with "specific and essential interests," but he did concern himself with his *craving* for these things and with the import that a contact with them might be supposed to have. Thus, there was never an actual departure from the life of reflexive self-consciousness.

The position Hegel describes as irony was certainly not confined to the theories and expressions of the German Romantics, nor was it, in its later appearances, confined only to avowed artists, like Eliot and Stevens. In the second half of the twentieth century, it had become practically the dominant position of literary and philosophical intellectuals alike. Richard Rorty and Harold Bloom both agreed that a postreligious, postphilosophical culture had been emerging ever since the early nineteenth century, and, without explicitly saying so, they both subscribed to the principles laid out in "The Oldest Systematic Program of German Idealism." Rorty understood that there was an analogy to be made between nineteenth-century idealism and twentieth-century textualism,[38] but he failed to press the analogy because he interpreted idealism as a particular set of arguments or theories to be promulgated as dogma rather than as the absolute egotism exhibited by the followers of Fichte and described by Hegel under the rubric of irony. Bloom, on the other hand, by concentrating his attention on the literary intellectuals instead of on the technical philosophers, saw clearly that the triumph of autonomous sensibility in the late twentieth century had been announced, or prepared for, by a host of nineteenth-century writers whom he called "the Prophets of Sensibility."[39] These "precursors of modern cultural thought" included such figures as Ruskin, Arnold, Carlyle, and Pater (along with many others), and they created what Bloom describes as a "blend" of "moral reflection, prose poetry, psychological portraiture, art and literary criticism, cultural history and a

curious kind of mythopoeic fiction . . . an amalgam that defies conventional description." Such writing, says Bloom, "mixes perception and sensation into a new kind of sensibility, one that is still with us today":

> Difficult to describe, this sensibility emphasizes a continuum haunted by
> intimations of mortality punctuated by brief bursts of radiance-privileged
> moments in which a peculiar vividness gives the illusion of redeeming
> life. It may be the stigma of the nineteenth-century Prophets of Sensibil-
> ity that (except for Pater) they sought to combat this climate of the spirit
> but oddly fostered it implicitly (even as Pater did so overtly). The in-
> creasing internalization of the self depended upon an augmentation of
> estrangement from the object world, and what was intended as prophetic
> warning and lament as to this estrangement became instead a subtle sug-
> gestion of an inevitable movement in elite sensibility.

Thus, it was a "strange anomaly" to Bloom that Nietzsche should now be
given so much credit for fathering the future at the expense of these other
precursors:

> They could not save or even preserve the post-Christian spirituality they
> sought to imbue in society, but they fostered in its place a pragmatic tri-
> umph of literary culture, beyond religion and beyond speculative phi-
> losophy. Psychoanalysis, despite its scientism, is only another form of
> that literary culture. So, in another way, are the textualist literary criti-
> cism and the language-oriented "human sciences" that are vivid parts of
> Structuralist and post-Structuralist formulations.

The "pragmatic triumph of literary culture" over science, philosophy,
and religion was explicated at length by Rorty, who even revived the term
"irony" in order to designate the new self-consciousness of thinkers in
relation to their own projects and the projects of others. Rorty explained
that what Bloom had described as "an inevitable movement in elite sensibility" was, in fact, the steadily growing acceptance, by intellectuals, of
the arbitrariness, or groundlessness, of "final vocabularies." A "final vocabulary" was a particular way of conceiving and expressing one's sense
of oneself or one's sense of the world. There were many such vocabularies, and there was no way to justify them or to resolve their differences.
They did not correspond to anything objective but were themselves instead the basis for claims about objectivity. Thus, Rorty defined the "ironist"
as "someone who fulfills three conditions":

> (1) She has radical and continuing doubts about the final vocabulary she currently uses, because she has been impressed by other vocabularies, vocabularies taken as final by people or books she has encountered; (2) she realizes that argument phrased in her present vocabulary can neither underwrite nor dissolve these doubts; (3) insofar as she philosophizes about her situation, she does not think that her vocabulary is closer to reality than others, that it is in touch with a power not herself. Ironists who are inclined to philosophize see the choice between vocabularies as made neither within a neutral and universal metavocabulary nor by an attempt to fight one's way past appearances to the real, but simply by playing the new off against the old.[40]

Ironists, in Rorty's sense, shared an elite realization "that anything can be made to look good or bad by being redescribed." They had in common the fact that they were "never quite able to take themselves seriously" because they were "always aware that the terms in which they describe themselves are subject to change, always aware of the contingency and fragility of their final vocabularies, and thus of their selves."[41]

The world as Rorty described it was composed of individuals who either knew the vanity of all possible conceptions (including their own) or else failed to know it. Those who failed to know it were still, as Hegel would say, in *earnest* about what they considered to be true or important:

> For genuine earnestness enters only by means of a substantial interest, something of intrinsic worth like truth, ethical life, etc.,—by means of a content which counts as such for me as essential, so that I only become essential myself in my own eyes in so far as I have immersed myself in such a content and have brought myself into conformity with it in all my knowing and acting."[42]

Earnestness, in this sense, was precisely what was banished by the new ironical sensibility. The only project left for such a sensibility, according to Rorty, was the project of "self-creation," undertaken in terms "necessarily private, unshared, unsuited to argument," and rooted in beliefs and desires acknowledged to be "ungroundable."[43] Society would be saved, implied Rorty, by the freely extended kindness or benevolence or condescension of ironist intellectuals to those engaged in rival projects and to those who were otherwise impaired by material or intellectual disadvantages. In all of these activities, the beliefs and desires of the ironists would not be supported by knowledge or understanding; rather, whatever passed for knowledge and understanding would be supported by belief and desire, regarded as irreducible and absolutely primal. Right spirits—those who knew the true nature of spirit—would work tirelessly for the liberation of all spirits, especially those in physical or intellectual bondage, and they would do so on the basis of their own inexplicable power to envisage "an endless, proliferating realization of Freedom"[44] through the cultivation of imagination and sympathy. It was almost a perfect revival of "the oldest systematic program of German idealism," and yet, to intellectuals in the 1980s, it seemed fresh and new. The very fact that there was no way to reconcile theoretically the demands of self-creation and the demands of human solidarity became, in Rorty's account, a testimony to the power of the spirit to *will* the simultaneous establishment of both self and community, by "[dropping] the demand for a theory which unifies public and private, and [being] content to treat the demands of self-creation and of human solidarity as equally valid."[45] The decision to *drop* theory and to *be content* with apparent contradictions was, at bottom, an expression of ironic freedom and therefore appropriately, and gloriously, arbitrary.

In France, Jacques Derrida and Michel Foucault were among the age's chief ironists, and their influence was considerable, particularly with respect to literary intellectuals. Derrida labored to show how an interest in the processes of signification might be substituted for an interest in objectivity, with the result that the agonistics of writing and reading became more important than the signified contents of books, which were accordingly reduced to the level of being considered virtual realities or mere appearances. It was not appropriate, from Derrida's point of view, to regard writing as a reflection or representation of anything prior to itself, whether it be some actually existing situation or an idea in the writer's mind. Thus, there was no access to, no contact with, a reality over and beyond what writing itself produced. "To write," said Derrida, was "to be incapable of making meaning absolutely precede writing."[46] "To write [was] to know that what has not yet been produced within literality has no other dwelling place, does not await us as prescription in some *topos ouranios,* or some divine understanding."[47] Writing thus became, for Derrida, the supreme spiritual gesture whereby the ordinary self of the writer and the signifiable character of reality were generated out of nothing, *ex nihilo.* "The literary act thus recovers its true power at its source."[48] And, because it "is inaugural, in the fresh sense of the word," it is also, with respect to the writer, "dangerous and anguishing," and especially risky: "There is . . . no insurance [remarked Derrida] against the risk of writing."[49] Significations were "always enveloped within the regional limits of nature, life and the soul," but in the moment that Derrida calls "the moment of the attempt-to-write," "the play of meaning can overflow signification," eluding its regional limits:

> The attempt-to-write cannot be understood on the basis of voluntarism. The will to write is not an ulterior determination of a primal will. On the contrary, the will to write reawakens the willful sense of the will: freedom, break with the domain of empirical history, a break whose aim is reconciliation with the hidden essence of the empirical, with pure historicity. The will and the attempt-to-write are not the desire to write, for it is a question here not of affectivity but of freedom and duty. In its relationship to Being, the attempt-to-write poses itself as the only way out of affectivity. A way out that can only be aimed at, and without the certainty that deliverance is possible or that it is outside affectivity.[50]

In passages like these, Derrida imagined a Fichtean world of spiritual shadowboxing that was full of Romantic drama. It was a place where the willful sense of the will might be reawakened, where deliverance from affectivity might be hoped for, and where a reconciliation with Being might be sought after. None of these strivings could he said to make a direct, unambiguous appearance in the literary works that proceeded from them. They could not be objectified "without becoming absurdities, and the structure proper to them must escape all classical categories."[51] Instead, they were to be understood as belonging "to the internal historicity of the work itself, in its relationship to a subjective origin that is not simply psychological or mental."[52]

Terms like "danger," "risk," "deliverance" (from affectivity), "reconciliation" (with the hidden essence of the empirical), "uncertainty," and "anguish" seemed to suggest the hellish spirituality of Eliot's ironic personae, but in fact Derrida turned more in the direction of the endless adventurousness of Wallace Stevens. He greeted the overflow of the play of meaning in the works he interpreted with a spiritual affirmation of his own playfulness. He called it "the Nietzschean *affirmation,*" which he defined as "the joyous affirmation of the play of the world and of the innocence of becoming, the affirmation of a world of signs without fault, without truth, and without origin which is offered to an active interpretation," and he contrasted it with "the saddened, *negative,* nostalgic, guilty, Rousseauistic side of the thinking of play," which "dreams of deciphering a truth or an origin which escapes play and the order of the sign, and which lives the necessity of interpretation as an exile."[53] Curiously, he admitted, "we live [these two interpretations of interpretation] simultaneously and reconcile them in an obscure economy," even though they are, in truth, "absolutely irreconcilable."[54] The more one read Derrida the clearer it became that he was constantly tracking a spiritual drama wherein nostalgia for "the lost or impossible presence of the absent origin" was in the position of either mastering, or being mastered by, the acceptance of "absolute chance" through a surrender "to *genetic* indetermination" and "the *seminal* adventure of the trace."[55] These were absolutely primary, absolutely fundamental, spiritual gestures. Writers and readers were finally to be judged in terms of which gesture had been predominant in the works they produced. The will to meet the play of the world with a corresponding gesture of playfulness was constantly, however, being subverted by the tendency of its own structured expressions to suggest, in spite of themselves, "the lost or impossible presence of the absent origin." Just as constantly, then, this will-to-play, this Nietzschean affirmation, would be required to resist all definitions or determinations of itself, including those made previously on its own behalf or by its own agency. This was the reflux action of irony, the action whereby it cancelled its constructions or returned them to the genetic indetermination of its own infinite spontaneity. All concepts were required to be volatilized or, by fiat, declared to be non-concepts. All designations of the infinitely proliferating power of dissemination were to be interpreted by the adept as non-designations thereof, and so on. When Derrida sounded like Heidegger, he was, as his translator explained, not "simply adopting Heidegger's ideas," rather he was "gradually putting Heidegger into question."[56] Irony permitted, or required, a constantly mutating formula whereby former positions might be abandoned or discarded as restrictions of the playfulness of the spirit.

Foucault's irony took the form of an exposé of the fake objectivity of modern science. Like Derrida, he wished to pass beyond man and humanism, and he spoke of the arbitrary nature of the concept of "man," which had almost run its course and whose disappearance would betoken "the death of man." Consequently, he made it his ambition to produce a criticism of the "discursive practices" that were responsible for creating the illusion that man could be known objectively or that man could be regarded appropriately as the "object" of the human sciences. If the determinations produced by these sciences could be shown to be contingent upon the historical occasions and situations wherein they were spawned, then the determined "knowledge" of man might be delegitimated or, at least, rendered problematic. Freedom was always Foucault's goal, freedom from being pinned down or categorized. In renouncing essentialism and the effort made by phenomenology to explain the transcendental structure of subjectivity, Foucault wished to clear the way for new conceptions of human nature and human knowing that "would permit the individual to modify himself according to his own will."[57] As a Romantic ironist, he knew that it was man's burden and glory to be an infinite spirit, never to be known but always in the process of becoming other than itself. Occasionally, readers got the impression that "man," "human nature," "the subject," "the self," "humanism," and so on, were all being cast aside as useless concepts, but nothing could be further from the truth. Freedom as pure egoism, as what Foucault toward the end called "the care of the self," which he defined as "an exercise of the self on the self, by which one attempts to develop and transform oneself, and attain to a certain mode of being,"[58] was simply a romantic redefinition of human nature as the inherently infinite task of self-construction. As he explained to Trombadori in 1978, the chief characteristic of man is that he has, like Keats's ideal poet, no character but instead a capacity for endless mutation. Thus, it was perfectly possible for Foucault to indulge in large-scale meditations on the nature and destiny of man, provided "man" was understood in a Romantic sense. In the entire course of their history, he would muse,

> [M]en had never ceased constructing themselves, that is, to shift continuously the level of their subjectivity, to constitute themselves in an infinite and multiple series of different subjectivities that would never place us in the presence of something that would be "man." Man is an animal of experience, he is involved *ad infinitum* within a process that, by defining a field of objects, at the same time changes him, deforms him, transforms him and transfigures him as a subject.[59]

Foucault was fascinated by Bataille's theme of the "limit-experiences" wherein "the subject reaches decomposition, leaves itself, at the limits of its own impossibility." That was "the way out," said Foucault, "the chance to free myself from certain traditional philosophical binds."[60] To be always in transition was precisely the ironist's method of being truly spiritual. Accordingly, Foucault noted with approval the development in France of a sort of "from-philosophy-to-activity" philosophy which was in the process of displacing traditional philosophy. From philosophy in its newer form, he believed,

> comes the movement through which, not without effort and fumblings, dreams and illusions, one detaches oneself from what are the received truths and seeks other rules of the game. From philosophy [in its new sense] comes the displacement and transformation of the limits of thought, the modification of received values and all the work done to think otherwise, to do something else, to become other than what one is.[61]

A new kind of intellectual seemed to be called for, one who knew how to pass beyond the old models of wisdom, one who was capable of destroying all determinations of truth, including his own:

> The Greek sage, the Jewish prophet, and the Roman legislator are still models that haunt those who practice today the profession of speaking and writing. I dream of the intellectual destroyer of evidence and universalities, the one who, in the inertias and constraints of the present, locates and marks the weak points, the openings, the lines of power, who incessantly displaces himself, doesn't know exactly where he is heading nor what he'll think tomorrow because he is too attentive to the present. . . .[62]

Irony, as practiced and thematized by Derrida and Foucault, became (as Hegel predicted) a perpetual undermining of anything that offered itself as an objective determination of the spirit, including all cultural formations and all pretended "knowledge." This was to be accomplished by "showing forth what has worth and dignity for mankind as null in its self-destruction," or by showing "that there is nothing in what is lofty and best, since, in its appearance in individuals, characters, and actions, it contradicts and destroys itself and so is ironical about itself."[63] The self-annihilation of all determinations was sometimes imagined idolatrously as Being's own tendency to be other than itself (Derrida's "play of the world"), but more often it was conceived along the lines of Rorty's insight that "anything can be made to look good or bad by being redescribed." As Hegel says, "Irony loves this irony of the loss of character."[64] Writing on Orwell in *Contingency, Irony, and Solidarity,* Rorty demonstrated the subversive power of redescription by constructing a new interpretation of *1984,* according to which *doublethink* became good and the pursuit of truth became bad. When it came to truth, Rorty observed that there was nothing in the nature of it that might prevent a facsimile of it from being used to any end or purpose. Orwell convinced us, said Rorty, that "all the intellectual and poetic gifts which had made Greek philosophy, modern science, and Romantic poetry possible might someday find employment in the Ministry of Truth."[65] But if the truth could not save us, what could save us was invincible rationalization. To have a self, in Rorty's reading of the novel, was to be capable "of weaving a coherent web of belief and desire."[66] To become irrational was not to lose contact with reality, it was to lose the ability to rationalize or justify oneself and one's actions by losing the capacity to go on weaving a coherent (or self-gratifying) web of belief and desire. The fact that Winston cannot "weave a story" around his betrayal of Julia, the fact that his betrayal of her *is* a fact which he cannot permanently forget or conveniently redescribe, is interpreted by Rorty, not as a vindication of the truth over all evasions, but as a consequence of Winston's having lost, through torture, the power to sustain a face-saving rationalization of his own behavior, the power to go on weaving for himself a coherent web of belief and desire. *Doublethink* would save Winston from facing the truth, allowing him to retain his coherence. Thus, in Rorty's interpretation, the point Orwell is trying to make in *1984* is that the worst thing that can happen to one is that one's capacity for *doublethinking* (or supreme fiction-making) should be disrupted. That *doublethink* should turn out to be a good thing after all, and that the spirit of Greek philosophy should turn out to be fully at work in the Ministry of Truth (and thus a bad thing after all), was a brilliant piece of virtuoso irony and a perfect demonstration of irony's power to make every determinacy waver and dissolve, not unworthy of the Ministry of Truth itself.

For his part, Foucault admitted to Trombadori that the coherence of his own project of being always other than himself had not been incompatible, at least for a time, with Stalinism. The attractiveness of Stalinism (during his brief stint in the Communist Party) had been, for Foucault, the very fact that it required continuous and unremitting *doublethinking* in order to stay abreast of official Party policy and thus permitted one to be constantly changing: "No matter how unconvinced we were, we still forced ourselves into believing what they told us. This was part of an attitude— I'd call it disastrous, but it was mine and it was my way of staying in the Party—of being obligated to sustain the opposite of what's believable; this was part of that exercise of 'the dissolution of the self' and of the search for a way of being 'other.'"[67] In this way, the complete loss of character might be ironically construed as the perfect achievement of character. Foucault's later attitude toward politics was characterized by avoidance of commitment to particular programs or schemes of action, largely because *ordinary* politics required a narrow single-mindedness or a holding-fast to a particular set of aims and purposes, which promoted sameness of character rather than the volatilization of character.

The success of irony in the twentieth century was nothing short of spectacular. The chief ironists of the age followed Heidegger in imagining that the Hegelian judgment concerning art might be set aside, or indeed had been set aside, by their own artistic manipulation of intellectual and cultural materials. In fact, the judgment remained in force precisely because it had predicted and accounted for, in advance, all the gestures of which the ironists were capable. The judgment was not that art should not *be* this; it was that *this* is what art has come to, this is what art *will be* henceforth. The more irony shows itself to be capable of making mincemeat out of philosophy in general (or out of Hegel's philosophy in particular), the more the judgment locks into place as an accurate description of the range and extent of ironic spirituality, already placed, by philosophy, within a larger, more comprehensive range of spiritual possibilities.

CHAPTER 3

WILLIAM CARLOS WILLIAMS AND
THE ART OF INFINITE SPIRITUALITY

> There is only one good art in any age; it is that which uses the sensible terms of that age fully with widest application to its needs for liberation of the whole man.
>
> —Williams, "The Poet in Time of Confusion"

In recent years there has been a great deal of interest in the impact of the visual arts, especially the art of painting, on William Carlos Williams. Most of this interest has focused on Williams's considerable familiarity with the major movements of modern art and on his personal associations with such important artists as Marsden Hartley, Charles Sheeler, and Charles Demuth. As a result of the scholarly investigations first of Bram Dijkstra and, more recently, of Henry M. Sayre and Peter Schmidt, we have become accustomed to the idea that Williams's poetic techniques were largely inspired by the techniques of modern painting, or by the various styles associated with Cubism, Dadaism, Photo-Realism, or Abstractionism.[1] Accordingly, we have learned how to recognize those poems by Williams that employ painterly methods, and we have come to identify Williams's work as a whole (or in its various parts) with the aims and purposes of one or more of the different schools of modern art. Dijkstra, for example, describes Williams's early poem "Spring Strains" as "an elaborate attempt at painting a Cubist picture in words,"[2] while Sayre finds an analogy between what he calls the "visual text" of Williams's late poetry and "the monumental drip canvases" of Jackson Pollock.[3] Most interesting of all perhaps is Schmidt's observation that Williams was simultaneously attracted to the irreconcilable tendencies of Precisionism, Cubism, and Dadaism.[4]

These discussions of Williams's indebtedness to the goals and methods of modern art have, on the whole, been most illuminating, but they have not sufficiently emphasized an important truth concerning Williams's attitude toward modern art or indeed toward art in general. The truth is that Williams's attitude was never servile with respect to art because he never regarded art as an end in itself. He always regarded it as a means to an end, and the end was liberation—the liberation of the human spirit from every particular representation of itself that tends to hamper it or restrict it, including perhaps especially those representations of itself that are fixed or congealed in works of art. For Williams, the particular virtue of modern art lay in its volatility, by means of which (he thought) it managed to intimate the artist's freedom with respect to the constraints imposed by any particular content or method. Indeed, the genius of modern art lay in its peculiar determination to resist, or to reconfigure, all determinate forms of vision and presentation, making it, as Hegel had predicted, "the self-transcendence of art but within its own sphere and in the form of art itself."[5] Without any particular awareness of Hegel, Williams concluded that art in the twentieth century had reached its endstage, wherein artists might use shapes and forms in order to depict something that eludes all shapes and forms, namely, the spiritual subjectivity of the artists themselves. For obvious reasons, this basic conclusion about art tends to be overlooked whenever Williams's use of a particular painterly method is under discussion, and the result is that his reliance or dependence on that particular method may be overestimated.

Such a mistake is made, for example, when Sayre attempts to explain Williams's conception of art in terms of a fixed opposition which is supposed to exist in Williams's mind between "formal design" and reality (conceived of as "recalcitrant and disorderly").[6] In other words, Sayre makes the mistake of assuming that Williams is more or less bound by, or committed to, the view that art is pure form or pure design imposed contrastingly on a real world that is extra-artistic. If that is the case, says Sayre, "a dissonance always exists between the realms of the abstract and the real, between the form the poem takes and its subject matter."[7] But the fact is that Williams did not restrict his definition of art in such a way as to equate it with abstract design; he includes under the rubric of art even those modes of representation that may be described as "realistic" because of their fidelity to whatever is "recalcitrant and disorderly" in reality. Art *may* be abstract, but it may also be realistic. The crucial thing is that it not be considered as restricted by any particular, narrow conception concerning what it must include or exclude.

The source of Sayre's view that there must be an *absolute* opposition between an interest in pure form and an interest in empirical reality appears to be his interpretation of Wassily Kandinsky's ideas concerning the problem or the question of form in art. Having assumed that Williams's allegiances must necessarily be divided between "the abstract pattern of his mind" and "the real chaos of his world,"[8] Sayre finds the prototype of Williams's divided allegiance in Kandinsky's famous distinction between the two extremes of modern art, which are, according to Kandinsky, "total abstraction" and "total realism." Sayre states erroneously that Kandinsky regarded these two extremes as "irreconcilable,"[9] but it is clear from Kandinsky's discussion that both extremes are to be regarded ultimately as expressions of the same essential content. In Kandinsky's own words, "These two poles [of "abstraction" and "realism"] open *two roads* which lead finally *to one goal.*"[10] Like Williams, Kandinsky believed that "a great spiritual epoch" was expressing itself in the widely divergent, highly self-conscious styles of modern art, all of which were capable of embodying what Kandinsky refers to as "the same inner resonance": "And just as in realism the inner resonance is strengthened by the removal of the abstract, this resonance is also strengthened in the abstraction by the removal of the real."[11] Thus, "we see that as a matter of principle it has *no significance at all whether a real or abstract form is used by the artist,*" since, for the purpose of expressing "my inner experience," "*both forms are internally equal.*"[12]

Because of its emphasis on the priority of "the inner resonance" and because of its view that "today the whole storeroom [of real and abstract forms] is at the *spirit's* disposal,"[13] Kandinsky's essay "On the Problem of Form" may be regarded as, in part, a restatement of Hegel's claim nearly a century earlier that artists in the future will be able to shuttle freely back and forth between extremes of realism and unrealism precisely because they will have realized that the true content of their art is their own "inwardness" and not the particular forms (real or abstract) that may be used to express that "inwardness." As we saw in the preceding chapter, according to Hegel's analysis, when "subjective inwardness of heart becomes the essential feature to be represented, the question of which specific material of external actuality and the spiritual world is to be embodiment of the heart is . . . a matter of accident."[14] In this sense, the choice of "total abstraction" is not irreconcilable with the choice of "total realism": "The aspect of external existence is consigned [says Hegel] to contingency and abandoned to the adventures devised by an imagination whose caprice can mirror what is present to it, *exactly as it is,* just as readily as it can jumble the shapes of the external world and distort them grotesquely."[15] In this sense, as Kandinsky puts it, *"there is no question of form."*[16]

Williams was practically the perfect embodiment of the modern artist, as conceived and described by Hegel and Kandinsky, because he refused to acknowledge the authority or privilege of particular artistic styles. For him, as for them, the meaning of the new self-consciousness concerning art boiled down to a matter of pure artistic freedom in the speculative contemplation of the different possibilities of expression. He makes this point clearly in his essay on the painter Emanuel Romano:

> It must be understood, before going further, what has occurred in painting during the past seventy-five years [Williams is writing circa 1951]: During that time (the resources of painting,) the means of seeing and placing colors and shapes upon the canvas have been enormously expanded (, mainly by the French school). Every avenue open to human ingenuity has been explored. (Today there is no school that one need follow. There is no longer any closed circuit to painting. Today, knowing the resources, anyone can do anything. Cézanne was a great realist—Van Gogh did something else—I pick them at random. They all added to the breaking of the bounds. Light was let in.) It was a true French Revolution. The modern masters, mainly the French, have given us painting, painting itself free from all restrictions. They said to us in effect: There it is. Now see what you can do with it.[17]

"The proof that I am I," as Williams had written more than thirty years prior to his piece on Romano, "is that I can use anything, not a special formula but anything."[18] This, I think, goes a long way toward explaining the apparently contradictory tendencies of Williams's aesthetic sympathies. At one time or another he expressed enthusiasm for just about all the major movements or schools of modern art, in spite of their seemingly irreconcilable differences. But he never gave any of them his complete or exclusive approbation. Always, at some point, he would express a reservation or a hesitation, which enabled him to retain a sense of his own independent authority. Like a good pragmatist or like a romantic ironist, Williams *used* aesthetic theories and aesthetic styles; he did not succumb to them. The conception he retained on his own spiritual centrality took precedence over each and every one of them.

Nevertheless, the tendency was strong, among those critics who favored a particular style or a particular set of poetic devices, to distinguish between those of Williams's poems that seemed "in character" according to what might be imagined to be his preferred style and those that seemed perversely "out of character." For example, critics who enjoyed the Cubist (or Dadaist) inclinations exhibited by the poems (and prose) of *Spring and All* (1923) were frequently put off by the meandering meditations of *The Desert Music* (1954) or *Journey to Love* (1955), and so they might conclude that Williams's later poetry had departed from or betrayed the demands of his own aesthetic. Sometimes it was suggested that a "characteristic" poem by Williams was a poem that eschewed rhetorical figures, such as similes and metaphors. Then, when a poem was found that *did* make use of such figures, it might be regarded as an exception or as an "uncharacteristic" poem. But every attempt to identify the workings or principles of a proper Williams poem was belied by the fact that, on principle, there could be no such thing as a proper Williams poem. In the largest sense of the term "artistic," there could be no such thing as a poem that was not "artistic." And yet this is what Sayre seems to imply when he associates "art," on the one hand, with objective descriptions set forth in poems governed by consistent stanzaic patterns and "the chaos of the world," on the other hand, with a looser kind of poetry consisting of "unpatterned, more personal poems" that are "generally longer, more emotional, and less controlled than the patterned objective ones."[19] While admitting that Williams was attracted simultaneously to the tighter configurations of artistic poetry and the looser configurations of what might be considered inartistic poetry, Sayre clearly implies that, although Williams hoped that these opposing attractions might be reconciled in a sort of super-poetry which would effect an ideal union of them, in fact his best poems were those that remained rooted in a sense of the irreconcilable distinction between art and reality, or between the abstract and the realistic. Thus, despite the concession that is made to the presence of variety in Williams, we are still compelled to accept a narrower definition of art than Williams's own definition, and we are still compelled to sort out Williams's poetry into those poems that reflect his own deepest insights and those that attempt, failingly, to resist just these insights. If, as Sayre asserts, it is unfortunately true that "most of the poems in which the variable foot occurs in a visually consistent staggered tercet" are based on the false premise that order and chaos can be made to coexist in an "ideal union," nevertheless we can be grateful that "the formal schemes of *Pictures from Brueghel* [Williams's last volume of short lyrics] . . . restore Williams's poetic to the heterogeneity upon which it is founded. . . ."[20] Of all the critics, it is Schmidt who seems most accepting of the variety or multiplicity of Williams's entire body of work, informed as it is by conflicting aesthetic criteria and exhibiting the poet's disdain for the confines of any fixed orientation toward the task of composition.

The function of all art was, as Williams saw it, to liberate the spirit from fixations and impositions. Sometimes it was art itself that imposed its own conventions upon us, from which liberation was required. Sometimes it was the conventionality of ordinary perception that created an imposition. Gestures would have to be various in order to meet the complexity of the problem. If the problem took the form of what Williams referred to as "our fearful bedazzlement with some concrete and fixed present,"[21] then *any* sort of re-shaping or re-creating of the sensory world might produce relief. Otherwise, "the senses witnessing what is immediately before them in detail" will tend to see "a finality" which they will "cling to in despair, not knowing which way to turn."[22] This "finality" is in fact a sort of illusion or, as Williams termed it, an "apparition," whose power over us can best be minimized through the manipulations of art. On the other hand, even the achievements of art tend to impose themselves upon us by offering their own finalities, in the form of modes of perception or ways of thinking that interfere with our own free spiritual power. Without a new art that is constantly turning away from or else reconfiguring the old art, the old art too becomes a paralyzing "apparition." And so art, in the largest sense of the term, exists not only to produce an alternative to what the ignorant worship as "reality" ("the so-called natural or scientific array" that has become "the walking devil of modern life")[23] but also to produce an alternative to what the ignorant worship as "art." "By this," as Williams said, "we understand the escape of man from domination by his own engines."[24]

It is easy to see why Williams was so fascinated by the possibilities of which art is capable when it has reached its endstage. Endstage art had acquired the freedom to be anti-representational or anti-mimetic and thus it was able to mock or evade the traditional requirement that art be subservient to that which it might be said to depict or represent. Also, because it offered the array of stylistic options that Williams celebrates in his essay on Emanuel Romano, endstage art had acquired the freedom to mock or evade the traditional requirement that art be subservient to the proprieties of a particular aesthetic approach. To the extent that it always countenanced the production of work that, according to one convention or another, must be regarded as "inartistic," endstage art truly deserved to be called what Hegel in fact called it, namely, "the self-transcendence of art." Certainly, when Williams offered to present a minute description of something "exactly as it is," or a fragment of spontaneous conversation, or a verbal document such as a letter or a newspaper clipping like those he put into *Paterson,* he was thumbing his nose at "art" and at the same time engaging in one of the licensed gestures of endstage art. The self-transcendence of art was finally a matter of the endstage artist's power to communicate the fact that he could do anything he wanted to do, even if it meant abandoning art itself in its familiar forms.

Williams understood perfectly that endstage art was an art that was dependent upon, or reflective of, a particular concept of human spirituality or a particular philosophy of human freedom. It could only be produced in connection with this concept or this philosophy. As he explained in a letter to John Riordan (dated October 13, 1926):

[M]y failure to work inside a pattern—a positive sin—is the cause of my virtues. I cannot work inside a pattern because I can't find a pattern that will have me. My whole effort . . . is to find a pattern, large enough, modern enough, flexible enough to include my desires. And if I should find it I'd wither and die.[25]

The gestures of Williams's art, like those of endstage art in general, could only be produced on the basis of a metaphysics of infinite subjectivity, such as we have already described in connection with the work of Foucault (in chapter 1) and such as Hegel described in his *Aesthetics* in connection with "the decay and dissolution of art itself."[26] Thus, it could not be said that a certain view of human nature and of human possibility was the *fruit* of Williams's artistic activity. Rather, it was the platform or the springboard for that activity. Everything Williams produced was *grounded* in the view that, by virtue of his spiritual power, the artist determines, and therefore exceeds, both natural and artistic forms, despite the fact that an enormous amount of human activity (both artistic and otherwise) seems to reflect an ignorance of such power. However great our bedazzlement with these forms, there is always the possibility of a knowing return to the ground of infinite subjectivity:

> The mind always tries to break out of confinement. It has tried every sort of interest which presents itself, even to a flight to the moon. But the only thing which will finally interest it must be its own intrinsic nature.[27]

CHAPTER 4

THE METAPHYSICS OF DECONSTRUCTION

> The feeling of something *queer* here comes from a misunderstanding. The kind of misunderstanding that is produced by a thumb-catching of the intellect—to which I want to call a halt.
>
> —Wittgenstein, *Remarks on the Foundations of Mathematics*

The special charm of deconstruction for intellectuals in the 1970s and the 1980s probably had a great deal to do with the fact that it seemed to represent an enormous advance in sophistication over other methods of textual interpretation. Whereas most critics of literary and philosophical texts were used to assigning specific, definite meanings (however subtle or complex) to the works they encountered through the exercise of what were called "readings" of those works, the deconstructors gave the appearance of having transcended mere reading by having grasped in a superior way aspects of textuality that frustrate reading or make it, in a strict sense of the term, impossible. Though he often admitted his own inability to "escape from the blind alleys of language"[1] not recognized as such by his less knowing counterparts, and though he openly confessed that his own interpretations could not possibly do justice to the plethora of meanings that texts actually contained, still, by saying as much, the deconstructor could not help but give the impression that he knew something deep about the inner workings of texts. Other critics seemed, by comparison, to be filled with metaphysical illusions associated with the belief—impossible to substantiate— that texts must be grounded in extratextual or extralinguistic realities, or somehow assignable to extraliterary causes. The deconstructor seemed to smile at this belief in the full knowledge that literature (or language) itself had produced it. Metaphysics, he knew, was a sort of optical trick, or an aftereffect of verbal play, wherein a ghostly set of fictions was simultaneously created and subverted by the operations of language. While other critics unwittingly revealed their own metaphysical biases or ideological prejudices by wrongly attributing these operations to a source of meaning outside the texts they studied, such as the consciousness of an author or the spirit at work in a particular age or culture, the deconstructor seemed to know exactly what it was that prevented a text from attesting unambiguously to any such source. In sum, it appeared that the deconstructor, in some sense, had gone beyond metaphysics, thereby transcending the principles that governed Marxists, formalists, psychologists, phenomenologists, structuralists, and indeed virtually every other kind of critic. The truth was, however, that deconstruction itself was metaphysical in its orientation and in its biases, as may be seen from an examination of two important essays written by the foremost American proponent of deconstruction, J. Hillis Miller. The first of these essays, entitled "Stevens' Rock and Criticism as Cure," appeared originally in 1976 in the *Georgia Review*.[2] The second, entitled "The Critic as Host," appeared in 1979 in a volume called *Deconstruction and Criticism,* which was, in effect, a sort of manifesto issued by the Yale deconstructors, including (besides Miller's essay) a group of related essays by Harold Bloom, Paul de Man, Jacques Derrida, and Geoffrey Hartman.[3]

In "Stevens' Rock and Criticism as Cure," Miller explains that deconstruction is part of a "new turn" in criticism "characterized by a focus on language as the central problematic of literary study.[4] While it is true that many of the so-called human sciences have been affected throughout most of this century by the implications of semiotics and linguistics, nevertheless, as Miller demonstrates, the deconstructionist attitude toward language represents an extreme view to the extent that it makes language an absolutely ungrounded, unconditioned given, not to be explained in terms other than those provided by itself. From the point of view of deconstruction, works of literature or philosophy cannot be explained by reference to any sort of extralinguistic situation from which they may appear to have been generated, nor can they be explained by reference to the supposed intentions or designs of the human beings who ostensibly caused them to come into being. They can only be accounted for by considering them as microcosms of the whole phenomenon of language, imagined in all its complexity and multiplicity. In effect, every specimen of language activity, from the slightest lyric to the weightiest philosophical tome, may be said to have a meaning which consists of all the implications that now attach, or ever have attached, to all the significances of all the words of which it is composed. That is to say, every instance of the use of language is known from the beginning, by hypothesis, to be infinitely complex because of the irreducible multiplicity of the patterns made by its component words and phrases. This is not something that just happens to be discovered through inquiry, something that turns up unexpectedly through an investigation that might have ended otherwise. It is something that is known to exist in advance, something demanded or expected by the deconstructionist mode of analysis.

Miller makes this clear in his analysis of the word "cure" from Stevens's poem "The Rock." The "cure of the ground" that Stevens calls for in this poem could mean, as Miller suggests, "a caring for the ground, a securing of it," while at the same time it could also mean "an effacing of it." It could even mean the finding of "proper names" for it, if one considers the word "cure" in terms of its rootedness in the Greek word *kuriologia*.[5] It could mean all of these things and more, because these and other meanings may be teased out of it etymologically and thus may be regarded as suggested by it. Since not all of these meanings are mutually compatible, it seems impossible to fix on a single interpretation either of passages that make use of the word "cure" or of Stevens's poem as a whole:

> The multiple meanings of the word "cure," like the meanings of all the key words and figures in "The Rock," are incompatible, irreconcilable. They may not be organized into a logical or dialectical structure but remain stubbornly heterogeneous. They may not be followed, etymologically, to a single root which will unify or explain them, explicate them by implicating them in a single source. They may not be folded together in a unified structure, as of leaves, blossom, and fruit from one stem. The origin rather is bifurcated, even trifurcated, a forking root which leads the searcher for the ground of the word into labyrinthine wanderings in the forest of words.[6]

On the basis of his own analysis of the word "cure," Miller speaks of Stevens's "cunning wordplay" in his "sagacious and somewhat covert use of the full etymological complexity" of the word, observing that such wordplay is typical of Stevens.

Later in his discussion of "The Rock," Miller explains that the poem's never-to-be-resolved incoherence can be attributed to the fact that "all the terms in the poem . . . are at once literal and figurative"[7] since each is really a catachresis or, in other words, a "violent, forced, or abusive use of a word to name something which has no literal name."[8] "Each term in 'The Rock,'" he argues, "including 'rock' and 'ground,' is a catachresis for something which has not, cannot have, a proper name." That something, according to Miller, is the abyss, the *Abgrund* or *Ungrund,* which the poem as a whole both calls attention to and conceals through the act of attempting to speak about it properly or appropriately. As an interpretation of Stevens's poem, Miller's analysis seems plausible precisely because it situates the wordplay of the poem in relation to Stevens's own attitude toward the philosophical problems posed by meaning and reference, or, in other words, because it explains the wordplay in terms of the poem's thematic or intentional concerns. But, in fact, the point of Miller's analysis is not to show that wordplay is instigated by authors; the point is to show that the volatility of language is beyond authorial control. That Stevens himself seems to have thematized this insight is certainly convenient but not really crucial. What is crucial is to recognize that all words, not just the key words and figures in "The Rock," are ambiguously literal and figurative, or appropriate and inappropriate, with respect to that which they appear to designate. Apart from any use they may be put to, they must all be regarded as bearing within themselves "the full etymological complexity" of words like "cure," and thus all employments of words may be said to be, like "The Rock," "incapable of being encompassed in a single logical formulation."[9] Stevens's poem is simply one instance of the fact that language has a mind of its own, that it is always "to some degree irreducibly idiosyncratic":

> The most unexpected words . . . may become momentarily nodes, at once fixed rock and treacherous abyss of doubled and redoubled meanings, around or over which the thought of the poet momentarily swirls or weaves its web. Such words are not the equivalents or substitutes for other terms. Each has its own proper laws and so may not be made an example of some general law. Such words may not be translated, thereby made transparent, dispensed with, evaporated, sublimated. They remain stubbornly heterogeneous, unassimilable, impervious to dialectical elation *(Aufhebung),* rocks in the stream, though the rock is air. The vocabulary of a poet is not a gathering or a closed system, but a dispersal, a scattering.[10]

The idea here is that, although words may be *analyzed* in such a way as to reveal the complexity of their origins and associations, they may not be *synthesized* in such a way as to produce the simplicity of a sentence or a paragraph or a book-length argument. But this idea is a function of the decision to regard the word as the right unit or the only real unit of literary investigation. It would be like regarding the atom as the only real unit of physical investigation or the cell as the only real unit of biological investigation. On the basis of these decisions, it might be concluded that, in contrast to the integrity and complexity of cells and cellular processes, organs and whole bodies ought to be regarded as only virtual realities or as gross oversimplifications of their own heterogeneous components. Or, similarly, it might be concluded that, in contrast to the actual indeterminacy of atomic behavior or the lawless volatility of subatomic particles and forces, visible, tangible structures (like those apparent to the naked human eye) might best be regarded as gross caricatures of the subtler details and finer adventures invisibly occurring within them. Unless one has a metaphysical preference for the relatively "small" as opposed to the relatively "large," there seems to be no essential reason to regard the study of words or the study of atoms or the study of cells as capable of invalidating, or relegating to the level of the mystical, the study of genres or the study of geology or the study of ecology.

The effect of making the "reality" of words subversive of the "ideality" of genres is, as Miller rightly indicates, to vaporize genre distinctions. Thus "the boundaries between literature and criticism are broken down . . . not because the critic arrogates to himself some vague right to be 'poetical' in his writing, but because he recognizes it as his doom not to be able to be anything else."[11] In amplifying his own definition of "dissemination" as a term representing "the affirmation of . . . the empty and remarkable place of a hundred blanks *[cent blancs]* to which one cannot give meaning," Derrida, says Miller, "provides a commentary on 'hundred blanks' *(cent blancs)* by making it one link in a chain generating a complicated multiple pun":

> It is a phrase, like the word "cure" in Stevens' poem, which is a node or knot of irreconcilable or undecidable meanings: *sens blanc, sang blanc, sans blanc, cent blancs, semblant.* Such words, says Derrida, "are not *atoms,* but points of economic condensation, necessary stations along the way for a large number of marks, for somewhat more effervescent crucibles. Then their effects not only turn back on themselves through a sort of closed self-excitation, they spread themselves in a chain over the theoretical and practical whole of a text, each time in a different way." These proliferating supplements and substitutions are the other possible words, none equivalents of one another, which may express the chasm of the

alogical, each time in a different way. Each term has its own systematic play of concepts and figures folded into it, incompatible with the self-excitation of any other word.[12]

Though it is possible to say that words have a degree of integrity as "stations along the way" or as "points of economic condensation," still it is evident on this view that one can never step into the same text twice, or even the same word twice.

Finally, what is gained by demonstrating that this kind of complexity is inherent in *every* use of language or that "all referentiality in language is a fiction"?[13] One result is that it becomes possible to volatilize or overturn every single conceptual distinction, so that no matter how simple or obvious or unambiguous such a distinction may seem, it can always be looked at more and more closely until it becomes blurry or indeterminate. In response to M. H. Abrams's approval of Wayne Booth's assertion that deconstructive readings are necessarily "parasitical" with respect to plain or obvious readings, Miller responded in "The Critic as Host" by demonstrating that the full etymological complexity of the term "parasite," together with that of its counterpart "host," makes it impossible to arrive at a completely unambiguous distinction between the concept of a "parasite" and the concept of that on which a "parasite" feeds. As it turns out, "a parasite was originally something positive, a fellow guest, someone sharing the food with you," whereas a "host," rightly considered, is someone who "contains in himself the double antithetical relation of host and guest [host in the bifold sense of 'eater and eaten'], guest in the bifold sense of friendly presence and alien invader."[14] In fact, it seems that a "guest" is a kind of "host" and a "host" is a kind of "guest," if for no other reason than because the words "guest" and "host" may be traced back to the same etymological root, as Miller determines in the course of his analysis. He concludes:

> The uncanny antithetical relation exists not only between pairs of words in this system, host and parasite, host and guest, but within each word itself. It reforms itself in each polar opposite when that opposite is separated out. This subverts or nullifies the apparently unequivocal relation of polarity which seems the conceptual scheme appropriate for thinking through the system.[15]

Instead of considering that some version of the distinction remains the basis for determining the uncanniness of each merger of the roles thus propounded, without which perception of the merger would be impossible, Miller draws the opposite inference that even the most innocent-seeming concept is dependent upon the antithetical concept to which it is opposed, but only in such a way as to be finally indistinguishable from it. The upshot is that Wayne Booth's proposition concerning the "parasitical" relation between deconstructive readings and readings that are not deconstructive is itself deconstructed by being subjected to what Miller refers to as "an extreme interpretation," according to which one goes "as far as one can with the terms" one has to work with.[16] Summing up the consequences of his own deconstruction of the concept of the term "parasite," Miller observes:

> To get so far or so much out of a little piece of language, context after context widening out from these few phrases to include as their necessary milieux all the family of Indo-European languages, all the literature and conceptual thought within those languages, and all the permutations of our social structures of household economy, gift-giving and gift-receiving—this is an argument for the value of recognizing the equivocal richness of apparently obvious or univocal language, even the language of criticism.[17]

If "richness" is thus discernible in particular words and phrases, whole works may be regarded as similarly "rich" by virtue of their infinitely various associations with the entire contents of Western culture, or indeed world culture. And so:

> If the literary work is within itself open, heterogeneous, a dialogue of conflicting voices, it is also seen as open to other texts, permeable to them, permeated by them. A literary text is not a thing in itself, "organically unified," but a relation to other texts which are relations in their turn. The study of literature is therefore the study of intertextuality. . . .[18]

The concept of "intertextuality" makes it possible to postpone indefinitely all questions concerning the non-linguistic origins of texts, or, more precisely, it rules out the possibility of raising such questions at all. If the origin of verbal phenomena is more of the same verbal phenomena, then, strictly speaking, verbal phenomena have no origin. In the absence of reciprocal relations with anything other than itself, language becomes, strictly speaking, the Absolute. No external world can be recognized to which language corresponds or within which language can be situated, nor can the intentions of rational agents be adduced as causes or determining factors with respect to language activity, since both the external world and the intentions of rational agents can be shown to have only a thematic existence *within* language. By absolutizing language in this fashion, deconstruction simply carries forward the Copernican Revolution of Kantian idealism, as I have already suggested in chapter 1. The idea that the external world is reducible to, or produced by, the conceptions of it that have been formed concerning it leads plausibly enough to the related idea that these very conceptions are themselves reducible to, or produced by, the expressions of them that have been formed to convey them. If the world is constituted by thought, why shouldn't thought be constituted by language? Why shouldn't it be the case, as Wittgenstein declared in the *Tractatus,* that the limits of my world just *are* the limits of my language? If nothing can be said to constitute language apart from its own "self-excitation," there is nothing to stop it from filling the slot previously occupied by the Absolute Mind. Just as each particular thought might be regarded (in the old form of idealism) as an expression of Mind Absolute, so each particular word or phrase might be similarly regarded as an expression of Intertextuality, or Language Absolute. Deconstruction's philosophical parentage in the old form of idealism can be seen very clearly when Miller refers, in "The Critic as Host," to "the law that language is not an instrument or tool in man's hands, a submissive means of thinking." On the contrary: "Language rather thinks man and his 'world,' including poems, if he will allow it to do so."[19] As the generative source of all ideas and thereby also of the "things" to which ideas were formerly thought to correspond, Language (with a capital L) replaces Mind (with a capital M).

By constantly breaking down or dissolving the distinctions between concepts, deconstruction might be said to run the risk of turning "richness" into meaninglessness. It is certainly a good thing to know that words are layered with meanings like palimpsests and thus, in a sense, deeply or densely metaphorical. But it is also well to remember that meaningful distinctions are themselves the basis for perceiving equivocal significations. A clear, unambiguous distinction between the concepts of "host" and "guest" is preserved or maintained each time both concepts are discovered to be implicated in a *word* for "host" or a *word* for "guest." That is to say, a *word* may be determined correctly to be ambiguous (because it is suggestive of incompatible meanings, each governed by a different concept), but the concepts themselves *cannot* be ambiguous for the simple reason that it is precisely their difference that creates the incompatibility between meanings. After examining the full etymological complexity of the *words* "host" and "guest," the various types of relationship that may exist between a host and a guest, including every possible role-variation or role-reversal, are clearer than ever. Rather than being uncannily merged, they are quite cannily sorted out. Each type of relationship, however complex, remains clearly distinguishable from the other types. Thus, while it may be true that *words* are ambiguous, the conceptual distinctions rolled up into words are quite otherwise. If every conceptual possibility suggested by a word were taken to be a functional part of the meaning of that word whenever the word was used, and if all the words in a text seemed worth pursuing equally throughout their various ranges of nuance, it would be impossible to read a text, for, in reading a text, it is necessary to give an unequal emphasis to different aspects of the text, even to ignore some aspects for the sake of noticing others. To achieve a "total" reading—to attempt to notice every aspect at every level of interest—would be to fly off in several different directions at once, and the result could only be that the text would appear incoherent.

The question, then, is whether it is appropriate to say that the text itself *is* "incoherent" or "anomalous" or "indeterminate." One way to answer this question would be to say that the "incoherence" or "richness" spoken of by the deconstructor is not necessarily incompatible with the meaningful patterns detected by other critics. And that is because complexity on one level of analysis is not incompatible with simplicity on another level. A complete analysis of the full etymological complexity of every single word in *Lycidas* might be practically impossible or, at least, infinitely long in coming. It might seek to be cognizant, as it went along, of "all the family of Indo-European languages" and "all the literature and conceptual thought within those languages," or it might despair of knowing even a fraction of all this and thus despair of ever coming to understand what it regards as the "necessary milieux" of Milton's poem. On this level, the poem might be said to be "unreadable," or full of never-to-be-exhausted possibilities. On another level, it might be said that the poem is a pastoral elegy, and a reading of the poem might be produced that focused on Milton's handling of the conventions associated with pastoral or elegiac poetry. To read the poem on the first-mentioned level is not necessarily to read it more discerningly, any more than to look at things through a microscope is necessarily to see them more discerningly. The patterns that one can see close up to, or far away from, a thing may be strikingly different but they do not simply cancel each other out, nor do they render the object seen mysteriously incoherent.

If I were to study all the paintings in the Louvre under a high-powered microscope, I might reach the conclusion that each painting is really an abstraction consisting of mere splotches or swirls of color, or I might be tempted to say that what appears in each case to be simply a splotch of blue or a splotch of red is really a kaleidoscopic jumble of several different colors, blurred together by the naked eye. But, upon reflection, I should not feel entitled to say that, when others talk of figures in these paintings or speak of an artist's use of a particular color (such as red or blue), they are speaking only of fictions, not having observed the true complexities that I alone have seen with my microscope. Nor should I feel entitled to say that all the paintings are really abstract designs simply because I have found a way *not* to see what the so-called representational paintings appear to be representing. For the same reasons, it would not seem appropriate, even if one could manage it, to allow an accurate perception of the biochemical dramas at work in the body of a great actor to disrupt or displace a perception of that actor's dramatic performance in the role of Hamlet or Lear, even though it might be considered that the biological dramas constitute the actual substance of that which appears to be occurring on the stage.

Nevertheless, the charm of deconstruction has much to do with the fact that it seems capable of undermining or interfering with other kinds of analysis. As Miller explains it, the art of deconstruction consists in demonstrating that the apparently coherent structures observed by other critics are really incoherent:

> Deconstruction as a mode of interpretation works by a careful and circumspect entering of each textual labyrinth. The critic feels his way from figure to figure, from concept to concept, from mythical motif to mythical motif, in a repetition which is in no sense a parody. . . . The deconstructive critic seeks to find, by this process of retracing, the element in the system studied which is alogical, the thread in the text in question which will unravel it all, or the loose stone which will pull down

the whole building. The deconstruction, rather, annihilates the ground on which the building stands by showing that the text has already annihilated that ground, knowingly or unknowingly. Deconstruction is not a dismantling of the structure of a text but a demonstration that it has already dismantled itself. Its apparently solid ground is no rock but thin air.[20]

All of this may happen as Miller describes it, except for the part about the whole building falling down as a result. To suppose that a deconstructive analysis seriously affects the kind of coherence or solidity that other critics have attributed to literary or philosophical works is to make the sort of mistake Wittgenstein describes in *The Blue Book,* which consists in supposing that an analysis of material objects in terms of sense-data or in terms of component atoms in some way reveals the incoherent status of the objects themselves as objects. Wittgenstein's account of this mistake pertains equally to the implications that are attributed to the analyses produced by deconstruction:

> We seem to have made a discovery—which I could describe by saying that the ground on which we stood and which appeared to be firm and reliable was found to be boggy and unsafe. —That is, this happens when we philosophize; for as soon as we revert to the standpoint of common sense this *general* uncertainty disappears.
>
> This queer situation can be cleared up somewhat by looking at an example; in fact a kind of parable illustrating the difficulty we are in, and also showing the way out of this sort of difficulty: We have been told by popular scientists that the floor on which we stand is not solid, as it appears to common sense, as it has been discovered that the wood consists of particles filling space so thinly that it can almost be called empty. This is liable to perplex us, for in a way of course we know that the wood is solid, or that, if it isn't solid, this may be due to the wood being rotten but not to its being composed of electrons. To say, on this latter ground, that the floor is not solid is to misuse language. For even if the particles were as big as grains of sand, and as close together as these are in a sandheap, the floor would not be solid if it were composed of them in the sense in which a sandheap is composed of grains. Our perplexity was based on a misunderstanding; the picture of the thinly filled space had been wrongly *applied*. For this picture of the structure of matter was meant to explain the very phenomenon of solidity.
>
> As in this example the word "solidity" was used wrongly and it seemed that we had shown that nothing was really solid, just in this way,

in stating our puzzles about the *general vagueness* of sense-experience, and about the flux of all phenomena, we are using the words "flux" and "vagueness" wrongly, in a typically metaphysical way, namely without an antithesis; whereas in their correct and everyday use vagueness is opposed clearness, flux to stability, inaccuracy to accuracy, and *problem* to *solution*.[21]

Another way to put this would be to say that, as soon as the deconstructor informs us that *all* texts or *all* uses of language are incoherent or self-contradictory, or that *all* apparently logical structures are actually, upon closer inspection, alogical or absurd, we can be sure that the operative descriptive terms are being used "in a typically metaphysical way, namely without an antithesis." We can be sure that a mistake has been made of the sort that Wittgenstein describes in this remark from his *Philosophical Investigations:*

> "If it is possible for someone to make a false move in some game, then it might be possible for everybody to make nothing but false moves in every game." —Thus we are under a temptation to misunderstand the logic of our expressions here, to give an incorrect account of the use of our words.
>
> Orders are sometimes not obeyed. But what would it be like if no orders were *ever* obeyed? The concept 'order' would have lost its purpose.[22]

To know in advance, by prescription, that "any reading can be shown to be a misreading on evidence drawn from the text itself"[23] is to use the term "misreading" in a metaphysical way, without an antithesis. It is like knowing that all the moves in every game can be regarded as false moves, from a certain perspective. Or rather it is like saying that, since I can never see all the sides of a house at any given moment from any actual angle of vision, whenever I *do* see a house from *one* particular side, I should call that "not really seeing the house," or I should say, "I have *mis*seen the house." I might even reach the conclusion that the house I have seen is really "unseeable" or that the house as a whole is actually a fiction since no one can ever "see" it as a whole. In such a conclusion, the metaphysical propensities of the deconstructive view make themselves apparent.

The novelty of deconstruction seemed very great when it first appeared in the late 1960s, although as Miller rightly observed in his essay on Stevens, "it can always be demonstrated that the apparent novelty of any new development in criticism is the renewal of an insight which has been found and lost and found again repeatedly through all the centuries of literary study since the first Homeric and Biblical commentaries."[24] Luther, for example, speaks out against deconstruction with his usual bluntness in *The Bondage of the Will,* when he cites approvingly, on the subject of Scriptural interpretation, Hilary's principle that "the knowledge of what is said is to be gained from the scope of what is said, not from certain detached words only."[25] In his controversy with Erasmus, Luther accuses Erasmus of assuming that we may "turn the words of God backwards and forwards according to our own lust," and he adds: "if that were the case, what is there in the whole Scripture, that might not be resolved into the philosophy of Anaxagoras—'that any thing might be made from anything'?"[26] While it might be argued that Luther simply fulminates against deconstruction, at least he gives an indication that he knows something about its methods and consequences, as for instance in this passage, where he accuses Erasmus of trope-hunting or trope-inventing:

> Let us [says Luther] come to the text itself, for the purpose of seeing, what I agreement there is between the text and the trope. For it is the way with all those who elude arguments by means of tropes, to hold the text itself in sovereign contempt [the text not being a thing in itself, as Miller says], and to aim only, at picking out a certain term, and twisting and crucifying it upon the cross of their own opinion, without paying any regard whatever, either to circumstance, to consequence, to precedence, or to the intention or object of the author. Thus the Diatribe, in this passage [Ex. 4:21], utterly disregarding the intention of Moses and the scope of his words, tears out of the text this term, "I will harden," and makes of it just what it will, according to its own lust: not at all considering, whether that can be again inserted so as to agree and square with the body of the text. And this is the reason why the Scripture was not sufficiently clear to those most received and most learned men of so many ages. And no wonder, for even the sun itself would not shine, if it should be assailed by such arts as these.[27]

Ironically, from the deconstructive point of view, it is the traditional critic who exhibits willfulness or lust, by ignoring the self-excitation or Brownian movement of a text's verbal elements, and by plucking instead out of the text scopes, designs, and intentions, in an effort to make the text stand still. Indeed, from the deconstructive point of view, scopes, designs, and intentions are essentially problematic, because they must be inferred. But how can it be otherwise when it comes to envisioning "the full etymological complexity" of particular words? Why must it be assumed that I cannot know the meaning of a word when I encounter it in the present in one particular context but I *can* know the variety of its meanings in a whole array of different contexts stretched across history, according to the reconstruction of that history by etymologists? If scopes, designs, and intentions are inferred with respect to whole texts by traditional critics, they are also inferred with respect to the various employments of particular words by the deconstructor. If arguments of one kind or another are required to get a text to stand still, they are also required to get it moving. The idea that traditional critics must work vigorously to produce textual simplicity, whereas deconstructors have only to sit back and receive textual complexity, without engaging in inference, is simply false. Whereas traditional critics feel compelled to make particular terms "agree and square" with the body of a text (and ultimately to make whole texts "agree and square" with a principle or ground outside themselves), deconstructive critics feel similarly compelled to make disparate meanings "agree and square" with the particular terms in which they are imagined to coincide, just as they are similarly compelled to make the terms themselves "agree and square" with the semantic possibilities constituted by the family of Indo-European languages. The work of "agreeing and squaring" is no less a work for the deconstructor than it is for the traditional critic. To complain that the latter has wrongly construed a text by taking it to be the product of an author's intention is, furthermore, precisely to construe the latter's criticism in terms of its own exhibition of scope, design, or intention, since the *words* making up this criticism would themselves be nothing to complain about, being instances, in keeping with all other instances, of the semantic possibilities of the Indo-European family of languages. The oppositions or differences between seemingly incompatible interpretations of the same text disappear as soon as they are seen to be equally suggestive of these possibilities. In fact, if every text is to be regarded as implying nothing less than "all the literature and conceptual thought within" the Indo-European language family, it is hard to see how any one text might be differentiated from another. The richness and complexity imagined to characterize all this literature and conceptual thought would have to be attributed to the combined effect of texts utterly lacking in distinctiveness and particularity.

The truth is that there *is* an intention that governs the exercise of the deconstructive reading strategy. It is the intention to show that all efforts to express the truth of things in language are misguided. As Miller says in his essay on Stevens, "There is no 'truth of things,' as such, to be represented."[28] But if this is so, then the ego of the interpreter must be adduced as the only explanation of an otherwise inexplicable industry: the industry of creating nonrepresentational interpretations of things having, in themselves, no intrinsic nature but falsely imagined to exhibit such a nature by other egos. This would make the deconstructor, as I have already argued in chapter 2 with respect to Derrida, a practitioner of what Hegel calls irony, for whom "nothing is treated *in and for itself* and as valuable in itself, but only as produced by the subjectivity of the *ego*."[29] The only way to avoid the Romantic idealism implicit in such an attitude would he to opt, as Miller seems to do in the essays we have just considered, for some sort of Absolute Idealism, or rather Absolute Linguisticism, in which the deconstructive exercise is itself grounded in, or generated by, the play of Language, taken as the Absolute Mind. This, as I suggested earlier, may ultimately be the import of the Heideggerian sentiment that "language thinks man and his 'world,' including poems, if he will allow it to do so."

CHAPTER 5

IDEOLOGY AND THE NEW PRAGMATISM

> No more than the works of Apelles and Sophocles, if Raphael and
> Shakespeare had known them, could have appeared to them as simple
> preparatory exercises for themselves—but rather as a kindred power
> of the spirit—just as little can Reason glimpse in earlier forms of
> itself only useful preparatory exercises for itself. And if Virgil re-
> garded Homer as such a preparatory exercise for himself and his
> refined age, so has his work remained a postscript for his predecessor.
>
> —Hegel, *The Difference Between the Fichtean
> and Schellingian Systems of Philosophy*

As most of us are no doubt aware, the new vogue of pragmatism can be
attributed, at least in part, to the excellent rhetorical skills of its leading
proponent, Richard Rorty. In *Philosophy and the Mirror of Nature* (1979)
and especially in the collection of essays entitled *Consequences of Pragmatism* (1982), Rorty has advanced the thesis that pragmatism is more
than just "the chief glory of our country's intellectual tradition."[1] It is also
(he claims) the most correct or the most acceptable form of that critique of
Western thought which has been the main project of philosophy on both
sides of the Atlantic since about 1900. Thus, according to Rorty, the Anglo-
American tradition of analytic philosophy and the Continental tradition
that runs from Nietzsche through Heidegger to Derrida may be regarded
as having converged, in the fullness of time, on a position already occupied by the pragmatists. As Rorty puts it in one of his most stunning sentences, "James and Dewey were not only waiting at the end of the dialectical road which analytic philosophy traveled, but are waiting at the end of
the road which, for example, Foucault and Deleuze are currently travel-
ing."[2] Suddenly pragmatism has become the latest thing, and we can see
something of its newly acquired prestige and power in the fact that it became the focus of an important debate on the status of theory, which raged
in the pages of *Critical Inquiry* back in the 1980s. The debate was initiated
by two pragmatists, Steven Knapp and Walter Benn Michaels, who in their
paper "Against Theory" argue that theory has no power to govern the practice of making judgments (as, for example, in the making of judgments
concerning the meaning of a literary text) for the simple reason that theory

is always situated in, and therefore governed by, the exigencies of practice itself. The significance of this argument can best be seen if one remembers that theory has been accorded a very high status indeed in most English departments ever since the decline of formalism about thirty years ago. Phenomenology, structuralism, and poststructuralism were taken up in quick succession during the sixties and seventies because each promised to provide a new and exciting "theory" of literature, a more philosophical view of it, that could change our way of reading particular texts. Theorists have been in high demand because they are the ones who are supposed to have the deepest insights into the nature of meaning or the nature of language or the nature of textuality. Their philosophical sophistication (derived mainly from an acquaintance with the latest French and German theorists of interpretation) supposedly gave them an edge over mere "close readers" who were ignorant of philosophy. Now, according to the pragmatist argument of Knapp and Michaels, it is clear that theory has no work to do at all since the issues theorists concern themselves with are already resolved in the course of those elementary acts or practices of interpretation that necessarily occur before the act of theorizing about interpretation can itself commence. In this way, the pragmatist (the critic who understands the priority of actual practice in relation to all those attempts to stand outside of practice in order to govern it by means of theory) emerges as the most sophisticated antimetaphysician of all, waiting at the end of the road for his weaker brothers who will come along presently still huffing and puffing about the implications of Heidegger's critique of the Western onto-theological tradition or Derrida's critique of the metaphysics of presence. The pragmatist does it right, gets it straight, and so now *he* has the edge.

The paper "Against Theory" provoked nine responses[3] including an important essay by Stanley Fish called "Consequences" and a short piece by the leading pragmatist Rorty called "Philosophy without Principles." The interesting thing is that, with a few notable exceptions, most of the contributors to the debate seem to be intent not on refuting the pragmatist thesis but rather on getting it stated in the clearest, most correct fashion. This alone is perhaps enough to suggest that pragmatism is today having an impact far beyond what it once had when it was regarded as an American version of British empiricism or as a mere rationalization of the principles of common sense. Indeed, as the *Critical Inquiry* debate indicates, pragmatism has become a force to reckon with not only on the philosophical scene but also on the literary scene, especially the so-called New Pragmatism as expounded by Rorty and Fish. Formidable though it may be, however, I want to argue here that this New Pragmatism must finally fail: first, because in a very important sense it has not accomplished the radical break with tradition that Rorty and the others think it has (which is to say, it has misconceived both itself and the tradition it seeks to break with); and, second, because on its own terms it cannot solve the problem of values, despite the fact that it likes to see itself as particularly sensitive to values and imagines itself to be "value-oriented."[4] Indeed, the nullity of the pragmatist theory of value is such that it leaves a vacuum, and into this vacuum ideology comes rushing, making all sorts of claims and demands which pragmatism is powerless to answer. In order to show how this happens, I would like to focus attention on three essays. The first is the very brilliant essay by Rorty that serves as the introduction to his volume *Consequences of Pragmatism.* The second is the essay I have already mentioned by Fish, which was Fish's contribution to the *Critical Inquiry* debate, and the third is an essay by Jonathan Culler on William Empson, which appeared in November of 1984 in the *Times Literary Supplement.* I shall use the first two essays for the purpose of demonstrating the inadequacies of pragmatism (particularly with respect to the problem of values), and I shall use Culler's essay in order to demonstrate the ideological messes we are left with after pragmatism has done its work—the "consequences," as it were, of pragmatism.

Rorty's essay is a splendid overview of pragmatism that tries to set it in relation to all previous philosophy (at least in the West) stemming from Plato. Rorty calls this prepragmatist philosophy "Philosophy," using a capital "p" to distinguish it from the kind of philosophy he expects to see practiced in the "post-Philosophical culture" which is just around the corner and which the pragmatists are doing their best to usher in. The trouble with Philosophy, says Rorty, is that it failed because it was too pretentious, too overweening. It tried to do metaphysics, it tried to ground our knowledge and experience by establishing absolutes, it tried to say big, important things about Truth or Goodness or Beauty that would always be true. Indeed, it tried to provide a sure foundation for all the rest of our living and thinking, and the task was simply too much for it. The virtue of philosophy (as distinguished from Philosophy) is that it has soberly and humbly renounced these pretensions. The new "philosopher," according to Rorty, will be a sort of "all-purpose intellectual" who will have abandoned the grandiose, quixotic projects of Philosophy in favor of the much more modest one of trying "to see how things, in the broadest possible sense of the term, hang together, in the broadest possible sense of the term." Here is Rorty's account, for example, of the failure of Philosophy, which has made it necessary for us to move on to something different:

> Pragmatists think that the history of attempts to isolate the True or the Good, or to define the word "true" or "good," supports their suspicion that there is no interesting work to be done in this area. It might, of course, have turned out otherwise. People have, oddly enough, found something interesting to say about the essence of Force and the definition of "number. They might have found something interesting to say about the essence of Truth. But in fact they haven't. The history of attempts to do so, and of criticisms of such attempts, is roughly coextensive with the history of that literary genre we call "philosophy"—a genre founded by Plato. So pragmatists see the Platonic tradition as having outlived its usefulness. This does not mean that they have a new, non-Platonic set of answers to Platonic questions to offer, but rather that they do not think we should ask those questions anymore.[5]

This is a very telling passage, I think, because it makes use of a ploy which is used again and again by philosophers who feel that it is necessary to debunk the Western tradition in order to make a really fresh start in philosophy. The ploy consists in claiming that all those old philosophers got bogged down in endless and fruitless wrangling over problems that could never be resolved because they admitted of no solution, or because they admitted of too many solutions. For every position there has been a counter-position; for every school there has been a rival, opposing school. And so it has gone on, pointlessly and relentlessly, like a perpetual-motion machine, until finally, out of sheer boredom or exasperation, we start looking around for a method that will enable us (as Wittgenstein puts it) to stop doing philosophy. In a word, the history of philosophy shows that it hasn't paid off, that it hasn't been able to deliver the goods, that it is bankrupt. (B.F. Skinner, by the way, uses this argument with wonderful effect in the first chapter of *Beyond Freedom and Dignity*.)

There are a number of things wrong with this ploy, it seems to me, and most of them have to do with the fact that it is based on too hasty an impression of philosophy's development, such as one might get from glancing quickly at some of the older textbooks on the history of philosophy. Thus, from such a glance, one might conclude that philosophy consists of lots of different opinions on a certain number of topics or subjects. Philosopher A believes that truth is this, Philosopher B believes that truth is that, Philosopher C believes that it is some third thing, and so on. (Tolstoy, for example, demonstrates in chapter 3 of *What Is Art?* that aesthetic philosophy can be made to look silly by merely listing, in rapid-fire order, the different definitions that philosophers have given of the term "beauty.") On the other hand, it is possible that one might arrive at the slightly different conclusion that every philosopher has been successfully refuted by his immediate successor and that this has happened so many times that it is extremely unlikely that any philosophy will ever be produced which will not, in the course of time, be successfully refuted. That Rorty himself subscribes to this latter view seems evident from his remark that "Nobody is so passé as the intellectual czar of the previous generation. . . ."[6] In other words, philosophy at a quick glance is either a huge sea of conflicting opinions or an endless chain of refutations wherein each philosopher simply neutralizes or cancels out the work of his predecessors.

Both of these versions of the history of philosophy are, I think, too glibly pessimistic. There is no reason to suppose, in advance, that every philosopher has necessarily gotten things wrong. Here or there, one or another of them just may have gotten something right. How can I tell if I don't pore very carefully over the tradition to find out? Maybe Kant and the other Enlightenment philosophers *did* demonstrate the impossibility of doing natural theology, but then again maybe they didn't. How can I tell if I don't pore over all the relevant texts in order to see who really won the debate? It may be that various sorts of misunderstandings have prevented the success of a particular philosophical view and that these misunderstandings have unfortunately become accepted by later generations which have allowed them to become the basis of views less adequate (or simply wrong) by comparison to the view they have replaced. On the face of it, I should say, it is no more likely that all philosophers have gotten things wrong than it is that one or two of them should have gotten them right. No overview of philosophy can tell me this; I have to go and find out for myself. And this means that I can't afford to junk the whole Western tradition just because I keep hearing voices saying that it didn't pan out or that it has "outlived its usefulness." For that matter, there is no reason to suppose that the truth, if it *were* found by a philosopher, would necessarily be met with instantaneous and universal acclaim, though it is the absence of such acclaim that persuades many pessimists that it has not, therefore, been found.

Given at least the bare possibility that a philosopher somewhere, somehow, may have gotten things right, one of the most distressing things about Rorty's position is that it discourages careful scrutiny of the tradition to find out whether this is so by making the tradition seem uninteresting and misguided. To take the tradition seriously, to get caught up in its questions, is to get entangled with it in such a way that we will never be able to extricate ourselves, and so we had better just let it alone and drop the questions. Instead of looking back at our predecessors with respect and awe in an effort "to preserve the elements of every intellectual tradition," which effort (says Rorty) will be "self-defeating," we ought rather to look back on them "with the amused condescension typical of later generations looking back at their ancestors."[7] If we are sometimes tempted to think that the questions that occupied these predecessors were important or deep, we need to disabuse ourselves of the temptation and repress, if possible, the intuitions that make such questions seem worthwhile:

> *Of course* we have such intuitions. How could we escape having them? We have been educated within an intellectual tradition built around such claims—just as we used to be educated within an intellectual tradition built around such claims as "If God does not exist, everything is permitted," "Man's dignity consists in his link with a supernatural order," and "One must not mock holy things." But it begs the question between the pragmatist and realist to say that we must find a philosophical view which "captures" such intuitions. The pragmatist is urging that we do our best to *stop having* such intuitions, that we develop a *new* intellectual tradition.[8]

Thus, in response to the suggestion that we look at the tradition to see what truth may be found in it, Rorty counters with the observation that that is precisely the sort of attitude that the tradition itself has fostered and that, consequently, needs repressing. Such an attitude must be extirpated, along with the intuitions and vocabularies with which it is associated and wherein it finds its home. It is for this reason, then, that the pragmatist does not recommend that we examine the philosophical tradition but instead busies himself trying to find "ways of cautioning the public against the Philosophical tradition."⁹ And yet, Rorty assures us, "his *only* argument for thinking that these intuitions and vocabularies should be eradicated is that the intellectual tradition to which they belong has not paid off, is more trouble than it is worth, has become an incubus."¹⁰ So around and around we go in a circle. First, we are told that the tradition is merely a record of futility and error. Then, when we feel inclined to go back and see whether or not this is so, we are told that the impulse to do this is tainted and ought to be "deliberately repressed."¹¹ If we ask why it is tainted, we are told that it is so because it is associated with ways of thinking that stem from tradition. If we ask what is so bad about tradition, then we hear once again that it is merely a record of futility and error. Evidently, we should stop being recalcitrant and simply allow ourselves to be retooled for the coming "post-Philosophical culture."

If we hold out long enough, though, we shall eventually notice something very curious about Rorty's suggestion that we shift from Philosophy to post-Philosophy. Indeed, we shall notice that it is oddly similar to Plato's suggestion that we shift from pre Philosophy to Philosophy. The reasons for making both shifts are substantially the same upon examination. Like Rorty, Plato too is worried about the fruitlessness, the futility, of all those pre-Philosophical opinions that go swirling around in our minds and form the basis of interminable debates that never seem to go anywhere or accomplish anything. I think that courage is *x,* you think that it's *y,* some other fellow there thinks that it's another thing, and so on. The only way to get out of this dilemma (says Plato) is to find a method that will enable us to sort things out so that we can arrive at better, more adequate ideas. Notice, too, that Plato does not come down from the mountain with the Forms already inscribed on tablets of stone. He merely says that if we are willing to operate within the constraints of a certain method, the method of dialectic, then and only then will we be able to make real *progress* toward finding what things are true and good. (All the "positive" or "metaphysical" elements of what is usually regarded as Platonism come afterward as a result of reflecting on the implications of what it means to have such a method.) This, I think, is essentially what is involved in the shift from pre-Philosophy to Philosophy, but it seems to me that the same thing is involved in Rorty's shift from Philosophy to post-Philosophy. The point is that, at last, a method has been found, although it is, of course, for Rorty, the pragmatic method. At last, we can see how our biases and prejudices (rooted as they are in spurious intuitions inculcated in us by tradition) have prevented us from making real progress by creating the conditions for interminable discussions. By adopting the pragmatic method (which is based on a true insight into how our ideas are formed, what makes them work, and what their limitations are), we can disabuse ourselves of these biases and prejudices (or at least short-circuit them) and get down to the real business of building up a body of truths that are really interesting and serviceable. They won't be like Plato's truths, they won't be the Truth, but that's just the point. They will be the kind of local. contingent truths that really are true—at least for the moment. At last, inquiry will be on a new footing. The scales of error will fall from our eyes, up out of the cave we'll come, knowing for the first time, as it were, the real limitations and, therefore, the real weight and power of our ideas. If they don't seem to be worth very much for a very long time, still it's something even to know that. Indeed, it is precisely this knowledge that enables us to look back with "amused condescension" at our ancestors, who wasted all that time trying to make their ideas true forever.

We have heard all this before, haven't we? Isn't this Plato's story? Up from slavery, into freedom; up from error, into Enlightenment? In fact, if Lévi-Strauss and structuralism were still in fashion, we could probably demonstrate that Plato's story and Rorty's story have the same "deep" structure, despite the fact that they seem to hold doctrines that are the mirror opposites of each other and are couched in somewhat different vocabularies. How, then, are we to choose between them? Which one of them is right? That, of course, is an unfair question, prompted by one of those intuitions that needs repressing. There is no such thing as the "right" version of this story. We can only ask which one seems preferable, which one is likelier to give us a better culture or a better life. If the Platonic tradition has failed us, says Rorty, then we need to construct a new and better one. But notice this: the pragmatist does not think

> that there is anything isolable as "the purposes which we construct vo-
> cabularies and cultures to fulfill" against which to test vocabularies and
> cultures. But he does think that in the process of playing vocabularies
> and cultures off against each other, we produce new and better ways of
> talking and acting—not better by reference to a previously known stan-
> dard, but just better in the sense that they come to *seem* clearly better than
> their predecessors.[12]

In what sense will our new ways of talking and acting be better than our old ways? It can't be because they'll be truer, nor can it be because they'll conform to the purposes for which we produce them. These purposes are themselves dependent on our ways of talking and acting. So all we can do is wait and see what our new ways of talking and acting look like or sound like and hope, meanwhile, that they'll strike us as clearly better than our old ways. If our purposes have changed (as indeed they must) in the course of our transition from Philosophy to post-Philosophy, then we have every right to expect, on the basis of history, that our new purposes will be better than our old ones. As Rorty puts it:

> If Philosophy disappears, something will have been lost which was central to Western intellectual life—just as something central was lost when religious intuitions were weeded out from among the intellectually respectable candidates for Philosophical articulation. But the Enlightenment thought, rightly, that what would succeed religion would be *better*. The pragmatist is betting that what succeeds the "scientific," positivist culture which the Enlightenment produced will be *better*.[13]

Once again, the obstinate questioner who keeps asking what "better" means is advised to change the subject. You'll know it when you see it, he is told. But how will I know that the new culture really is better? Wrong kind of question, comes the answer; you'll know it because it will *feel* better. But what will make it better? Well, it'll suit our new purposes and needs in a fashion inconceivable to the old culture. Will these new purposes and needs be really worth pursuing and ministering to? Of course. Their value is established by the fact that they will seem more important to you than the ones you've left behind. Or, to put it slightly differently, their value depends on the fact that, when the time comes, they simply *will* be the purposes and needs that you *do* happen to value.—In other words, the new culture will be better than the old one because, when the time comes, it will strike me as clearly better than the old one. I should now call it "good" (to use an old-fashioned term) because it's the sort of thing I'm then likely to call "good."

At this point, we have arrived at what I call the Trobriand Islander fallacy after a little passage in B. F. Skinner's *Beyond Freedom and Dignity* where I first encountered it. Arguing from a point of view very similar to Rorty's, Skinner tells us in this passage that we do not have to worry, in the old-fashioned way, about what is really good or really valuable:

> What a given group of people calls good is a fact: it is what members of
> the group find reinforcing as the result of their genetic endowment and
> the natural and social contingencies to which they have been exposed.
> Each culture has its own set of goods, and what is good in one culture
> may not be good in another. To recognize this is to take the position of
> "cultural relativism." What is good for the Trobriand Islander is good for
> the Trobriand Islander, and that is that.[14]

One imagines a group of these islanders, gathered together in council,
trying to decide which of several courses of action to take in a very important matter, trying, that is, to decide the "right" thing to do or the "good"
thing to do, given a certain set of circumstances. What would be the effect
if one of them stood up and said, "I know, we've only got to do what a
Trobriand Islander would do in these circumstances, and that will settle
it"? The suggestion would most likely be regarded as null and void, for the
simple reason that it is no help at all to be told, when one is in a quandary,
that one ought to regard as good the very thing one *does* regard as good. In
other words, the only person who cannot take comfort in the remark "What
is good for the Trobriand Islander is good for the Trobriand Islander, and
that's that," is the Trobriand Islander faced with the problem of trying to
decide what is good. Or, to put it in the simplest possible terms, when I am
confronted with the problem of how to behave in a certain situation, I
cannot appeal for a *reason* to behave one way or another to that which
causes me to behave as I do. The pragmatist can tell me, after the fact, that
I have necessarily acted in accordance with my true values. He can also
advise me to try to behave in the future so that my actions will remain in
accordance with these values once they have been identified (though this
will be rather peculiar advice because there is really no way I can *not* act
in accordance with the values that really do guide my behavior). What the
pragmatist cannot do is to help me determine *what* to value. If ever I should
wonder what is good, or what is important, or what is right, the pragmatist
tells me cheerfully that, of course, what is good is what I believe to be
good, and what is important is what I believe to be important, and what is
right is what I believe to be right. But that's no help at all, unless I can
count on never being in a state of doubt about these things. Here we can
see the nullity, the impotence, of pragmatism in every situation where value
judgments are problematic. In every such instance, it seems to me, we are

compelled to fall back not only on the values we have learned from our tradition but also on the traditional ways of justifying and interpreting those values. Unfortunately, the only tradition we have to work with is the bad one, the Philosophical one, which has become "an incubus" and needs to be "repressed." The new tradition, the better one (which is to say, the one we'll all agree *is* better *after* it arrives), is, just as unfortunately, not yet with us. Thus, we find ourselves in a very sad case, "living between a repudiated past and a dimly seen post-Philosophical future."[15] We are, in fact, a little like those Trobriand Islanders, sitting in council trying to decide between the claims of the old tradition and the claims of the new. We are on the cutting edge where all kinds of attitudes and values, of one type or the other, are at stake. And the pragmatist is like the islander who arises, full of celerity, to announce that the problem doesn't exist since all we have to do is be ourselves and act accordingly.

Rorty is apparently not afraid that a vacuum will result in a culture in which nobody any longer feels obligated (or even able) to isolate "the purposes which we construct vocabularies and cultures to fulfill." Such a culture strikes him as potentially much more open, much more democratic, than the one that, up till now, has been oppressing us like an incubus:

> The question of whether the pragmatist is right to be so sanguine is the question of whether a culture is imaginable, or desirable, in which no one—or at least no intellectual—believes that we have, deep down inside us, a criterion for telling whether we are in touch with reality or not, when we are in the Truth. This would be a culture in which neither the priests nor the physicists nor the poets nor the Party were thought of as more "rational," or more "scientific" or "deeper" than one another. No particular portion of culture would be singled out as exemplifying (or signally failing to exemplify) the condition to which the rest aspired. There would be no sense that, beyond the current intra-disciplinary criteria, which, for example, good priests or good physicists obeyed, there were other, transdisciplinary, transcultural, ahistorical criteria, which they also obeyed. There would still be hero worship in such a culture, but it would not be worship of heroes as children of the gods, as marked off from the rest of mankind by closeness to the immortal. It would simply be admiration of exceptional men and women who were very good at doing the quite diverse kinds of things they did. Such people would not be those who knew a Secret, who had won through to the Truth, but simply people who were good at being human.[16]

One's first reaction to this paragraph may very well be to wonder just who is going to bother paying any attention to those "good priests" and "'good physicists," since, as Rorty has told us in the preceding paragraph, the Enlightenment did well to weed out our religious intuitions (enabling the new secular spirit to displace the old religious one) just as what is about to follow the Enlightenment will do well to displace the Enlightenment concept of "science." Thus, if anyone is tempted to regard priests and physicists as good, it won't be because priests and physicists have anything important to tell us. But perhaps that's just the point. We won't have to pay attention; we can just appreciate them for being good at being human. If the priest says that Nature is one kind of thing and the physicist says that actually it's a very different kind of thing, we can just smile very approvingly at both of them and say, "Yes, that's a splendid priestly sort of conception of it all right, and, yes, *that's* a splendid sort of physicist's conception of it, too. No need to choose, because they're both very interesting and very human." If the priest and the physicist object that there's something important at stake in choosing between them, we shall likely become a little disappointed in them (a little less inclined to call them "good") because we shall have caught them invoking, by implication, something other than "the current intra-disciplinary criteria." Here, at last, we see the purpose of the new "all-purpose intellectual." It will be his business to enjoy the views of other intellectuals (who will be gently reminded, when they need it, to stay within the boundaries of their own disciplines' criteria) without ever having to take any one of them seriously. Every view will be to the "all-purpose intellectual" aesthetically interesting, particularly if it gives expression to some aspect of what it means to be human, and it will be very difficult to think of a view that isn't able to do that.

But now suppose a Hitler comes to power (though how this could happen in a post-Philosophical culture may be hard to imagine). Suppose I am faced with two different views regarding the question of whether I should support him as my country's leader or oppose him by joining the underground resistance movement. Which view should I countenance? Which should I act on? If I am an "all-purpose intellectual," I can say: "Yes, this National Socialist program *is* wonderful in its way, a very striking expression of at least one part of what it means to be human. On the other hand, the resistance program makes sense too, if you look at it from a certain point of view. So what is there to choose? This man Bonhoeffer is certainly impressive, but then Goebbels is no slouch, either, as a minister of propaganda. In fact, when it comes right down to it, Hitler himself makes a damn fine torturer. Unless I want to appeal to some sort of 'transdisciplinary transcultural, ahistorical criteria,' I'd better just admit right off that all three of these men are outstandingly good at being human, each of course in his own way." It is pretty clear, I think, that the struggle for or against National Socialism will not be fought by men who think like the "all-purpose intellectual." Indeed, given the volatility of the passions that are likely to be generated in these other men, such an intellectual would do well to keep a low profile when the police vans roll by.

So there we are. What' s good for a Trobriand Islander is good for a Trobriand Islander, what's good for a Christian is good for a Christian, what' s good for a Marxist is good for a Marxist, and what's good for fellows like Hitler and Stalin is good for fellows like Hitler and Stalin. And that's that. My point is, however, that while the "all-purpose intellectual" is enjoying his ride on what Rorty (approvingly) refers to as "the literary-historical-anthropological-political merry-go-round,"[17] his less-enlightened counterparts (those more ordinary intellectuals who still happen to believe that one or another position is really important or really true) will be busy working for the success of their respective ideological programs, and the rest of us will get no help from the pragmatist in trying to decide how to respond to the claims of these ideologies. We shall either have to sort them out in the old-fashioned way (by deciding, for example, that Christianity is right and Marxism wrong, or vice versa) or else sit back and expect that we shall like whichever one of them happens to succeed. Interestingly enough, we can see this situation already shaping up even in a field as comparatively harmless as that of literary criticism by simply comparing the easygoing pragmatism of Stanley Fish with the ideological fervency of Jonathan Culler.

As I mentioned earlier, Fish's contribution to the debate on the New Pragmatism in *Critical Inquiry,* which appears in an essay entitled "Consequences," is essentially a defense of the pragmatist point of view. Thus, Fish begins by accepting what he calls the "antifoundationalist" argument according to which there is no point in trying to find reasons in order to ground our behavior because we shall never be able to do anything other than what we actually do anyway. Since literary theory (or indeed any theory) is just such an attempt to work out reasons for doing one thing or another in advance, it is obviously a hangover from the old-fashioned days of Philosophy and had better be discarded or, at least, smiled at with amused condescension for being essentially unavailing and inconsequential. In other words, Fish subscribes to the Trobriand Islander fallacy. He knows in advance that theory will always fail because he knows that what it's trying to do is simply impossible. What it tries to do is to reform practice "by substituting for the parochial perspective of some local or partisan point of view the perspective of a general rationality to which the individual subordinates his contextually conditioned opinions and beliefs."[18] Impossible, cries Fish. That's like trying to appeal to all those transdisciplinary, transcultural, ahistorical criteria nobody believes in anymore. It simply can't be done. It's like asking Hitler to think like somebody other than Hitler or like asking a Trobriand Islander to think like somebody other than a Trobriand Islander. We're simply stuck with our particular community's values, and whenever we try to think about those values in order to justify them or criticize them, all we shall ever be able to do is to produce rationalized expressions of them. In Fish's own words:

> This then is why theory will never succeed: it cannot help but borrow its terms and its content from that which it claims to transcend, the mutable world of practice, belief, assumptions, point of view, and so forth. And, by definition, something that cannot succeed cannot have consequences, cannot achieve the goals it has set for itself by being or claiming to be theory, the goals of guiding and/or reforming practice. Theory cannot guide practice because its rules and procedures are no more than generalizations from practice's history (and from only a small piece of that history), and theory cannot reform practice because, rather than neutralizing interest, it begins and ends in interest and raises the imperatives of interest—of some local, particular, partisan project—to the status of universals.[19]

There we have it in a nutshell. I'm going to do a certain kind of criticism not for any particularly good reason (certainly not for the reasons I vainly imagine) but for the same sort of reason that cows chew their cud and frogs catch flies. And you are going to do a different kind of criticism for the same sort of reason that cats meow and dogs bark. Sure, we'll talk big, give all our fancy, universalizing reasons for why we're doing what we're doing, but the pragmatist, or the "all-purpose intellectual," is going to be standing there all the time smiling, enjoying the spectacle, as he watches us demonstrate various aspects of what it means to be human.

Fish, then, accepts the fact that we are all governed by ideological imperatives—the imperatives generated in us by our conditioning—because he doesn't think there is anything we can do about it. Certainly there is no point in trying to escape this conditioning. We might as well sit back and enjoy the fun while the parade of fools passes by. There they'll be—Marxists and fascists, Christians and atheists, or (if one prefers) formalists and phenomenologists, structuralists and poststructuralists—all contending, one against the other, while we look on with amused condescension. And if anyone tries to criticize us for being so easygoing about it all, we can always reply that, in fact, we're only doing what we ourselves *have* to do since clearly *our* conditioning has dictated that we spend our time being "all-purpose intellectuals." So what's there to choose?

Underneath it all, of course, is ideology. But what can we do about that? We can't meet ideology with argument because argument itself is only an expression of ideology. As Fish says, "rather than dictating or generating arguments, theoretical positions are parts of arguments and are often invoked because of a perceived connection between them and certain political and ideological stands."[20] Thus, "every argument is already interested and political no matter what its theoretical trappings,"[21] and no argument succeeds because of its cogency. If it wins, it just wins, and that's that. Fish puts it this way:

> [J]ustifications are always interested and acquire their intelligibility and force from the very practices of which they are a public defense. That is, if both parties could be brought to see that political justifications are the only kind there is and that this fact does not render argument nugatory but necessary, they might fall to recommending their contrasting agendas for the frankly political consequences they would be likely to have and not for a theoretical purity they could never achieve.[22]

The whole thing, then, is a struggle for power. Will Christians rule or will Marxists rule? Will structuralists get the most jobs or will they be beaten out by poststructuralists? On the one hand, there's not much point in listening to what all these persons have to say, but, on the other hand, the ones who come up with the most ingenious arguments deserve perhaps to be our bosses for having put in so much effort. Whoever puts in the most effort is likeliest to succeed anyway, and we've got every reason to expect that they'll be *better* than their predecessors—just as the Enlightenment was better than the old religious culture it destroyed and just as whatever follows the Enlightenment is going to be better than the Enlightenment.

Meanwhile, maybe literary critics would do better just to mind their own business instead of confusing themselves by appealing to "transdisciplinary criteria." After all, it's obvious, isn't it, that "philosophy is one thing and literary criticism is another."[23] Since there's nothing to be gained by appealing to theory ("which is another name for philosophy"), we can now get back to analyzing poems and novels in the simple, unpretentious way we just happen to do that sort of thing:

> A literary critic already knows what to do simply by virtue of his being embedded in a field of practice; it is hard to see why his performance would be improved or altered by bringing to bear categories and urgencies of another field of practice.[24]

In Fish's version of pragmatism, as in Rorty's version, there are just lots of interesting people doing lots of interesting things for no particular reason except that that's what they do. There are philosophers, there are literary critics, there are dictators, and so on. And there's really no point in trying to impose criteria from one sphere of activity on persons who are already engaged in another sphere. Everybody already knows what to do simply by virtue of the fact that he or she is already doing it.

Ideologues, of course, see the whole matter rather differently. They take themselves, and their opponents, very seriously, as witness Jonathan Culler's passionate defense of William Empson in a piece published in *TLS*.[25] Culler calls Empson "the greatest English critic of the century" for the simple reason that Empson takes writers' ideas seriously. If they have the right ideas, Empson likes them; if they don't, he doesn't. But, more importantly, Empson attacks other critics who *don't* take writers' ideas seriously. Indeed, he suspects (as does his defender Culler) that there has been a conspiracy in modern criticism to ignore the eccentricities of writers who oppose Christianity or who hold views incompatible with those of Christianity. Such writers have been "appreciated" or "admired" in terms of an aesthetic that neutralizes (from a secretly Christian point of view) their ideological thrust. Thus, according to Culler,

Empson sees himself as defending authors against a professional academic criticism which eliminates idiosyncratic views that authors may have held so as to interpret their works in the terms of a general aesthetic ideology: a marriage of Eliot and Frye, in which the meaning of a work is a symbolic structure related to a typology heavily informed by Christian doctrine. Most of the biographical essays [in Empson's *Using Biography*], like the uncollected essays on Donne and Coleridge, combat the imperative that underlies so much criticism: interpret works as reflections on or of ideologically respectable themes and overlook authors' idiosyncratic views.[26]

In other words, whereas most critics may have thought that they were doing pure criticism (the sort of activity that just comes naturally to a literary critic) or, on a higher plane perhaps, the work of the "all-purpose intellectual" (which is just seeing how things hang together in the broadest possible terms), in fact they have been stumping for Christianity all along, quite unconsciously. (This will come as news indeed to Rorty and Fish, who probably have never dreamed that their neutrality with respect to all systems of belief could ever be construed as a sort of fellow-traveling with Christianity.) It's all got to stop. says Culler. No more fake neutrality, no more seeing how authors hang together. You've got to choose sides. Either religion is right or it's wrong. If it' s wrong, then it's got to be eliminated from the curriculum in every one of its manifestations, both subtle and unsubtle. And so we have the following passage wherein Culler boldly assumes his own ideological stance

It could be argued that despite its beneficent effects in certain times and places, religion is historically one of the greatest sources of evil in the world, but we [English teachers, literary critics] pass over this in silence. We have no evidence for the existence of God, but we do not speak out against idolatry. Religion is the most potent repressive force in America today, but teachers of literature do not raise their voices against it—thinking it irrelevant but all the while honoring the Hartmans and Fryes who promote religious values and attitudes. Religion provides the ideological legitimation for anti-feminist politics and other movements of political reaction, yet feminist critics do not attack religion itself, only its patriarchy. In America politicians of all stripes now appeal to God without fear of ridicule. Arguments about prayer in the schools never attack religion itself, and priests call, without fear of reprisals, for laws to conform to their religion. How much responsibility for this state of affairs lies with schools and universities, which have abandoned the task of combating superstition and failed to foster a critique of religion? If universities are at fault, then much blame must fall on teachers of literature, for they, not the scientists, historians, or philosophers, are the ones who have been assigning Milton and Eliot and teaching students not to question their religious values.[27]

What will the "all-purpose intellectual" say to that? If my analysis of the New Pragmatism is correct, he won't be able to say anything—except, perhaps, that that's just the kind of thing that fellows like Culler *do* say. He might, in a spirit of fun, be tempted to quote a sentence or two from *Areopagitica* on the subject of censorship, or he might, just in time, remember the word of caution given by Reginald Fitz Urse in *Murder in the Cathedral* to the effect that the audience should disperse quietly to their homes without loitering in groups at street corners. But if he goes to the library to check these passages, he may very well find that Milton and Eliot have disappeared from the shelves. Chaucer won't be there, either. Nor will Spenser. Nor will Donne or Wordsworth or Coleridge, except in their eccentric parts. Personally, I can't decide which I like least: Rorty's "amused condescension" toward the whole tradition or Culler's efficient elimination of the parts of it that are "wrong." It seems to me that the only solution is to examine the entire tradition, trying to take as much of it as we can as seriously as we can and encouraging others to do the same. Neither Rorty nor Culler, neither the pragmatist nor the ideologue, is quite willing to do that, and. to me, that means that they both must count among those philosophers who have gotten things wrong. Nevertheless, I do take them seriously, and I don't want their books burned. The right attitude, it seems to me, is evidenced by Hegel, whom Rorty not quite accurately enlists as a historicist prototype of the "all-purpose intellectual" when he observes that Hegel's "temporalization of rationality" was "the single most important step in arriving at the pragmatist's distrust of Philosophy."[28] But compare this with what Hegel himself says about the attitude of the "all-purpose intellectual":

An age, which has put behind itself as a past such a quantity of philosophical systems, seems to have to arrive at that indifference which life reaches when it has tested itself in all forms. . . . If it moves out of itself to a state of curiosity, there is nothing more urgent for this sort of indifference than to give a newly-developed philosophy a name. As Adam expressed his dominion over the animals by giving them names, it expresses its dominion over a philosophy by finding a name for it. . . .

No philosophical system can remove itself from the possibility of such assimilation; each is capable of being dealt with historically. Just as every living form belongs, at the same time, to the realm of phenomena, so a philosophy, as phenomenon, has delivered itself over to that force which can transform it into a dead opinion and into something past from the very beginning. The living spirit which resides in a philosophy needs to be brought forth by a kindred spirit in order to manifest itself; it passes by the historical attitude *(dem geschichtlichen Benehmen),* which issues from some interest in the knowledge of opinions, as an alien phenomenon and does not reveal its inner character *(sein Innres)*. . . . The historical attitude holds fast to its own standpoint, remaining indifferent to truth; and it retains its independence, regardless of whether it accepts opinions, casts them aside, or makes no decision. It can have no other relationship to philosophical systems outside of their being viewed as opinions; and, since such accidents as opinions can make claim against it, it has not recognized that there is truth.[29]

Hegel, in fact, despised the "all-purpose intellectual," and he describes him with unmistakable severity as a disbeliever in the quest for truth who believes instead in the incapacity of science. But how should I ever know this—indeed, how should I ever know that, in this respect, Rorty has got him wrong—if I didn't feel encouraged to go back and look at Hegel for myself, and where should I find him (Hegel being a Christian) if Jonathan Culler were Librarian at my university?

CHAPTER 6

THE SELF-CONTRADICTIONS OF PRAGMATISM

At this point, I would like to consider more closely what seems to me to be a perverse, unintended consequence of the pragmatist theory of knowledge, which has come to the fore again and again in the writings of such leading proponents of pragmatism as Stanley Fish and Richard Rorty. The consequence I mean is simply this: in explaining the phenomenon of knowledge, both Fish and Rorty are obliged to posit the existence of real conditions or real processes which are themselves beyond knowledge and therefore, strictly speaking, unknowable. Since one of the chief ambitions of pragmatism is precisely to overcome the opposition between knowing and being, or the opposition between knowledge and whatever might be supposed to exist outside of, or independently of, knowledge, any appeal to conditions or processes taken to be, not the *product* of knowledge, but rather the *ground* of knowledge (unknowable in itself) would seem to be an embarrassing lapse back into metaphysics, the very thing pragmatism wants most to avoid. If this is the case—and I hope to show that it is the case—then the arguments put forward by both Fish and Rorty must finally be recognized as self-contradictory or self-defeating.

Let me begin by calling attention to the problems that beset Stanley Fish's leading concept, i.e., the concept of the interpretive community. Fish very helpfully tells the story of how he arrived at this concept in the introduction to his book *Is There a Text in This Class?* (1980). It all began with the problem of deciding how to determine what books mean. At first, says Fish, he was under the impression that "linguistic and textual facts" ought to be regarded as objects to be understood or as objects *for* interpretation. It seemed to him natural to believe that questions about these facts were rightly constrained by the nature of the objects themselves offered up for interpretation, by the nature of the literary field itself as populated by "texts, facts, authors, and intentions." Eventually, however, it became clear to him, through a long examination of the processive nature of literary interpretation, that he was putting the cart before the horse in trying to do justice to the independently existing phenomena of literature. "I now believe," he explains at the end of his essay, "that interpretation is the source of texts, facts, authors, and intentions. Or to put it another way, the entities that were once seen as competing for the right to constrain interpretation (text, reader, author) are now all seen to be the *products* of interpretation."[1] In effect, by abandoning the New Critical focus on texts as self-subsisting or self-constituting entities, and by focusing instead on readers' experiences of texts, Fish simply rediscovered idealism. Before his very eyes, the "primary qualities" that pertained to literature, and indeed to everything associated with literature, took on the character of "secondary qualities" whose true origin was experience or consciousness itself. Instead of regarding the field of inquiry as a real world waiting to be interrogated, Fish at last realized that "the relationship is exactly the reverse: the field of inquiry is *constituted* by the questions we are able to ask because the entities that populate it come into being as the presuppositions . . . of those questions."[2] Or, in other words, "it is the reader who 'makes' literature" what it is by perceiving it according to beliefs and interests that absolutely determine what can, or cannot, be perceived with respect to it.[3]

In saying that interpretation in itself "produces" or "makes" or "constitutes" all the "facts" that can be spoken of in connection with all literary matters whatsoever, Fish knew he was flirting with what sounded like "the rankest subjectivism," and so he hastened to add that, of course, individual readers are not themselves personally responsible for the readings they produce. In Fish's scheme, "the reader is identified not as a free agent, making literature in any old way, but as a member of a community whose assumptions about literature determine the kind of attention he pays and thus the kind of literature 'he' 'makes'":

> Thus the act of recognizing literature is not constrained by something in the text, nor does it issue from an independent and arbitrary will; rather, it proceeds from a collective decision as to what will count as literature, a decision that will be in force only so long as a community of readers or believers continues to abide by it.[4]

Thus Fish arrived at his notion of the interpretive community. Different communities authorize different kinds of reading, or different kinds of interpretation, according to the different sets of beliefs or assumptions that characterize them. The individuals who belong to these communities do not themselves determine or freely control the communal mind-set that informs their own acts of perception and interpretation. Instead, they themselves are in the grip of this mind-set. Or, as Fish puts it, "since the thoughts an individual can think and the mental operations he can perform have their source in some or other interpretive community, he is as much a product of that community (acting as an extension of it) as the meanings it enables him to produce."[5] Instead of having to choose between the objectivity of textual facts and the subjectivity of some particular reader's consciousness of those facts, Fish thought he had found a third thing which accounted in a superior way for both facts and experiences of facts without itself being either clearly subjective or clearly objective. Indeed, said Fish,

> the claims of objectivity and subjectivity can no longer be debated because the authorizing agency, the center of interpretive authority, is at once both and neither. An interpretive community is not objective because as a bundle of interests, of particular purposes and goals, its perspective is interested rather than neutral; but by the very same reasoning, the meanings and texts produced by an interpretive community are not subjective because they do not proceed from an isolated individual but from a public and conventional point of view.[6]

The existence of interpretive communities seemed obvious to Fish. It explained both agreement and disagreement in terms of community location. Members of the same community agree on things because they "see (and by seeing, make) everything in relation to that community's assumed purposes and goals." By the same token, "members of different communities will disagree," because, having different sets of purposes and goals, they will see the facts differently or, more precisely, see different sets of facts.[7] Further than this one could not go. Everything that could be thought of could be thought of only as the product of an interpretation, and interpretations themselves could be thought of only as the products of interpretive communities. With respect to interpretive communities, the only thing that could be said was that, on the whole, they were multiple in number and relatively stable in character, albeit not unsusceptible to change. The interpretive community was, so to speak, the end of the line or bedrock, depending on whichever metaphor one preferred.

But consider, for a moment, what a curious conclusion this was. It might be said that one had started out by trying to understand the world, by trying to understand what was true or what was real. But soon one realized that, in order to have knowledge of the world, one had to have knowledge of books. But in order to appreciate or appropriate books, one had to know what books were, one had to know the facts about literary or textual meaning. And in order to understand the way in which these facts are constituted by the mental dispositions of those who produce such meaning, one had to understand that the producers of meaning are themselves intelligible only as members of interpretive communities, which must be imagined as existing in some sort of temporal or spatial array in relation to each other. One wondered, finally, if anything had been gained by going through all these steps, since, at the end of it all, one was still facing the objective reality or factual status of the communities themselves. The dramas associated with the formation, the opposition, the coalition, the perseverance, the evolution, or the extinction of these communities, seemed to be thought of by Fish as matters of objective fact, while, at the same time, it was clear that he wanted to regard all such matters—all so-called facts— as the contingent expressions of the communities whose "interests" and "purposes" had spawned them. It seemed that one was going round and round in a circle. On the one hand, interpretation was declared to be constitutive of anything that might be proposed as factual, but on the other hand, the fact of interpretive communities was adduced as the proper explanation of the variety of interpretive practices. Was it possible to have it both ways at once by maintaining both positions simultaneously?

Apparently, in the beginning at least, Fish thought that it was. In the text we have been considering, which was published in 1980, he seems just on the verge of realizing that the rootedness or situatedness of every particular thinker might very well rule out the possibility of that thinker's having anything at all valuable to say about the general conditions of rootedness or indeed about anybody else's particular kind of rootedness. But not quite yet, for he still imagines that he might somehow be in a position to envision disagreements arising from *rightly apprehended* differences between community perspectives. That is to say, he imagines that "the business of criticism" is "to determine from which of a number of possible perspectives reading will proceed." Or again, as he puts it, "the business of criticism" is "to establish by political and persuasive means . . . the set of interpretive assumptions from the vantage of which the evidence (and the facts and the intentions and everything else) will hereafter be specifiable."[8] This implies, of course, that it is possible to know the deepest things about one's own mind-set and the mind-sets of others. There is, says Fish, "a stability in the makeup of interpretive communities and therefore in the opposing positions they make possible" which "explains why there are disagreements and why they can be debated in a principled way."[9] In phrases like these, Fish seems to imply that the general structure and behavior of interpretive communities may be contemplated in such a way as to compel the conviction that no community is "right" or "wrong" in relation to the others but that each is equally valid in terms of its own deepest assumptions and beliefs. This is clearly a big thing to know, and it is just as clearly being put forward as the "right" picture of the whole situation.

On the other hand, even in 1980, it was beginning to dawn on Fish that, if he was right about the nature of interpretive communities, it might follow that it is impossible to know anything really fundamental about one's own mind-set or the mind-set of others. The idea that we can get a handle on our own deepest beliefs and assumptions or attain any sort of vantage point whereby we might survey the variety of possible interpretive perspectives seemed somehow at odds with the idea that was also forming in Fish's mind that consciousness is, in fact, "wholly informed by conventional notions," so that "any 'decision' to affirm this or that belief would itself be enabled by beliefs" that are not themselves chosen.[10] Throughout the 1980s, it was this second idea that began to take precedence in Fish's thinking, as the essays collected in *Doing What Comes Naturally* (1989) plainly show.

Indeed, the more he thought about it, the more convinced Fish became that rootedness in a particular historical or social situation simply precluded the possibility of developing good ideas *about* rootedness. Obviously, foundationalist thinkers were wrong, because they kept trying to find good reasons for thinking one way or another, or the right method of inquiry so that knowledge might be uniform or well-grounded. But even antifoundationalist thinkers were wrong, in Fish's view, to the extent that they kept trying to work out the theoretical implications of fully grasping the contingency or situational character of all possible knowledge. Fish recanted nothing concerning his own theory of the importance of interpretive communities, but he began to insist that nothing followed from it of any consequence other than a bare recognition that whatever it is "you think to do," it "will issue from you as naturally as breathing" without benefit of theory, "unreflective actions" being the only kind there is.[11]

It is particularly fascinating to watch Fish reprove his fellow anti-foundationalists, as he does, for example, in his essay "Anti-Foundationalism, Theory Hope, and the Teaching of Composition," because in his reproof he makes it clear that reliable, authoritative knowledge of one's own situation and of the situations of others must be rejected as the last, most insidious vestige of the foundationalist urge to "ground inquiry and communication in something more firm and stable than mere belief or unexamined practice."[12] The danger is that antifoundationalism tends to betray its own "correct picture" of the human situation whenever it tries to maintain a consciousness of this picture or whenever it tries to induce actions more in keeping with the truth of it than other actions might be supposed to be. According to Fish, this is what happens when Kenneth Bruffee suggests that students in schools be made aware of the fact that knowledge is always relative to knowledge communities. First, Bruffee wants students to "recognize that they are already members of communities of knowledgeable peers," and then he wants them to inquire into the belief-structures of all sorts of different groups and communities, including those they themselves belong to and those that others belong to. In Bruffee's own words, "people from potentially every conceivable community would become aware of what the beliefs of their own communities are, what the beliefs of other communities are, what distinguishes the beliefs of their own communities from the beliefs of other communities, and in what respects the beliefs of most communities are identical."[13] Instead of being pleased that Bruffee is attempting to incorporate the theory of interpretive communities into actual school practices, Fish simply declares that Bruffee's project "is incompatible with anti-foundationalism because it assumes the possibility of getting a perspective on one's beliefs, a perspective from which those beliefs can be evaluated and compared with the similarly evaluated beliefs of others." But, says Fish,

> what anti-foundationalism teaches . . . is the inescapability of situatedness, and if situatedness is inescapable, students could not possibly identify in nonevaluative ways their own beliefs, because as situated beings some set of beliefs of which they could not be aware would be enabling any identification they might make; and, therefore, the act of identification would from the very first be "evaluative" through and through. One could escape this logic only by saying that while the operations of the mind are always a function of context, in one operation—the identification of its own context and that of others—it is independent. Such an exemption is

obviously contradictory and marks a return in Bruffee's discourse of the foundationalism he has supposedly banished.[14]

I take it that what Fish is saying here is that you can't *know* your own situation (you can only *be in it*) and you can't *know* anybody else's situation, because whatever you may think you *know* about these things is always a conditioned product of your own situation-bound categories. The knowledge that your own particular situation enables you to have ought never to be criticized or tempered or leavened by means of a supposed knowledge of the limits of that situation or a supposed knowledge of the varieties of situated knowing, because such criticizing, tempering, or leavening is strictly impossible, given what we know about the constraints of situated knowing. The only thing to do is to "dumb down" into your own situation, with perfect confidence that, within the limits of your own professional practice and by means of the rules of decorum governing that practice, you can do whatever you want to do as naturally as you please. Everything will take care of itself and all things will happen just as they do happen, without theoretical props or advice from philosophers. In a sense, Fish's knowledge of the whole situation is precisely that which enables him to tell others that there is no such thing as "a knowledge of the whole situation," and so they had better stop trying to factor such a knowledge into their own already adequate, already situated knowledge practices.

This, as I say, has been the principal leitmotif in Fish's writings since 1980. The absolute ground of all our knowing and doing is the actually existing structure of interpretive communities, which, precisely because it is the *ground* or *condition* of knowing, cannot itself be known. But this is a form of transcendentalism, a form of knowledge that cannot be accounted for in terms of any of the actually situated knowledges that Fish approves of and declares to be alone valid. It is hard to see how Fish can invoke the existence of an unknowable knowledge structure for the purpose of issuing admonitions to other intellectuals to keep within the boundaries of their own limited knowledges. In order to do this, it would seem that he would have to be in a position to act as a sort of umpire of the games of knowledge, with the power to declare which moves are within bounds and which moves are out of bounds. At the same time, and from exactly the same position, he would have to assure his fellow intellectuals that it is unseemly—indeed impossible—for anyone to take upon himself the umpire role. It is rather like the situation in *Animal Farm* where those who abolish the old class structure helpfully preside over the new structure, making sure that it remains classless and nonauthoritarian.

Fish would certainly deplore being called a positivist, but there is nevertheless something in his doctrine that is powerfully reminiscent of the old positivist desire to distinguish between appropriate propositions, developed according to the rules, and all other propositions, which might look appropriate but, being developed without reference to the rules, are in fact meaningless. An amazing number of intellectuals, from Fish's point of view, are guilty of forgetting themselves in such a way as to imply that they can actually envision fundamental criticisms of their own or other people's situations. But, in terms of guild decorum, their own proposals for change are simply indecorous or, more precisely, meaningless. As Fish puts it:

> [I]f all knowledge is situational and we are always and already in a situation, we can never be at any distance from the knowledge we need. Anti-foundationalism cannot give us the knowledge we seek because its lesson is that we already have it.[15]

The whole practice of trying to think about how it is that we think about things, with the hope of making future recommendations for improvement, is misguided, being a sort of rogue practice without benefit to any other existing practices. Everybody already knows how to think about things in ways that are appropriate, as is evident from the fact that he or she is already practically engaged in whatever it is that is being done. Hence there must be no talk of deep reforms issuing from essential criticisms of existing cultural practices.

How then does anything change? How do cultural practices evolve or become extinct? Easy, says Fish; they just do, unpredictably and uncontrollably, as a consequence of their inherent dynamism. One reason why we can't criticize our own (or anybody else's) situated knowledge is that we can't neutrally or non-parochially know anything, but another reason is that knowledge situations are in constant motion. They won't stand still long enough for us to scrutinize them. That is because, according to Fish, a community practice or a knowledge situation is essentially not "a new kind of object to which we could now turn our attention"; it is not "an entity, but a bundle of tacit or unspoken assumptions that is simultaneously organizing the world and changing in response to its own organizing work."

Thus we may say that "a situation is always on the wing, and any attempt to capture it will only succeed in fixing it in a shape it no longer has."[16] If one were to ask how even this much could be determined concerning the volatile character of the invisible, inaudible assumption-bundles that organize the world, the answer is that, of course, there is nothing at all determinate about them (if we thought there was, we would be guilty of "substituting for the discredited notion of determinate facts the finally indistinguishable notion of determinate situations"), and therefore the suspicion that situations are volatile should not be construed as knowledge capable of "rendering unproblematic our relationship to these newly determining entities."[17] When we turn to look at these entities that are not really entities, it is like looking at particle-trails in a cloud chamber. Indeed, since whatever we look at must be seen through the categories of a particular community's mind-set, it is rash to say that change is absolutely a property of anything. "No fact is self-evident," Fish reminds us,

> and therefore it is a mistake to think of change or its absence as being verifiable by a simple (unmediated) act of empirical observation; rather it is only within the perspective of some interpretive descriptive system that change is or is not a feature. That is to say, the fact of change, like any other fact, is irremediably interpretive; its specification cannot be made independently of the way a community conceives of itself, of the story it tells about itself and lives out in the actions of its members.[18]

Thus, it cannot be known clearly that interpretive communities have any sort of history or any particular position *in* history, since historical knowledge itself is entirely a matter of whatever it is that the communities happen to think it is, and no actual view of the real situation of these communities is possible. Knowledge being situated *inside* the communities, they themselves are unknowable.

In the final analysis, the purpose of Fish's metaphysics of knowledge is not to produce curiosity with respect to the unknowable features of the nonentities it persistently calls our attention to; rather, it is to persuade us that there is no option other than to mind our own business and to do what comes naturally. What is ironic is that so much persuasion is required to keep everyone on task. It almost seems as if it comes naturally to people not to respect the boundaries of the various interpretive communities or the limits of their own particular knowledge situations. But instead of being content with the actual practices of intellectual poachers and rustlers, Fish continues to urge in his latest work (*Professional Correctness* [1995]) that the essential characters of distinctively different practices be recognized and respected for what they are, not blended together or blurred indiscriminately. In effect, this means that the function of theory (or at least Fish's theory) is to make sure that practice continues to be the simple unreflective thing it was always meant to be, without succumbing to the temptation to be more enlightened philosophically or more relevant politically. Instead of disappearing "in the solvent of an enriched notion of practice," as Fish announced it would in the preface to *Doing What Comes Naturally,* interpretive theory is required to maintain an eternal vigilance in order to ensure the purity of distinctively different practices. If this is pragmatism, it is, one might say, a sort of "policed" pragmatism.[19]

In this respect particularly, Rorty's version of pragmatism seems more easygoing than Fish's. The advantage of knowing that all ideas and all possible descriptions of things are merely contingent expressions of the interests or needs of those who have developed them is, from Rorty's point of view, that it liberates us from having to think that we are bound to work in terms of any particular set of them. We don't have to "dumb down" into one professional position, restricting ourselves to the categories that are "natural" to just that position. Indeed, Rorty likes to range freely over all that he knows, picking and choosing whatever he needs according to his own purposes, thus availing himself of the pragmatist idea that ideas themselves are only instruments or tools, to be selected or scrapped as one sees fit, rather than ineluctable categories that cannot be dispensed with, like a pair of glasses that cannot be removed. Knowing that there is no such thing as the way things really are, and knowing that alternative descriptions have been offered for just about everything, Rorty assumes that the essential questions are, simply, what do we require, and what ideas will help us meet our requirements?

People who try to think in terms of one or another of the different theories or different descriptions that have been proposed by various thinkers would do better to think of such things as "convenient divisions within a toolbox—divisions between batches of linguistic tools useful for various different tasks."[20] When it comes to describing anything or thinking about anything, whatever we need can be found *in* the toolbox or can be added *to* the toolbox. Thus:

> The pragmatist thinks that the tradition needs to be utilized, as one utilizes a bag of tools. Some of these tools, these "conceptual instruments"— including some which continue to have undeserved prestige—will turn out no longer to have a use, and can be just tossed off. Others can be refurbished. Sometimes new tools may have to be invented on the spot.[21]

This seems to make everything rather easy and straightforward. "Thinghood, identity, is itself description-relative."[22] A description is only a linguistic tool, and language itself is entirely a matter of the various ways we have of talking about it. We can't just say

> that language *really* is *just* strings of marks and noises which organisms use as tools for getting what they want. That Nietzschean-Deweyan description of language is no more the real truth about language than Heidegger's description of it as "the house of Being" or Derrida's as "the play of signifying references." Each of these is only one more useful truth about language—one more of what Wittgenstein called "reminders for a particular purpose."[23]

At first, it seems that it might be very helpful to look at things this way—very empowering, very liberating. The content of every possible view of every conceivable matter ceases to be compelling, ceases to hold the mind captive, because we can locate it somewhere in the toolbox or the tool bag. The world itself ceases to be compelling, because it is reducible to such conceptions as there may be of it, and the whole array of conceptions is at our disposal, waiting to be picked over in accordance with our particular purposes. But if reality in all its parts is only conceivable as that which is constructed according to human needs and purposes, it is hard to see how human needs and purposes can be thought of as real, or be thought of at all. If everything conceivable is socially or humanly constructed, then the *basis* or *ground* of all this constructing is itself inconceivable. (This is actually a serious problem, though at first glance it may appear to be trivial.) Indeed, if reality is whatever I end up saying it is, how shall I determine what to say about it? I might have purposes of one sort or another if I lived in a world that had a character of one sort or another, but if I live in a world whose character will be determined by the things I choose to say about it or think about it, on what basis can I choose to say or think anything about it? What can my purposes be without reference to any actually existing, actually known situations?

Rorty gets around this problem by assuming that social or human realities are just obvious, without having to take their cue from the clever descriptions or conceptions of them arrived at by philosophers. What to do in the world is also obvious: we should work for a better world, a safer world, a more comfortable world, a happier world. It is only ideas *about* the world that are tricky, variable, contingent, and either helpful or obstructive to our purposes. These purposes cannot be determined by consulting the truth of things, because the truth of things is determined by our purposes. Thus, Rorty speaks approvingly of "Heidegger's dissolution of philosophical pseudo-problems through letting social practice be taken as a primary and unquestioned datum, rather than an explanandum."[24]

Politics, then, is a large part of what is obvious. From Rorty's point of view, there is no way to justify or find good grounds for one's political or social attitudes: one is either reactionary or progressive, one is either sympathetic or unsympathetic to the goals and tendencies of the French Revolution. If one is a pragmatist in the tradition of Dewey, one will simply turn away from those who are trying to get things "right" in science or philosophy and throw in one's lot with "the engineers and the social workers—the people who are trying to make people more comfortable, and to use science and philosophy as tools for that purpose."[25] That is to say, if one is a good pragmatist, one will make oneself useful by working to eliminate suffering and to promote happiness, without waiting for proofs and reasons.

Of course, to say that all this is obvious is also to say that it can't be explained. As with Fish's concept of interpretive communities, Rorty's concept of the social practices that determine all thinking to be either progressive or reactionary, useful or obstructive, is such that these practices must be taken for granted and, at the same time, declared to be unknowable. But is it really all that obvious which political activities are most likely to produce a better world for the largest number of people? Isn't it an exaggeration to suggest that half or more of all the political activity in the world is opposed to making people more comfortable, or more secure, or better off, while the rest of that activity is, in fact, devoted to promoting their well-being? Most political differences seem to have to do, not with whether people *ought* to be better off or *ought* to be free from suffering, but with how best to achieve these goals. Competing political systems, competing political policies, rest on different assessments of what human beings may be expected to do in various sets of circumstances, or of the right way to prioritize the components of social well-being or social security, or, finally, of the right strategy for attaining the greatest happiness for the greatest number of people. Without knowing something about political history, something about economics, something about the actual workings of existing political systems, and even something about psychology and ethics, it is hard to see how anyone could arrive at right estimates of political matters, or suppose themselves to be truly progressive in such matters. And yet, in Rorty's view, all this knowledge, which might be imagined as properly informing one's political views or one's sense of what is socially appropriate or desirable, is itself to be judged, and thus accepted or rejected as knowledge, in terms of whether it is socially expedient, socially obstructive, or socially irrelevant. Knowing what to do might seem to depend on the development of knowledge, but here knowledge itself seems to depend on whether or not it can fit into the already-constituted projects of the politically adept. This is Rorty's version of Fish's idea that we already know what to do simply by virtue of the fact that we are already doing it. Why this should be considered a progressive attitude rather than a conservative one, or even a reactionary one, is not clear.[26]

Appealing to the obvious or the inexplicable is evidently one of Rorty's principal strategies. Take, for example, his essay on "Freud and Moral Reflection." Here Rorty expounds the view that Freud's great achievement was to dethrone the imperial self, the monarch-like ego, and to raise to awareness all those marginalized elements or ingredients of the self that are normally excluded from consciousness but which lurk in the basements or dungeons of the sub-conscious mind. Rorty is particularly impressed by Donald Davidson's suggestion that one might regard Freud's insights as implying that there are two or more persons actually vying for attention or for dominance within us, rather than one person with repressed inclinations or imperfectly processed memories. The value of Davidson's suggestion, according to Rorty, is that it enables us to see that Freud's novelty is "his claim that our unconscious selves are not dumb, sullen lurching brutes, but rather the intellectual peers of our conscious selves, possible conversational partners for those selves":

> This suggestion that one or more clever, articulate, inventive persons are at work behind the scenes—cooking up our jokes, inventing our

metaphors, plotting our dreams, arranging our slips, and censoring our memories—is what grips the imagination of the lay reader of Freud. . . . It substitutes a picture of sophisticated transactions between two or more "intellects" for the traditional picture of one "intellect" struggling with a mob of "irrational" brutes.[27]

Indeed, Rorty is pleased to think of the self as consisting of multiple, component selves, with different points of view, different priorities, different stories to tell abóut the meaning and even the facts concerning one's own past, because it means that one has more material with which to make oneself larger, stabler, and more mature. It is as though we could watch our component selves pass in review, all on an equal footing, learning from each in turn, and becoming the better for it. The problem with this picture is that a reviewing self, sympathetic to the whole project, fairminded, eager to learn, has to be imagined as already constituted or already existing at the time of the review. It cannot be imagined as an automatic consequence of the mere existence of the component selves, for these are already present, creating whatever effect they can. If, as Rorty says, maturity consists "in an ability to seek out new redescriptions of one's own past," "new self-descriptions whose adoption will enable one to alter one's behavior,"[28] then maturity is a condition of carrying out the project rather than a consequence of its being carried out. In other words, in explaining Freud's discovery that the self is really a complex field of multiple seething selflets, and in trying to maintain that ultimate selfhood is really an achievement that results from attending to the various testimonies of these selflets, Rorty has to appeal to a self that has authority over its own components (rather than mere equality) and the power to contemplate its own renovation. Furthermore, he has to appeal to the phenomenon of the self itself in order to explain the dramas and adventures wherein the self is supposedly constituted, since the selflets that make up the self are themselves homuncular persons. The problem comes to a head when Rorty praises Freud both for "helping us see ourselves as centerless, as random assemblages of contingent and idiosyncratic needs" and, at the same time, for helping us "become increasingly ironic, playful, free, and inventive in our choice of self-descriptions."[29] Who or what, after all, is really capable of *choosing* anything if the self is really a centerless, random assemblage of needs? Throughout the entire discussion, the self is simply assumed rather than explained, in spite of all the effort expended to explain it.

Political change is likewise rendered inexplicable in Rorty's essay "Unger, Castoriadis, and the Romance of a National Future." Ideas concerning what ought to be done, or what can be done, to effect political change are seen as obstacles to change, impeding the real mechanism of change, which is spontaneous imagination of how things might look if they were actually other (and much better) than they really are. "As a Kuhnian," says Rorty,

> I have doubts about whether argument plays much of a role in scientific or political Gestalt-switches. Arguments (whose premises must necessarily be phrased in familiar vocabularies) often just get in the way of attempts to create an unfamiliar political vocabulary, a new *lingua franca* for those trying to transform what they see around them.[30]

Apparently, genuine change can't be theorized or developed on the basis of already existing views, because the content of these views must concern itself with that which has already happened. History holds thought tightly bound, unless we leap into novel, unpredictable positions without the aid of blueprints. (Throughout the essay, Rorty constantly intimates that the Western democracies, which he normally praises, have ceased to be exemplary as far as the Third World is concerned, because they have run out of new ideas and entered a period of exhaustion or stagnation.) Thus, if there is to be new political activity, it will have to be the result of bursting spontaneously into a new paradigm, constructed out of pure hope and without benefit of models. "If politics can create a new form of social life," says Rorty, "there will be time enough later for theorists to explain how this creation was possible and why it was a good thing."[31] No one should be deterred from imagining that welcome political change is likely to come from "something unforeseeable and passionate" just because Mussolini, Hitler, Lenin, and Mao were similarly spontaneous and passionate. Rather we should try to bear in mind "that the notion of 'argumentative procedures' is not relevant to the situation [most often noticed in Third World countries] in which nothing familiar works and in which people are desperately . . . looking for something, no matter how unfamiliar, which might work."[32] To suppose that "theorizing, or philosophical reflection, will help us sort out good from bad romantics" is to make the mistake of supposing that "philosophy can anticipate history by spotting 'objectively progressive' or 'objectively reactionary' intellectual movements."[33]

Having said all this, Rorty proceeds to conclude his essay "on a concrete note." That is, he attempts to imagine a profoundly radical, profoundly romantic social experiment that actually succeeds and that actually transforms everybody's ideas about politics. "Suppose," he says,

> that somewhere, someday, the newly-elected government of a large industrialized country decreed that everybody would get the same income, regardless of occupation or disability. Simultaneously, it instituted vastly increased inheritance taxes and froze large bank transfers. Suppose that, after the initial turmoil, it worked: that is, suppose that the economy did not collapse, that people still took pride in their work (as streetcleaners, pilots, doctors, cane-cutters, Cabinet ministers, or whatever), and so on. Suppose that the next generation in that country was brought up to realize that, whatever else they might work for, it made no sense to work for wealth. But they worked anyway (for, among other things, national glory). That country would become an irresistible example for a lot of other countries, "capitalist," "Marxist," and in-between. The electorates of these countries would not take time to ask what "factors" had made the success of this experiment possible. Social theorists would not be allowed time to explain how something had happened that they had pooh-poohed as utopian, nor to bring this new sort of society under familiar categories. All the attention would be focused on the actual details of how things were working in the pioneering nation. Sooner or later, the world would be changed.[34]

The most striking thing about this whole scenario is that it is both perfectly obvious and, at the same time, utterly inexplicable. Surely, only meanness of spirit or poverty of imagination could prevent a person from seeing how splendid all this would be. In fact, people *have* thought of such a scenario before, many times. The problems all seem to have to do with the practical mechanisms whereby its realization might be accomplished. It is odd, therefore, to hear a pragmatist, who might be expected to be interested in social engineering, dismiss considerations of the practicality of the arrangements thus imagined on the grounds that such considerations are likely to be theory-ridden or otherwise burdened with disabling recollections of previous failures. The truth is that Rorty wants to imagine a new political situation (which, of course, is not new at all in terms of what it aspires to) as the *basis* for theory rather than as the *product* of theory. Therefore, he has to imagine the actual achievement of social justice, or the actual achievement of the greatest happiness for the greatest number, as the only basis for thinking about the mechanisms for achieving these ends. Not having achieved them, they remain in the realm of the unthinkable obvious, unaffected by the knowledge that pertains to things as they now stand or as they have stood in the past.

Normally, Rorty defends the record of Western liberal democracy, and instead of charging it with stagnation, as he does in this essay, he praises it for its openness to change and revision. He is aware, however, that many intellectuals have been critical of Western liberal democracy, like Foucault, of whom he writes: "You would never guess, from Foucault's account of the changes in European social institutions during the last three hundred years, that during that period suffering had decreased considerably, nor that people's chances of choosing their own styles of life increased considerably."[35] In reading this remark, we are reminded of the fact that opposing descriptions of actually existing political and social institutions must give us pause whenever we feel inclined to celebrate them or denigrate them. Presumably our approbation or disapprobation ought to be based on a correct description of the institutions in question. If the true direction of our political course is not necessarily obvious (and even Rorty is not always sure that it is), then it might be the case that politics ought to depend upon knowledge, rather than having things the other way around. Ascertaining the true effects of actual institutions might be more important than Rorty wants to admit for the purpose of developing one's political views or of making political decisions.

How, after all, should one think about the greatest happiness of the greatest number? According to Leibniz, this is already the achieved condition of the whole creation. According to Mustapha Mond in Huxley's novel *Brave New World,* it is the inevitable result of a properly engineered caste system. According to Jeremy Bentham, it *would* be the result of phasing out paternalistic government. According to John Stuart Mill, it *would* be the result of phasing such government in. Certainly, it hardly helps to say, as Rorty does in one of his essays, that in a democratic utopia, properly conceived, "everybody can do what they want if they don't hurt anybody else while doing it,"[36] because this principle is compatible with virtually any number of personal restrictions, large or small, depending on how one interprets what it means to "hurt" other people or to interfere with them. The obvious ceases to be obvious when we descend from the region of platitudes and enter the region of actual practices. It is precisely there that pragmatism itself ceases to be practical (at least, as Rorty expounds it), for it is there that we need to know, as well as we can, what's what.

CHAPTER 7

POSTMODERN FANTASIES OF PLURALISM

Thinking of the key, each confirms a prison.
—T. S. Eliot, *The Waste Land*

Pluralism is, arguably, the central feature of postmodernist thought. In one way or another, almost every discussion of contemporary intellectual culture makes this clear. Consider, for example, the way in which Fredric Jameson chooses to discuss postmodernism in an essay published in *New German Critique*. Instead of trying to say what postmodernism is (or is not), Jameson wisely acknowledges, at the very beginning of his essay, that postmodernism may be interpreted in a variety of different ways, according to the political persuasions of its interpreters. Thus, the multiplicity of possible interpretations becomes the focus of his attention: "The various positions which can logically be taken on it [postmodernism], whatever terms they are couched in, can always be shown to articulate visions of history, in which the evaluation of the social moment in which we live today is the object of an essentially political affirmation or repudiation."[1] In other words, postmodernism is in the eye of the beholder, so let's look, first of all, at the beholders. This, I say, is a typically postmodern gesture in that it seeks to do justice to the plurality of possible interpretations of contemporary culture.

Indeed, postmodernism is very often described in terms of its resistance to univocal views of things. Thus, when a postmodernist attacks the traditions of Western culture, what he or she usually objects to most is the narrowness of those traditions. How silly to suppose as our ancestors did that there is only one reality or one truth to be known and that we can know it only if we submit to this or that "correct" method! Isn't this a form of intellectual totalitarianism, and hasn't nearly all of Western art and philosophy been infected with it up until our own enlightened age? When Richard Rorty, a leading postmodernist intellectual, tries to imagine what our new culture is going to be like (the culture that is just on the verge of displacing traditional culture), what he imagines is a culture "in which no one believes that we have, deep down inside us, a criterion for telling whether we are in touch with reality or not, when we are in the Truth":

This would be a culture in which neither the priests nor the physicists nor the poets nor the Party were thought of as more "rational," or more "scientific" or deeper than one another. No particular portion of culture would be singled out as exemplifying (or signally failing to exemplify) the condition to which the rest aspired. There would be no sense that, beyond the current intra-disciplinary criteria, which, for example, good priests or good physicists obeyed, there were other, transdisciplinary, transcultural, ahistorical criteria, which they also obeyed.[2]

In the new, postmodern age, Rorty goes on to say, there won't be any privileged authorities. There will just be a number of men and women who are very good at doing the quite diverse kinds of things they do. Rorty's vision of a burgeoning pluralism may be compared with Andreas Huyssen's description of what has been going on in our culture since the 1960s:

Since the 1960s, artistic activities have become much more diffuse and harder to contain in safe categories or stable institutions such as the academy, the museum or even the established gallery network. To some, this dispersal of cultural and artistic practices and activities will involve a sense of loss and disorientation; others will experience it as a new freedom, a cultural liberation. Neither may be entirely wrong, but we should recognize that it was not only recent theory or criticism that deprived the univalent, exclusive and totalizing accounts of modernism of their hegemonic role. It was the activities of artists, writers, film makers, architects, and performers that have propelled us beyond a narrow vision of modernism and given us a new lease on modernism itself.[3]

As this passage suggests, one way of distinguishing postmodernism from modernism is to minimize or ignore the disruptive, destabilizing procedures of the latter by assimilating it to one or another of the traditions it tried to transcend. Thus, the modernists may be taken to task for making art itself seem uniquely valuable or privileged, so that the artist can emerge as the true hero of society, bringing meaning and coherence to an otherwise meaningless and incoherent universe. If this is so, then the postmodernists may congratulate themselves for having recognized that even the artist has no special authority to establish the meaningfulness of things.

Another version of this maneuver is demonstrated by Christopher Norris in his book *The Contest of Faculties*. It is possible, as Norris at one point reminds us, to regard literary modernism not as a critique of the false pretensions of realism but as an effort to practise realism according to a new definition of it. Accordingly, we could say that "writers like Joyce, Woolf or Lawrence saw themselves as creating a new and better form of realism, one that discarded the circumstantial trappings of Victorian fiction and rendered the truth of subjective experience." On this view, it is the postmodernists, not the modernists, who understand that "reality is made, not found, and that novels had better draw attention to their own fictive devices, rather than trying to pass themselves off as chunks of real-life experience."[4] However questionable this may be as an interpretation of modernism, nevertheless it is clear that what postmodernists dislike about modernism is its pretentiousness and what they like about the newer art is its lack of pretentiousness. From the vantage point of postmodernism, it seems necessary to imagine that the modernists were engaged in trying to find the right way to represent reality, whereas it remained for the postmodernists to come to the conclusion that reality is whatever we take it to be or make it to be, that reality, in other words, is irreducibly plural just as we ourselves are plural in our various aims and methods.

If all of this sounds just a little bit odd, it should, because the literary modernists used to be given high marks for their sensitivity to the multiplicity of possible perspectives on reality. There was a time when it seemed that modernism was responsible for countenancing all manner of experimentation in the arts, especially experimentation designed to overthrow restrictive definitions of art and "official" conceptions of reality. Even those modernists such as Pound and Eliot who stressed the importance of an awareness of tradition usually had in mind the discovery or invention of a tradition much larger, much more inclusive, than their predecessors could possibly have known. Thus, the effort to make modernism itself seem narrow and restrictive is part of the effort to distinguish genuine pluralism from false pluralisms or limited pluralisms. Whoever can lay claim to having the most open, least exclusive, least restrictive view of things will clearly deserve the palm, while those who come up short will thereby confess their true spiritual affinity with the now-outmoded past and, in particular, with the various dogmatisms or monisms of the Western tradition.

Even among postmodernists themselves, the issue seems to be: who is more genuinely pluralistic than who? Sometimes we hear that there are two postmodernisms, one of which is weak and flabby and the other of which is strong and vigorous. Hal Foster, in his introduction to a collection of essays on postmodern culture, speaks of "a postmodernism of resistance and a postmodernism of reaction,"[5] by which he means, respectively, a postmodernism that resists authoritarianism both in politics and in culture and a postmodernism that is reactionary in the sense that it has no critical edge but simply accepts whatever it finds without argument. There are, of course, different ways of looking at these two different versions of postmodernism, but Foster is right, I think, in suggesting that there are two schools of thought about what it means to be postmodern, and the interesting thing about them is that each, in its own way, claims to be more pluralistic than the other. Each sees the other as being, in one sense or another, reactionary, while it sees itself as being more advanced, more actively opposed to the reigning orthodoxies and dogmatisms (or, at least, the remnants thereof that still exist in this period of transition out of the modern and into the postmodern). Each sees the other as being guilty of a sort of fellow-traveling with attitudes that more properly belong to the pre-enlightened past. And that means, necessarily, being less pluralistic.

Let us, for a moment, look at how the situation appears from the standpoint of those, such as Foster, who imagine that they represent the spirit of resistance or the spirit of critique. What do they see when they look at contemporary culture? They see, very often, a sort of easygoing acceptance of all styles and attitudes, a sort of "anything goes" eclecticism that is unable or unwilling to make distinctions and discriminations. They see a passivity that oscillates between "future shock" and what might be called "future delight" at the immense variety of experiences our culture now affords us. In short, they see what Denis Donoghue in the *New York Times Book Review* (22 June 1986) refers to as "the promiscuous cool of postmodernism." Donoghue, looking at the kind of postmodernism Foster calls "reactionary," remarks: "There is a certain weightlessness in postmodernism that makes it possible for an artist to do anything he chooses, but doesn't suggest that he should try for anything in particular: like a game without rules." The problem with this attitude, according to such different observers as Foster and Donoghue, is that it discourages resistance to cultural and political trends that are dangerous or destructive. The "lotus-eating" kind of postmodernist, so the argument goes, tends through his indifference to support the status quo, whatever it may be, and the result is that he loses his power to think of alternatives to the status quo.

By accepting everything that comes along as grist for the mill, he loses his ability to sense that culture as a whole, society as a whole, may be drifting in a bad direction toward the exclusion of divergent views, toward a repressive standardization of acceptable opinions, in short, toward a consumer mentality that is constantly being distracted from the ideological principles that have caused it to come into being in the first place and continue to operate without interference, behind the scenes as it were. In short, the "cool" postmodernist imagines that he really is living in an age that has seen the end of ideology, in a sort of wonderful awareness that all ideologies are merely fictions, whereas, in fact, one ideology or another is secretly governing every aspect of his life without his being aware of it. Thus it is left to the other kind of postmodernist—the "resisting" or "critical" postmodernist—to make this clear by restoring to our awareness the ideological bases of all our doing and thinking. If we think we live in a free society with equal opportunity for all, the critical postmodernist shows us all the "others" whom we have really (albeit unconsciously) excluded, such as women or non-Westerners. If we think that postindustrial consumer capitalism ought to be the model for a worldwide "free" society, he shows us the bitter truth about how such a model works and he informs us of alternatives. Even in the apparently innocuous domain of literature, if we think we have grasped the meaning of a text or group of texts, he shows us that we have systematically ignored aspects of that meaning that will forever disrupt our efforts to achieve a "complete" interpretation. Indeed, the critical postmodernist, whether in the guise of feminism, Marxism, or deconstruction, or in a combination thereof, promises to give us a deeper, richer, more inclusive view of things than we can possibly have without his assistance. By forcing us to notice all that we have repressed or overlooked, by bringing back again whatever (or whomever) we have shunted off to the margins, the critical postmodernist can claim to be the "true" pluralist, the "true" respecter of all the complexities of difference and divergence.

Now let us pause to look at how the situation appears from the other side. First of all, it should be clear that those who have made a good case for what Foster denounces as "a postmodernism of reaction" and what Donoghue dismisses as "promiscuous cool" do not see themselves as either reactionary or indifferent. They see themselves as advocates of the most pluralistic kind of thinking possible, and they see their fellow intellectuals—

feminists, Marxists, and deconstructionists—as well-meaning but essentially deluded allies in the collective project of building a better, postmodern world. Richard Rorty, as I take it, is a leading proponent of this side of postmodernism, and the gist of his argument (especially in *Consequences of Pragmatism*) is very simple: no one, he argues, is in a position to deliver the sort of authoritative critique that the feminists, Marxists, and deconstructionists seem to imply they are capable of delivering. True, says Rorty, these intellectuals do disassociate themselves from the dominant traditions of Western philosophy, but, in doing so, they may give the impression that they themselves are philosophers in possession of "deeper" or "higher" truths than those that were commonly entertained by their more naïve predecessors. How indeed can they possibly stand outside the cultural conditions in which they, like all the rest of us, are immersed? Aren't they too, like the rest of us, situated within their own particular contexts, subject to their own particular blindnesses and limitations? If they set themselves up as a special class of persons who know something big, something really important, that the rest of us don't know about the foundations of thought or culture, aren't they making the same sort of mistake that philosophers have always made? In a word, aren't they guilty of having metaphysical pretensions? If they were truly self-aware, they would see themselves as intellectuals alongside other intellectuals, pushing their own partisan projects just as those other intellectuals are pushing theirs. If they succeed, it will be because, through persuasion or force, they have captured our attention and held our interest; it will not be because their projects are intrinsically "better" or "truer" than those that fall by the wayside. In other words, from the point of view of Rorty's postmodern pragmatism, it is only pragmatism that can achieve a genuinely pluralistic awareness of the multiplicity of projects; it is only pragmatism that can give us a genuinely inclusive view of things. And, from this view, it is clear that the pluralist sympathies of the critical postmodernists are necessarily limited, however admirably intended.

This, then, is the essence of the standoff between the two different versions or variants of postmodernism. Each claims to be more far-seeing than the other, more liberated and liberating than the other. And that is because each imagines itself to be capable of detecting the seeds (at least) of a dogmatic authoritarianism in the other. When Rorty looks at a figure like Derrida, he sees a man whose heart is in the right place. After all,

Derrida is attacking the power and authority of Western philosophy; indeed, he is attacking the pretensions of all attempts to achieve a stable, rational conception of reality or to arrive at the truth of things. But, as Rorty suspects, there is a dangerous possibility, even in deconstruction, that it will try to pass itself off as a new sort of metaphilosophy, specifically, as the philosophy that knows the truth about representation or the truth about language or the truth about the metaphysics of presence. Strong deconstructionists, of whom Derrida himself is one, try to *show* that writing is just writing by refusing to play the game of argumentation with other philosophers, by choosing, instead, to write in a style that continually frustrates and subverts the conventions of rational demonstration. Weak deconstructionists, epigones of Derrida, make the fatal mistake of trying to *demonstrate the truth* of Derrida's insights into the nature of writing and so fall into the trap of becoming (against their own good intentions) philosophers or, as we now say, theorists. When this happens, the result is that deconstruction compromises itself and becomes just another view of things alongside other views, with hardly more to offer than a particularly intense delusion of explanatory grandeur. The best thing about deconstruction, as far as Rorty is concerned, is that it is capable of producing wonderfully outlandish prose-poems of mock-demonstration that have dumbfounded traditional philosophers in their attempts to understand and thereby master it. These philosophers need to be put in their places, and if deconstruction can succeed in doing this, so much the better.

Of course, there is something slightly patronizing about this view of deconstruction. The pragmatist (or "all-purpose intellectual,' as Rorty likes to call him) gives the impression that he can see all around deconstruction, that he can assess its strengths and weaknesses, appreciate its style. and, most importantly, measure the degree of its success or failure in relation to other styles. This puts the pragmatist in the position of being top-dog pluralist, weighing one partisan project against other partisan projects. The pragmatist can see more than any of the projectors, because he alone can see how they all stand in relation to each other without having to take sides and thus collapsing into narrowness or partisan blindness. No wonder that the ardent deconstructionist Christopher Norris bristles at Rorty's suggestion that pragmatism has got the jump on deconstruction. Norris, in his book *The Contest-of Faculties,* takes it for granted that Rorty's "appreciation" of deconstruction represents the most powerful alternative to deconstruction itself, and so he tries to meet the challenge by insisting not only that deconstruction is "a rigorous thinking-through" of the textual and epistemological consequences of traditional concepts (rather than just an absurdist exercise in stylistics) but also that Rorty's version of pragmatism "carries its own specific charge of ideological assumptions."[6] Specifically, Norris charges that Rorty assumes too easily that he has achieved a post-Philosophical, above-the-battle stance without partisan interests of its own. In fact, says Norris, Rorty's pretended neutrality may be seen as a way of "falling in all too readily with the interests of a present-day status quo."[7] This is very perceptive of Norris, since Rorty does indeed come close to defining "good thinking" or "right thinking" as whatever happens to reflect the status quo in intellectual matters at any given moment. Norris suspects a link here with political conservatism or, perhaps, some sort of naïve bourgeois liberalism. Deconstruction alone can save us from these and other ideological morasses, because, according to Norris, it is the most powerful instrument of ideological critique we have at our disposal. In allowing us to see more than the victims of ideology can see, in allowing us to see around or through everybody's ideology, it gets the jump even on pragmatism. Furthermore, it gets pluralism right by turning it into a matter not of counting noses or projects but of unmasking seemingly univocal views in such a way as to reveal their true complexity as incoherent amalgamations of eternally incompatible, eternally hostile elements. Awareness of this complexity gives us an alternative view of every partisan view of things and so liberates us from having to accept each view's erroneous view of itself.

What are we to make of this standoff between deconstruction and pragmatism, between these two different versions of pluralism, each claiming to be the *echt* version and thus the true representative of postmodern enlightenment? I, for one, should like to suggest that it is simply wrong to think that either deconstruction or pragmatism is genuinely pluralistic. Both of these fashionable ways of thinking see themselves as having transcended the struggle, the give-and-take, the clash, of contrary opinions which normally occurs in an atmosphere of genuine pluralism. Like most other philosophers, the deconstructionist and the pragmatist believe themselves to have arrived at an understanding of things which, in some sense, is "right" or "correct" or "true." Even though they have discovered how to undermine the concept of truth, in doing so they display a method and an attitude which they take to be "true" or "right." But more importantly, both of them have found ways of thinking and arguing that make it possible for them not to take their opponents seriously. Strictly speaking, they do not even have to listen to what their opponents are saying, because they already know in advance that, if what they're listening to is not informed by at least an implicit acceptance of the principles of deconstruction, or the principles of pragmatism, it cannot be anything other than an exhibition of the really *deep* or *fundamental* kinds of error that deconstructionists, or pragmatists, have been called to expose. This means not just that it is unnecessary to meet an opponent head-on in a clash of ideas but that it is impossible to meet him so. The situation is rather like that of a psychiatrist or a psychotherapist listening to patients. The principles of the therapy are never in question, nor does the therapist pay much attention to the superficial content of what his patients are saying. Instead he works through the superficial content in order to arrive at some notion of what has *caused* his patients to speak the way they do. (As Martin Buber once pointed out to Carl Rogers, under such conditions genuine dialogue is impossible and only a parody of dialogue can be achieved.) Since the deconstructionist and the pragmatist can never meet with other thinkers in the open marketplace of ideas without a keen awareness that these others are wrong from the start, they are closer to being solipsists than pluralists. For them, the Western tradition does not present a rich diversity of conflicting ideas and opinions. It is more like the Manhattan Project, although it has finally come to grief with the recognition that it was vitiated from the beginning by having incorporated one or two absolutely fundamental errors. Because of their inability to encounter significant "others" in the intellectual marketplace, the deconstructionist and the pragmatist have no alternative but to indulge in their own fantasies of specious pluralisms.

Let us consider more closely the case of deconstruction. The will to be pluralist is certainly clear in the apologias of its leading practitioners. As J. Hillis Miller observes in his essay "The Critic as Host," "The hypothesis of a possible heterogeneity in literary texts is more flexible, more open to a given work, than the assumption that a good work of literature is necessarily going to be 'organically unified'":

> Deconstruction attempts to resist the totalizing and totalitarian tendencies of criticism. It attempts to resist its own tendencies to come to rest in

> some sense of mastery over the work. It resists these in the name of an
> uneasy joy of interpretation, beyond nihilism, always in movement. . . .[8]

From this point of view, it appears that the superiority of deconstruction
with respect to other modes of literary analysis consists in the fact that it is
more sensitive to the complexities of the texts with which it deals. Instead
of forcing a text to produce an oversimplified account of itself, the
deconstructionist allows the full etymological and rhetorical complexity
of a given text to be made manifest by means of a minute examination of
the text's verbal details. The assumption behind his procedure is that it is
not *the author* that means but rather *the text* that means, and what the text
means is always, by definition, the sum total of what all its component
words now mean, or have ever meant, in all their possible uses and contexts. Any reading that does not take these into account may be regarded
as insensitive to "the possible heterogeneity" of the text. Since all texts,
including critical or philosophic texts, are amenable to the deconstructionist
mode of analysis, it follows that all of them can be shown to contain multitudinous elements, many of which are incompatible and, therefore, capable of rendering the texts in which they appear "incoherent" or "indeterminate." More importantly, it also follows, on the principles of deconstruction, that "literal" meaning or "referential" meaning is a kind of illusion, a sort of virtual image conjured up by a temporary suspension of the
verbal play that is always going on (usually unnoticed) at every textual
level. Naïve writers and naïve readers are constantly making the mistake
of assuming that they can suppress this play, either by suspending it altogether or else by domesticating it. In fact, they can only mislead themselves by constructing incomplete or false interpretations of whatever it is
they happen to be writing or reading. In particular, any writer who tries to
communicate a clear, unambiguous meaning by using carefully defined
concepts or carefully controlled figurative language can be shown to have
been subverted in his efforts *by his own words*. Language itself rises up, as
it were, and baffles us in the attempt to make it say our thoughts. Indeed, it
refuses to represent us but instead insists on shaping or determining the
very ideas we would like to think it is only transporting.

    One problem with this line of reasoning is that it leads, on the face of
it, to an infinite regress of what might be called enabling interpretations.
Suppose, for example, that I read a certain text by an author and imagine

(falsely) that I know what the text means in terms of what the author is driving at or referring to. Suppose that I further imagine that this meaning limits the text or, in some way, is responsible for the text's being as it is. The deconstructionist will insist that I am making a mistake about the text and will urge me to read an analysis of it that reveals the contradictory implications of its verbal details. Upon doing so, presumably, I shall revise my earlier conception of what the work means. All of this may very well occur as planned if it can be assumed that the explanatory text—the deconstructive analysis—is capable of referring me to the original text without itself requiring some sort of enabling interpretation. If I can read the deconstructive analysis in such a way that it helps me to understand the original text, then the assumptions behind deconstruction in general are false. For I might just as well have read the original text in such a way as to have understood what it referred to. If I truly need to be apprised of the verbal complexity of the original text, then, on deconstructive principles, I cannot apprehend the second text—the explanatory text—until *its* verbal complexity has been made manifest by a third text. Furthermore, I shall have to disabuse myself of the notion that the second text literally refers to the first text, because in order to think this I should have to disregard the verbal play that constitutes the reality of the second text. And so now I have three texts. But, if I can't read the first one without the second, or the second one without the third, how shall I read the third without a fourth? On the other hand, if I can read the second one without the third, why can't I read the first without the second? If all texts require interpretation, and all interpretations are themselves to be conceived as verbal texts, then no texts can be understood, even if there be world enough and time to produce an infinite number of them. However, if there is anywhere a text that is capable of producing insight into some other thing (even another text), it is because we have taken it as representationally significant and chosen not to deconstruct it. Indeed, whenever we read a deconstructive analysis that seems to us particularly illuminating with respect to the work it is ostensibly "about," it is clear that we can't be reading the analysis itself in a deconstructive fashion. We are reading it literally, naïvely.

We can draw a moral concerning this problem from Christopher Norris's attempt to explain Paul de Man's attempt to explain Rousseau's *Social Contract* in Norris's book *The Contest of Faculties*. At one point, Norris praises Paul de Man for "the exemplary rigour" with which he brings out . . . the consequence of reading texts (including 'political' texts) in the light of their rhetorical organization."[9] Norris quotes de Man's own comment on how one ought to proceed with Rousseau's text. "We are not here concerned," says de Man,

> with the technically political significance of this text, still less with an evaluation of the political and ethical praxis that can be derived from it. Our reading merely tries to define the rhetorical patterns that organize the distribution and the movement of the key terms—while contending that questions of valorization can be relevantly considered only after the rhetorical status of the text has been clarified.[10]

As Norris himself puts it, "if Rousseau's text could be read as political *theory* pure and simple, then it would serve as an unproblematical blueprint" for the setting-up of actual governments or actual constitutions. Indeed, *The Social Contract* would itself turn out to be a knowable entity, "an object of purely scientific knowledge." "That this is not the case," says Norris, "is explained, for de Man, by the *Contract's* literal 'unreadability' at the level of straightforward constative utterance." If this is true of all texts, as deconstruction implies—not just that they are ambiguous in their implications but that they are literally unreadable at the level of straightforward constative utterance—then what are we to make of Norris's remark (a moment later) that "we should not take too lightly de Man's statement that 'far from being a repression of the political, as Althusser would have it, literature is condemned to being the truly political mode of discourse'"? Should we take this remark at face value at "the level of straightforward constative utterance"? Isn't Norris making a claim about the significance of one of de Man's sentences, a sentence, moreover, which in itself appears to be making a claim about the nature of literature? And aren't these claims literally impossible to understand, literally unreadable, until after the rhetorical status of the texts in which they occur has been clarified? Why should I suppose that I can know what Norris and de Man are even talking about, if I may not suppose that I can know what Rousseau is talking about? It is touching indeed to hear Norris constantly pleading that deconstruction as an instrument of "enlightened critique" has genuine political implications, especially when we remember that, like *The Social Contract,* its texts are literally unreadable. According to Norris, "De Man's texts quite explicitly *ask* to be read in this 'political' mode. They insist that the field of rhetorical tension is always . . . a space where the politics of reading is inevitably brought into play." Indeed, as Norris would have it, we should deplore the fact that Marxist critics show a reluctance "to notice these passages of explicitly political reflection in de Man." On deconstructive principles, what should they notice except that their explicitness is an illusion, a smoke screen, temporarily covering the fact that they are, strictly speaking, unreadable or indecipherable?

It would seem, then, that a thoroughly consistent deconstructionist can never meet another text (much less another author) in the sense of being able to attend to what texts (or authors) appear to be saying. To do so would be naïve. He can only remain in a sort of solipsistic vacuum where all voices and all claims (including his own) are finally dissolved into one thing, namely, the play of language. If texts and authors have no independent status in relation to each other, nor any means of resisting the deconstructionist's technique of dissolving them into a huge sea of textuality, why should we continue to speak of deconstruction as though it constituted a genuine pluralism? Certainly this is not the sort of pluralism Matei Calinescu has in mind when he defines "the new (postmodern) pluralism" as "a plurality of world views, a plurality of conflicting beliefs that articulate themselves ever more forcefully and vigorously to become 'happy dwelling places of the mind.'"[11] It is more like the pluralism of Democritus, which renders the visible universe intelligible by regarding it as a large collection of atoms.

But now suppose we take Norris seriously and listen to what he is trying to tell us. Others, besides him, have claimed that deconstruction may be useful in detecting the latent ideology that governs a text. Christopher Butler, for example, claims this in his book *Interpretation, Deconstruction, and Ideology*. According to Butler, "Derridan analysis may reveal a use of concepts with hidden metaphorical levels which are *systematic* in some way that reveals the nature of those general beliefs about the world to which we appeal in interpreting metaphor, and of which we are hardly conscious, because they are so deeply encoded in the language we use to deal with the text."[12] But this means that all texts (including those that attempt to explain other texts) are caught in the grip of ideological motives and assumptions which their authors must express willy-nilly, apart from or within whatever their texts appear to be saying on the surface. Once again the gloomy prospect of an infinite regress looms on the horizon.

Writer A produces a text in which he makes a series of naïve constative utterances or in some other way tries to use language in order to say something. Writer B listens to Writer A's language and detects therein the nuances of certain ideological assumptions or biases of which Writer A may or may not be conscious. Writer B then produces a text in which he deconstructs Writer A's text in order to expose its ideological underpinnings. But how are we to take Writer B's text? Should we accept what Writer B is trying to tell us about Writer A at face value, on the level of straightforward constative utterance? Don't we find it necessary to deconstruct *his* utterances in order to expose *their* ideological underpinnings? And won't this have to go on forever if the really significant thing about every text is the latent ideology encoded in the author's rhetoric? If Writer B's observations about Writer A's rhetoric are not themselves vitiated or compromised by their own rhetoric, why must we assume that Writer A's observations are necessarily compromised by Writer A's rhetoric? Indeed, if all writing is imbued with traces of ideology, as deconstruction assumes, and if all writing could be deconstructed in such a way as to make these traces manifest, how should we proceed to deal with the ideologies thus detected? We shall have reached a point where there is no alternative but to deal directly with the beliefs, the biases, the assumptions or preconceptions, of the different writers with whom we have chosen to concern ourselves. We shall have to decide whether these beliefs or assumptions are true or false, right or wrong, valid or invalid. That is to say, once a hidden ideology has been brought into the light, we shall be forced to consider whether or not it has any merit. Having been exposed, it will cease to be the tacit foundation of one position or another, dictating from behind the scenes, as it were, the arguments of this or that group of intellectuals. It will be on the table, up for discussion. When this happens, we shall find ourselves talking in ways strikingly reminiscent of the ways old-fashioned intellectuals used to talk in the days before postmodern enlightenment. If we try to weigh the relative merits of Christian ideology versus Marxist ideology, we shall find ourselves arguing about the validity of the various propositions asserted by Christian and Marxist thinkers. It will be as though deconstruction had never existed, for we shall catch ourselves imagining that we can actually understand the straightforward constative utterances these thinkers are making.

If various ideologies really do lie at the foundation of all writing and thinking, what is the point of detecting them and exposing them by means of what Norris calls "the rigorous close reading of texts," if there is no way to justify them or refute them? To assume that we can choose or reject ideologies *for good reasons* is to play the old-fashioned game called Western philosophy, a game that is incompatible with the tenets of deconstruction. If, on the other hand, we assume that we can't choose or reject ideologies (because such decisions are themselves being dictated by ideological motives), then all we have left is the option to survey (from an always biased point of view) the whole panoply of ideologies, each one impervious to the others and inviolable in its isolation, like a windowless monad. Thus, when I read a given text, I will encounter not what the writer naïvely imagines himself to be saying (the superficial content of arguments, reasons, and the like) but rather an ideology, similar to my own or different. If different, no meeting of minds is possible. If similar, no meeting of minds is possible either, for we shall be of one mind, of the same mind. For whose benefit, then, does the powerful critique that deconstruction is supposed to be exist? In actual practice, I think, we tend to accept or reject the ideological positions we encounter, once we are made aware of them, for reasons that would be perfectly familiar to thinkers who flourished long before postmodernism. In fact, a genuine pluralism requires the tacit assumption that ideologies can be validated or invalidated by means of the writings we produce to justify them. If this is an illusion, then the point of both reading and writing has been obviated. We might just as well not talk to each other at all, if all our talking is going to be regarded as merely an egotistical display of assumptions impervious to criticism. Ultimately, I would suggest, the deconstructionist contemplates a world in which all discourse is vitiated by its necessary reliance on essentially unjustifiable assumptions. In such a world, it is impossible to encounter significantly different views of things, views that may legitimately claim our assent or dissent. In such a world, only the deconstructionist's relentless exposure of the groundlessness of views has genuine validity or value. Pluralism becomes a hollow show of meaningless differences.

What about the other version of postmodernism, the pragmatist version? Surely pragmatism does not fail to countenance the existence of different views of things. Does it not thrive in an atmosphere of differences, refusing to accord a special privilege to any one view so that all may flourish? Surely pragmatism is the one philosophy (or rather post-philosophy) that is capable of contemplating with unalloyed satisfaction what Calinescu calls "a plurality of world views, a plurality of conflicting beliefs that articulate themselves ever more forcefully and vigorously to become 'happy dwelling places for of the mind.'" But pragmatism too is open to the objection that it is really a sort of metaphilosophy, incapable of meeting, or of being met by, any of the views that come against it because it is so adept at arranging those views for purposes of aesthetic contemplation on a level or plane beneath itself. It denies, of course, that any philosophy it can think of can be in such a privileged position, but then it also denies having any pretensions of its own to being a philosophy. It proclaims itself to be not a way of looking at things, which might be relative to other ways of looking at things, but rather *the* way of looking at the ways of looking. Assuming that this is the most modest of all possible claims, the pragmatist looks at other intellectuals in the same way that an adult might look at children frolicking or squabbling on a playground. William James uses a similar image, borrowed from Giovanni Papini, in the second of his Lowell Institute lectures on pragmatism. Pragmatism, says James,

> lies in the midst of our theories, like a corridor in a hotel. Innumerable chambers open out of it. In one you may find a man writing an atheistic volume; in the next someone on his knees praying for faith and strength; in a third a chemist investigating a body's properties. In a fourth a system of idealistic metaphysics is being excogitated; in a fifth the impossibility of metaphysics is being shown. But they all own the corridor, and all must pass through it if they want a praticable way of getting into or out of their respective rooms.[13]

What James fails to acknowledge here is that if the atheist and the religious man come out into the corridor at the same time, they are likely to get into a furious argument. They won't see themselves as interesting character-types, such as "the atheist" and "the religious man." They will see themselves as being either right or wrong, and it will matter a great deal to each of them which one it is. Pragmatism is not the corridor in the hotel; it is a view *from* the corridor into each of the rooms, one after another. The pragmatist is a man like the other men, except that *his* room is the corridor from which he can view as he pleases the projects of all the others. His enthusiasm for each project is genuine in its way, but it is limited by his awareness that there are always equally interesting counter-projects going on at the same time. The delusion of each of the projectors—that his project alone is supremely important or absolutely valid—is smiled at by the pragmatist, who does not share it but rather tolerates it as a necessary condition of the project's being done at all. If this is not a privileged view of things— indeed, a totalitarian view—I can't imagine what is. The enjoyment of other people's views from an aesthetic point of view rather than from some consideration of their intrinsic merit or validity (which is what matters most to those who propound them) is, at the very least, extremely patronizing, and it is certainly not to be regarded as essentially different from the other projects that are going on in the hotel just because it is the project of watching how different people work at different projects. Indeed, pragmatism stumbles into self-contradiction whenever it tries to recommend itself as a position of advantage from which it is possible to see that there is no such thing as a position of advantage.

Norris is right, I think, to consider the possibility that pragmatism in its postmodern form (that is to say, in the form advanced by such recent thinkers as Richard Rorty and Jean-François Lyotard) *may* be a rationale for a certain form of political or social liberalism, which would mean, of course, that its above-the-battle stance could hardly be more than an illusion. As Norris puts it:

> The upshot in political terms would be a 'liberal' consensus forswearing the idea of social improvement through rational critique and relying instead on the free circulation of communal myths and values. Such thinking translates readily enough into the present condition of western 'liberal' democracy, where the appearance of open, pluralist debate (sustained by mass media) disguises the monopolistic interests of power.[14]

In other words, Norris is worried about pragmatism's ideological underpinnings, which is all well and good provided we can ascertain that the ideology of pragmatism really is "western liberal democracy" and provided we can come up with a valid argument to the effect that there really is something wrong with "western liberal democracy." Despite its illusion that it constitutes a particularly rigorous form of ideological critique, deconstruction, on its own terms, can do neither of these things. Only an old-fashioned intellectual, trained in the days before postmodernism, would have the naïveté to embark on these projects.

   The real problem with pragmatism (apart from questions concerning its unconscious ideological motives) is that, like deconstruction, it cannot take its opponents seriously enough to engage with them on the same plane. It is less interested in what its opponents have to say than it is in the various conditions that conspire to define where it is that they belong on the intellectual map. It is the philosophy *par excellence* that tries to account (in Calinescu's words) "not only for *what* is stated about the world or worlds and their reciprocal relations" but also "for *who* makes such a statement and *why* (for what purpose and in whose interest?), and *how,* and on the basis of what kind of *authority.*"[15] With answers to all these questions safely tucked away, it would appear that we have accounted for what a statement has to say about the world without having to determine the extent to which it is true. Indeed, the point of making such inquiries is to demonstrate that we have emancipated ourselves from the naïveté of believing in a correspondence theory of truth. But instead of entertaining for consideration those ideas about the world that our fellow intellectuals have invited us to consider, we have spent our time forming ideas of our own about what it is that these intellectuals are doing when they form their ideas. Whether we are right or wrong in our conclusions, it is certainly true that our ideas stand in relation to what they are doing in exactly the same way that their statements about the world stand in relation to the world. All of our statements in response to the questions *who, why,* and *how,* are really statements about the world; that is to say, they are statements about what these intellectuals are really like and what has caused them to think the way they do. If we value our own ideas about these things, we necessarily commit ourselves to the very correspondence theory of truth we are trying so hard to get rid of. Meanwhile, though, as I have just said, we have found a way of ignoring the content of those statements about the world our fellow intellectuals have placed before us. This content is, for us, the least interesting thing of all. Why, then, should we expect that others will be interested in listening to us? If they are good pragmatists, they will be too busy forming their own ideas concerning how we happened to arrive at our ideas. On pragmatist terms, it would be impossible anyway to determine whether our ideas are right or wrong. Indeed, the issue would be meaningless. However, if the pragmatist is unable to take other people's views at face value on their own terms, and if he has no right to expect them to take his views (or any views) at their face value, by what stretch of imagination does he arrive at the conclusion that he is living in a world where fundamentally different views of things are capable of meeting each other head-on, face to face?

Certainly the world of James's hotel is not such a world. In fact, it is not so much a hotel as it is an elegant madhouse. From time to time, the pragmatist looks into each of the cells like a kindly therapist checking on the progress of his patients. Perhaps he pauses for a moment to look at a page or two from the absolutely mad treatise on metaphysics that one of his patients is composing so earnestly. Yes, the book is coming along well, and it will constitute a fitting explanation of how the world actually looks from this particular madhouse cell. A word of encouragement, a pat on the shoulder, and the therapist is gone. Next he appears in the cell of a logical positivist, who is busily at work proving that metaphysics is impossible. It's an odd sort of view, thinks the therapist, but if it makes him happy, that's all that matters. Another word of encouragement is spoken, and the therapist steps quietly out into the corridor. Yes, they are all of them hard at work at their various forms of world-making therapy, spinning out their harmless fantasies, each according to his favorite delusion.

Back in his office, the therapist has a full case history that accounts for each of them. In reality, of course, none of them is getting any better, but they are, after all, harmlessly occupied, and each of them is enjoying himself immensely in his own mad way. With all due apologies to William James, who was himself a serious man with a genuine curiosity about the views of other people whose thinking happened to be different from his own, this view of the pragmatist as a sort of kindly warden keeping an eye on things in a home for the mildly insane seems to me not at all inapplicable to such latter-day, postmodern pragmatists as Richard Rorty or Stanley Fish. Whatever they espouse, it certainly isn't pluralism, for a genuine pluralism would require them to entertain at least the barest possibility that one or another of the madhouse occupants just might be right. The image of essentially isolated people carrying out their solipsistic activities in private cells under the watchful eye of the corridor's lone denizen—a postmodern pragmatist—can hardly be taken as the image of a pluralistic society wherein different ideas are respected enough to be thought worth contending against. Indeed, the postmodern pragmatist is a pluralist only in the sense that he has learned how to cultivate an aesthetic vision of an unusually large number of basically incompatible views, according to which all may be regarded as equally interesting because all are essentially nugatory.

We are forced to conclude, I think, that neither pragmatism nor deconstruction is capable of providing an adequate rationale for pluralism. Instead, they both constitute ways of thinking that make it possible to show that thinking itself is essentially blind or flawed. When the demonstration of this proposition itself explodes into self-contradiction, the deconstructionist and the pragmatist are not dismayed. Rather, they seize the opportunity to say, "Yes, yes! Exactly so. This is just what we've been saying all along. This proves that we are right." But once I recognize that all thinking is essentially handicapped or essentially flawed, I can never again regard the thought-projects of others in quite the same way I did before becoming thus enlightened. And this makes it impossible for me to take them even provisionally on the terms they demand or require. Conversation ceases and aesthetic enjoyment (or boredom) commences.

The project of demonstrating that thinking is handicapped or flawed, which pragmatism and deconstruction share between them, is, as I have been suggesting throughout this book, not an especially new phenomenon. It has been going on, in its various modern forms, ever since the Enlightenment. To know this is to know that postmodernism, in its theoretical ambitions, is simply the latest phase of the perennial effort made by postrationalism to construct a critique (or, in Norris's terms, "a rigorous thinking-through") of reason itself. Hegel's critique of this critique is as effective today as it was against the Kantians:

> The initial demand is that we should first investigate reason generally, the cognitive capacity or conceptual thought, before proceeding to cognition. . . . We picture the project of cognition as though it were something that came about by means of an instrument with which one wants to grasp the truth. On closer consideration, the demand that we should first cognize this instrument is inappropriate, however plausible it may seem. . . .
>
> Reason is to be investigated—but how? It must be investigated rationally, it must be cognized. This is possible only through rational thinking, through rational cognition; any other way it is impossible. This demand directly involves a requirement that annuls itself. If we ought not to begin philosophizing until we have cognized reason rationally, then we cannot begin at all, for in cognizing we are comprehending rationally; but we are supposed to relinquish this rational comprehension, since it is precisely reason that we are supposed to cognize. This is the same de-

mand as that Gascon makes who does not want to go into the water until
he is able to swim. To learn to swim one must go into the water. One
cannot make cognition into one's object without thereby behaving
cognitively at the same time.[16]

Instead of reaching the conclusion that reason can be shown *not* to have
passed inspection, we are forced to conclude just the opposite, namely,
that inspections are themselves rational performances. The determinations
of reason cannot be limited if, in fact, it is reason itself that determines
what shall be called limits. Or, as Hegel says elsewhere in a similar context, "since the investigation of the faculties of knowledge is itself knowing," it cannot be a preliminary exercise in advance of knowing, nor can it
be a preemptive determination that knowing is impossible, "because it is
that already—it cannot come to itself because it is already with itself."[17]
Perhaps, if we were really concerned about pluralism, we might go so far
as to say that a genuine pluralism (as opposed to a skeptical monadology)
is possible only if all thought-projects (including the project to undermine
reason) can be regarded as expressions of the same inherent rationality,
for only thus can it be said that their differences do make a difference.

THE CRISIS OF REASON IN CONTEMPORARY THOUGHT

> I am willing to have a maximum of "relativity," but I wonder if they have ever considered that if "relative" systems have no connexion, and no common object, each is absolute: and if they have a common object, or form a connected group of perspectives, then they are only relative views, like optical illusions, and the universe is not ambiguous in its true form.
>
> —Santayana, *Letters*

In general terms, what does one mean when one speaks of a crisis of reason in contemporary thought? What is this crisis? Surely it must have something to do with the belief, which we have been discussing, that reason has shown itself to be incapable of carrying out the tasks that were formerly expected of it: first of all, the task of building up a coherent view of things as they really are, and then the task of working out the political and ethical consequences of things as they really are. Nowadays, it is widely assumed that thought cannot perform these tasks, under the guise of reason or under any other guise. We have come to suspect—many of us—that reason's goals have always been unattainable, since they are a mere reflection of reason's hubris. The fact that we do not seem to have a coherent view of things as they really are is obviously explained by the fact that, outside of reason's dream, there is no such thing as "things as they really are." To suppose otherwise would presumably be naïve. Here we see the first stage of the crisis. As a result of making the discovery that reason is not only a constituting power but also a constituted product (which can be taken to mean that it is both a fabrication and a source of fabrication), the projects entertained by reason no longer seem to be viable. The second stage of the crisis comes when it dawns on us that, like it or not, we are still faced with the necessity of having some sort of sense of ourselves and the world we live in. If philosophy in the grand manner is no longer possible now that its engine, reason, has been exploded, then some sort of postphilosophical thinking will have to take its place, and the question is, what will this thinking look like and how will it proceed?

This is what I take to be the crisis of reason. In some versions of the

177

story, this crisis is supposed to have been brought on by the Enlightenment. Accordingly, the eighteenth century is often depicted as the time when reason reared itself up to its full height in order to contemplate the conquest of ignorance and superstition through an endless expansion of knowledge and the freedom that comes from knowledge. Trouble sets in only when reason starts taking a closer look at itself. In attempting to clarify reason's procedures, Kant succeeds paradoxically in paving the way, first, for the extravagant claims of the German idealists and, then, for the obliteration of those claims by subsequent thinkers. In the nineteenth century, Marx and Nietzsche seem to show that reason is interested or biased, because it is rooted in, and apparently shaped by, conditions of which it is unconscious or toward which it refuses to be properly deferential. In the twentieth century, such impressive thinkers as Freud, Wittgenstein, Heidegger, and Derrida continue to investigate the way in which seemingly rational thought is blind to its own irrational or prerational underpinnings, and the result is that the Enlightenment's vision of a "modern" world based on reason has given way to our own, more advanced vision of a "postmodern" world based on the critique of reason.

In recent years, many books have been written that assume that the crisis of reason, as I have just described it, is simply a fact of life. Sometimes these books elucidate what I call the first stage of the crisis; that is, they rehearse the various arguments that have been used to diminish reason's pretensions. Sometimes, however, they proceed to the second stage by attempting to describe what is now in store for us as a result of our having become aware of these pretensions. What I would like to do here is to examine very briefly two books that belong predominantly to the second category. The first is a book by Jean-François Lyotard called *The Postmodern Condition*,[1] and the second is a collection of essays, edited by Anthony J. Cascardi, called *Literature and the Question of Philosophy*.[2] These two books, for the most part, take for granted the fact that speculative philosophy has become obsolete. However, in trying to get on with the further business of describing what is to come next, they show themselves to be enmeshed in just this philosophy. More specifically, they reveal that the two philosophical narratives that Lyotard relegates, respectively, to the Enlightenment and to German idealism are still very much alive, even in the arguments of those who imagine themselves to be, as Lyotard would have it, incredulous toward them. Thus, in spite of itself, the critique of reason manifested in these books ends up looking like a vindication of reason, with the result that the "crisis of reason" narrative itself, as I have just outlined it, begins to appear somewhat doubtful or bogus.

Lyotard's book *The Postmodern Condition* may be described as an attempt to explain the evolution of contemporary society in terms of the relative fortunes or destinies of two basically different kinds of knowledge: narrative knowledge and scientific knowledge. Before the rise of Western science, all cultures everywhere understood themselves through myths, fables, and legends. That is to say, they understood themselves in terms of stories or narratives. These narratives were not regarded by the cultures that produced them as standing in need of proof or verification. By nature, they were formulaic or ritualistic, and their validity as knowledge was determined, not by their correspondence to the facts, but by their correspondence to the forms and rituals associated with their transmission. In this way, they were self-validating or self-legitimating, according to Lyotard. But then science came on the scene, with the demand that everything be proven or demonstrated. Science made knowledge a matter of inquiry and, from the very beginning, passed judgment against the "customary" or "traditional" knowledge contained in narrative. "The scientist," says Lyotard, "questions the validity of narrative statements and concludes that they are never subject to verification or proof. He classifies them as belonging to a different mentality: savage, primitive, underdeveloped, backward, alienated, composed of opinions, customs, authority, prejudice, ignorance, ideology" (*PC,* 27). Thus, the rise of scientific knowledge would seem to require a corresponding decline of narrative knowledge. Such a decline does occur, at least with respect to the narratives associated with the prescientific era. But then a curious thing happens. In order to validate itself, science "produces a discourse of legitimation with respect to its own status, a discourse called philosophy" (*PC,* xxiii) which is essentially narrative in nature rather than scientific. As Lyotard puts it, "scientific knowledge cannot know and make known that it is the true knowledge without resorting to the other, narrative, kind of knowledge, which from its point of view is no knowledge at all" (*PC,* 29). In Plato, for example, scientific discussions are situated inside stories that are "more closely related to tragedy than epic" (*PC,* 29), while in Descartes the legitimacy of science is demonstrated "in a *Bildungsroman,* which is what the *Discourse on Method* amounts to" (*PC,* 29). Since Descartes's time, the philosophical justification of science has taken the form of two different narratives. The first, which Lyotard calls the emancipation narrative, is a product of the Enlightenment. It views science as an instrument for liberating mankind from the compulsions of ignorance and superstition. The second, which Lyotard calls the speculative narrative, is a product of German idealism, and it focuses on the liberation of thought itself through the progress of scientific investigation and reflection.

These two narratives justify science, but they are not themselves justifiable by science. Each in its own way tries to situate science in terms of a metadiscourse which is incompatible with scientific discourse. By the end of the nineteenth century, the full extent of this incompatibility began to be appreciated by most serious thinkers, and the effort to ground science by such extrascientific means was abandoned. Nowadays the sciences are permitted to go their own separate ways according to their own separate logics, and it is no longer felt to be necessary or even possible to synthesize them by incorporating them within the schemes of the Enlightenment *philosophes* or the German idealists. According to Lyotard, one of the chief characteristics of postmodern thinking is that it is incredulous toward the metanarratives associated with these schemes. The only thing that now justifies science is its own performative power; it has become self-legitimating by virtue of its undeniable ability to produce new knowledge. Instead of conceiving itself in terms of the role it may be thought to play within a larger drama, it now conceives itself as a multiplicity of language games, each governed by its own set of rules. That is why there is no way to impose upon them the authority of a higher reason. Each of the games is subject to its own immanent logic, which can evolve or mutate in ways that are unpredictable and, therefore, nonrectifiable. There was a time, says Lyotard, when this situation seemed alarming, especially to those who still had a hankering for the moribund projects of philosophy. But the decline of these projects has coincided with an explosion of progress in the sciences, and thus it is better for science, in the long run, that things should have taken this particular turn.

There is still, however, one obstacle to the perfect autonomy of scientific knowledge, and that, ironically, is an obstacle for which science itself is partly responsible. Because its researches have had powerful technological implications, science has, ever since the Industrial Revolution, been allied with, and indeed dependent upon, the forces of capitalist production. The material progress of society makes possible the further progress of the sciences by means of large-scale funding, while, at the same time, the progress of the sciences makes possible the material progress of society. The two kinds of progress have become locked into a single system, wherein success is measured by the criterion of performativity. Society's capacity to meet the needs of science depends upon science's capacity to meet the needs of society, and vice versa. The result is that science runs the risk of being dictated to by the state bureaucracy, whose function it is to supervise the efficiency of the total system. Planners and decision makers, with the well-meaning intention of getting science to achieve maximum output, are thus in a position to establish goals for science, not long-range teleological goals such as the old philosophers envisioned, but immediate practical goals more in keeping with the projects that science itself is best at. In short, a systems approach to all the problems of social organization, and indeed to every aspect of our lives, seems to be the inevitable outcome of the triumph of scientific knowledge over, first, traditional knowledge and, then, over philosophical knowledge. Productivity and performativity, because of their close association with the only valid form of knowledge, establish a standard of meaningfulness by which to judge everything that goes on in society. Everything that does not function in some way in the building-up of the power made possible by science can be deemed meaningless and, in fact, is likely to be eliminated in society's quest for greater and greater performativity. The computerization of society, which Lyotard discusses at the beginning of his book, fits very nicely into this scenario. Conformity to the processes involved in the storage and retrieval of information from computer data banks will henceforth be required of everyone who wishes to have a position in the vast system of information exchanges that will dominate future social activity. It seems almost like a nightmare come true, with science calling the shots for everybody and the state calling the shots for science. As Lyotard candidly admits on the last page, the computerization of society "could become the 'dream' instrument of controlling and regulating the market system, extended to include knowledge itself and governed exclusively by the performativity principle" (*PC*, 67).

There is no doubt that Lyotard finds this an appalling possibility. He imagines, however, that it can be averted, not by trying to reinstate the authority of the old narrative knowledge (which would be futile) but by paying closer attention to the most recent developments in science, which are conspiring to undermine the deterministic model that systems theory seeks to impose upon us. As Lyotard puts it, "the pragmatics of postmodern scientific knowledge per se has little affinity with the quest for performativity" (*PC*, 54), and that is because, in dealing with a new variety of indeterminate phenomena, science has had to revise its own expectations so as to accommodate itself to "undecidables, the limits of precise control, conflicts characterized by incomplete information, *'fracta,'* catastrophes, and pragmatic paradoxes" (*PC*, 60). A systems approach to science is based on the supposition that science is a stable, predictable method of describing a reality that is similarly stable and predictable. In fact, as soon as science finds itself confronted with situations that are unstable and unpredictable, its own evolution becomes "discontinuous, catastrophic, nonrectifiable, and paradoxical" (*PC*, 60), so that a systems approach cannot be applied to it. Indeed, according to Lyotard, a careful study of postmodern science will show that "its pragmatics provides the antimodel of a stable system" (*PC*, 64). Dissension and novelty are the very essence of it, not predictability. To the extent, then, that it places a premium on the invention of new moves and even brand-new games, "contemporary science excludes the possibility of using [the paradigm of a stable system] to describe society" (*PC*, 61). It rules out conformity, and it rules in imagination. Thus, if science is to continue, a totally efficient, highly centralized state—the state conceived as an ecosystem or as a perpetual-motion machine—will have to permit the existence of a certain amount of freedom in its brain-cells or think-tanks. In the context of a fully computerized society, it is even possible to imagine (as Lyotard tries to do) that, if the public is given free access to the memory and data banks, freedom itself will be maximized through massive exchanges of information. For then every language game would be open to every person, and all the games would be "games of perfect information at any given moment" (*PC*, 67). The generation of new moves and new games could go on forever, since "the reserve of knowledge—language's reserve of possible utterances—is inexhaustible" (*PC*, 67). In this way, the alternative to Western philosophy is not the nightmare of Big Science. It is the prospect of being invited to participate in the exciting little dramas of the language games.

What is one to make of all this? One hardly knows where to begin. Perhaps the first thing to say about this book is that it is itself, most obviously, a master narrative, and, as such, it represents exactly the kind of knowledge that is now supposed to be meaningless. This, I take it, is a very bad form of self-contradiction. It makes me feel incredulous toward Lyotard's whole argument, which, of course, he himself says is the right response to make when one finds oneself in the presence of a grand philosophical narrative. But I feel incredulous, not because it *is* such a narrative, but because Lyotard doesn't seem to know that it is, or because he doesn't seem to care that the fact that it is means that something must be wrong with the thesis that such things are obsolete. As one reads along, one gets the uncanny feeling that the author of *The Postmodern Condition* has found, at least in principle, exactly the right kind of discourse for situating and interpreting all the things he is talking about, but, at the same time, it is also clear that he is declaring this very discourse an impossibility. The existence of such a discourse does not, I think, require us to accept each and every thesis that happens to be imbedded in it. But the acceptance of this particular thesis does mean that we cannot accept the existence of the discourse that produced it. As a consequence, the status of the thesis becomes radically ambiguous.

Consider, for a moment, the claim on which Lyotard's whole argument turns; I mean the claim that there is a fundamental difference between narrative knowledge and scientific knowledge. The distinction between these two different kinds of knowledge is what prompts the author to declare that there is an essential incompatibility between prescientific thinking and scientific thinking, just as there is an essential incompatibility between philosophical thinking and scientific thinking. The language games of science and narrative have different sets of rules, and, since they are structured differently, they are incommensurate with each other. That is why, according to Lyotard, "Science has always been in conflict with narratives" (*PC,* xxiii). It is not that science has come to a different set of conclusions; it is that science and narrative operate according to different sets of pragmatics. Lyotard puts it this way:

> [D]rawing a parallel between science and nonscientific (narrative) knowledge helps us understand, or at least sense, that the former's existence is no more—and no less—necessary than the latter's. Both are composed of sets of statements; the statements are "moves" made by the players within the framework of generally applicable rules; these rules are specific to each kind of knowledge, and the "moves" judged to be "good" in

one cannot be of the same type as those judged "good" in another, unless it happens that way by chance.

It is therefore impossible to judge the existence or validity of narrative knowledge on the basis of scientific knowledge and vice versa: the relevant criteria are different. All we can do is gaze in wonderment at the diversity of discursive species, just as we do at the diversity of plant or animal species. (*PC,* 26)

As soon as we read this, we feel prompted to ask, what is the species of Lyotard's own discourse? Since science and narrative are being presented throughout the entire book as the two fundamental thought-forms, we would like to know whether he is writing from the point of view of science or the point of view of narrative. If *The Postmodern Condition* is a work of science, then it seems unfortunate to admit that it is impossible to judge either the existence or the validity of narrative knowledge on the basis of scientific knowledge. On the other hand, if the book is a work of narrative, it seems equally unfortunate to have to admit that narrative knowledge is characterized by an "incomprehension of the problems of scientific discourse" (*PC,* 27). If science can't comprehend narrative and narrative can't comprehend science, but Lyotard's book *can* comprehend both of these things well enough to pronounce upon their incompatibility, it must be that Lyotard has found some third kind of discourse. It appears, in fact, that he has somehow managed to combine the two fundamental thought-forms. To have understood that these forms can be brought into relation by means of an analysis of them as language games, to have reduced them to this common principle, is to have made a scientific analysis of them. Alternatively, to explain the past, present, and future of Western culture in terms of the unfolding of these forms, or in terms of their encounters with each other, is to indulge in what Lyotard himself refers to as a master- or metanarrative. It seems that, somehow, Lyotard *has* managed to synthesize the incompatible language games, which is more than just to gaze in wonderment at their diversity. The truth is, he is practicing philosophy.

With respect to the narrative side of his book, what Lyotard has done is to blend together the two philosophical narratives that are supposed to be defunct: the emancipation narrative and the speculative narrative. No reader can fail to observe that the question of whether science is liberating or enslaving us is constantly being raised; indeed, it looms over the whole discussion. We notice fairly soon that, in Lyotard's eyes, all language games are equal in terms of their right to exist. But we are also invited to notice that Western science is typically aggressive in its attitude toward other forms of knowledge. When it encounters traditional or customary knowledge, it pronounces such knowledge backward and stupid. And since the Enlightenment narrative of emancipation carries with it the implication that it is only valid knowledge that can make us free, its effect has been to accelerate the process whereby "the traditional knowledge of peoples" has been destroyed. In a sense, then, to contemplate science is to contemplate "the entire history of cultural imperialism from the dawn of Western civilization" (*PC,* 27). Eventually, science turns a deaf ear even to the philosophical narratives, pronouncing them no less backward than the others. At approximately the same time, the situation has been reached wherein science begins to function as "a force of production" or as "a moment in the circulation of capital" (*PC,* 45). When this happens, the performance criterion of science becomes intertwined with that of the state, and the process whereby knowledge gets converted into power and power gets converted into knowledge comes under the supervision of planners and decision makers unduly impressed by systems theory. The story thus far seems to suggest that, with respect to the interests of emancipation, science has been villainous rather than heroic. But, just when things look darkest, it turns out that the most advanced science of all—postmodern science—encourages us to be adventurous instead of rule-bound, and provides us with the antimodel of a stable system, according to which diversity and dissension are preeminently valuable, not conformity and consensus. In short, science is our friend after all. In its innermost workings, it inaugurates, not a methodical determinism, but rather a pluralism. It sympathizes with all language games, not just one. It bids a thousand flowers to bloom. In fact, if the state will only take to its heart the implications that naturally follow from the antimodel of a stable system, especially the one about how helpful it will be to "give the public free access" to all its data banks, every citizen will be placed in a position to make "knowledgeable decisions" on a scale hitherto unprecedented, thereby enjoying a freedom of opportunity equally unprecedented. But surely this is precisely the goal envisioned by the emancipation narrative, which Lyotard relegates to the Enlightenment period, but which his own narrative cannot help but recapitulate.

The other narrative—the speculative narrative—is likewise recapitulated in Lyotard's discourse. It manifests itself there in a number of ways. For one thing, it is clear that the whole story is a description of the process whereby thought has become more and more conscious of itself. Originally, language-game activity was perfectly unself-conscious, and the principles of the games were not at all clear to their practitioners. In proclaiming the old narrative knowledge to be mythic or fabulous, the new scientific knowledge did, in fact, understand something about the narratives that they themselves could not understand. In this respect, an advance was made. But comprehension was still inadequate to the extent that, in its early phases, science falsely supposed itself to be benefited by the narrative grounding of philosophy, while, for its part, philosophy did not understand that it too would eventually be scrapped by science. Thus, a new stage of awareness was reached when the uselessness of philosophy's grounding activity began to sink in and philosophy could be sloughed off, leaving science all by itself as the only game in town. The whole story thus far is the story of a gradually deepening realization of the consequences attendant upon the incompatibility of science and narrative. Then suddenly, in our own time, a climax is reached. The conflict of the language games comes to an end because finally the principle of that conflict is completely grasped: the games begin to be perceived *as games*. It is at this point that thought finally grasps itself in its true form. Suddenly, everything can be reconceived or redescribed. The history of thought can now be properly reinterpreted as the history of language-game activity. All the old disputes take on a new meaning. In addition, now that thought is conscious of its own underlying principles, it has nothing to fear from the prospect of a plurality of games. Even if the games should mutate or evolve into quite different forms of language-game activity, there would be no cause for alarm, because thought is now in a position to comprehend such developments. Under the patient, watchful eye of the language-game umpire (who, in Lyotard's discourse, takes over the role of the speculative philosopher), every game is invited to prosper exactly to the extent that it accepts its status as a game and does not seek to interfere with other games, except perhaps by merging with them playfully or gamingly. In this way, thought's perfect self-awareness may be seen to coincide with the completest possible realization of the principle of freedom. The emancipation narrative becomes congruent with the speculative narrative, and both narratives achieve the status of incarnate fact, despite Lyotard's belief that he is being incredulous toward them.

But suppose we ignore for a moment the narrative component in Lyotard's book. It ought still to be obvious that the thought that has gone into the book is speculative in its nature. It is speculative in the sense that its ambition is to understand why it is that the fundamental thought-forms *are* heteromorphic or heterogeneous. To regard these forms as instances of language-game activity is, of course, to have found their common measure. To be able to account for the conflicts and misunderstandings that have marked their histories is, of course, to have achieved a single, overarching explanation of them, after the fashion of what German idealism refers to as speculative philosophy. The knowledge that language games are "subject to heterogeneous sets of pragmatic rules" (*PC,* 65) comes, not from *playing* the games according to these rules, but from *watching* them in detachment and noting their similarities and differences. To be able to pass in review the games of "customary" knowledge, the games of "modern" science, the games of philosophical knowledge, and finally the games of "postmodern" science, noticing in the process that each of these sets of games is characterized by its own particular purposes and strategies, is to be free of the constraints imposed by just these purposes and strategies. In fact, it is to be engaged in an exercise of what Hegel calls reason. Reason is not, for Hegel, a bland account of the way in which all thought-projects are consistent with each other on their own terms. Nor is it an effort to dictate in advance the procedures to be followed by the various departments of scientific inquiry so as to predetermine the harmoniousness of their results. Rather, it is an after-the-fact meditation, which focuses with special intensity on the conflicts and contradictions exhibited by thought-projects in their natural habitats, or, in other words, when they are left alone to pursue their own particular ends. Like Lyotard, Hegel knows that thought has evolved and that, in doing so, it has taken different shapes or forms with implications that are self-contradictory or mutually exclusive. Unlike Lyotard, he also knows that the thought that comprehends this fact has already engaged in an act of synthesis that is not within the province of any of the shapes or forms it is contemplating. Philosophy, conceived as the knowledge of knowledge, *is* possible for Hegel, because for him it is possible for reason to assess the distinctions generated by the understanding.

Similarly, philosophy in exactly the same sense *is* possible for Lyotard (even though he seems not to see that it is), because clearly he *can* synthesize contemporary thought in such a way as to show that it exhibits a characteristic tendency to be sensitive to the antinomies generated by the latest science. And notice, he does this despite the fact that the materials of his synthesis are supposed to have originated in language games that are heteromorphous. The more we hear about how these games are impervious to each, the more impressed we ought to be by the power of reason, regardless of Lyotard's disclaimers.

Having discovered that *The Postmodern Condition* is self-contradictory to the extent that it both practices philosophy and denies the possibility of philosophy, what is one to do? Which part of the book deserves to be saved? Should one say that there is proof enough that philosophy can still be done in the fact that Lyotard himself is still doing it, apparently without realizing it? Or, alternatively, should one hold fast to Lyotard's thesis about philosophy and, on the basis of that thesis, start looking for those aspects of his own discourse that are philosophical by nature and, therefore, quite properly the object of suspicion or incredulity? Many thinkers nowadays would opt, I think, for the second alternative. According to this point of view, the trouble with a book like *The Postmodern Condition* is not that its vision is wrong. After all, it does make an effort to show that both thought and reality (in our latest concepts of them) are intrinsically indeterminate or inherently unstable and, therefore, nonrectifiable in terms of any explanation that tries to pass itself off as the emanation of a higher reason. This—the content of its vision—is perfectly acceptable. The trouble is that, if things really are incoherent or unstable or indeterminate in their implications, then a powerfully explanatory, deeply coherent overview of things, which is capable of describing the thought-forms in their determinate natures as well as in their historical relations, seems rather embarrassing. If philosophical overviews could be shown not to have eluded the universal instability or incoherence or indeterminacy or relativity that we now know to be inherent in our thinking about reality (or, indeed, in reality itself), all would be well. If philosophy itself could be analyzed in such a way as to reveal in the very nature of its discourse the same kinds of phenomena postmodern science focuses on in its investigations—things like "undecidables, the limits of precise control, conflicts characterized by incomplete information, *'fracta,'* catastrophes, and pragmatic paradoxes"—then the presence of rational argument in a philosophical text could be exposed as a mere pretension or, more precisely, as an illusion. This, I think, is a sort of underlying premise of the other book I have mentioned, the essay collection entitled *Literature and the Question of Philosophy*.

Professor Cascardi, who edits this volume, is doubtless correct when he refers to himself and the twelve other contributors as "thirteen disparate voices," whose work "precludes ideological summary" (*LQP,* ix). Nevertheless, he tips the scale just a bit in the direction of a lurking agenda when he states that the reason for interrogating philosophy's relation to literature is that "philosophy is itself unable to produce a coherent theory of the differences that separate it from literature" (*LQP,* x). Most of the essayists, though not all of them, manage to convey the impression that they regard philosophy as though it were somehow illegitimate, as though it were a sort of usurping tyrant whose claims to authority over other modes of discourse have been found out. We may infer from the title of the book that literature is going to be treated as a given, without need of foundation or justification, whereas, with respect to philosophy, there is a question, a problem. Gradually, and in spite of individual differences in tone and doctrine, it becomes clear that a case *is* being made out, for the most part, against philosophy. From Plato to at least Hegel, so the argument runs, philosophy has tried to bully us into accepting certain methods and dogmas, without being in a position to pay due attention to the subtle processes that account for methods and dogmas. Fortunately, with the help of various antiphilosophers or postphilosophers dating from about the time of Nietzsche, we are now able to give these processes the recognition they deserve. For instance, we now know that philosophy could never become what it always wanted to be or imagined itself to be, namely, a mode of knowledge capable of transcending its own linguistic and/or experiential contexts. On the contrary, we now can see that these contexts are a fundamental reality of far greater significance than the conceptual chimeras they gave rise to. This being the case, philosophy's traditional preoccupations may be exposed as exercises in self-deception, the cure for which is to be found in the frequent demonstration of philosophy's containment within the matrix of literature. Thus, while it used to be that philosophers passed judgment on poets and fiction makers, postphilosophers now find themselves in a position to detect poetry and fiction making in philosophy itself. As a result, philosophy's stock is coming down in value, whereas literature's stock is going up, correspondingly. This, or something like this, is what the majority of Cascardi's contributors either take for granted or else seek to prove.

The proof, when it comes, often takes the form of a deconstruction that purports to show that a classic philosophical text can be seen to contain, within its own verbal materials, a host of implications, some of which must needs interfere with what is usually taken to be the text's main drift. The point, apparently, is to show that reason, even when it seems most at home in the writings of its principal defenders, is inevitably compromised by the indeterminacies or ambiguities inherent in the very nature of textuality. (Three of Cascardi's contributors—Dalia Judovitz, Peter McCormick, and Harry Berger, Jr.—try to show this using texts by Kant, Plato, and Descartes.) One way of responding to these deconstructions might be to observe that the "argument" of a text and the "text" of an argument cannot properly conflict with each other, since each of these things is a phenomenon that makes its appearance as a result of gestalting the same verbal object in a different way. A microscopic scrutiny of what a deconstructor regards as the "literary" level of a text—a review of its component figures of speech, for example—constitutes one way of gestalting this object, but so does the perception, on a different level, of what is meant by the term "argument." The perception of an argument depends upon construing a text in terms of what it may be taken to mean as a whole. The perception of a text's materials or literary devices depends upon construing a text in terms of what its component parts may be taken to mean, considered in themselves and without regard to context. Each perception has its own validity, and each is equally the product of an interpretation. The danger lies in supposing that an argument is simply made up or foisted off on a text, whereas textual materials are really there, waiting to be discovered. The truth is that the analysis of the import of the materials of a text is no more (and no less) a rational construction than is the analysis of a text's argument. If rational construction is itself disallowed, textual materials will become just as invisible as textual arguments. On the other hand, if it is permitted, then the existence of a design or pattern that may be supposed to govern the whole of a text is no more difficult to establish than the existence of those lesser patterns that are supposed to be discernible in its component parts. To suppose that the parts of a text are real, whereas the whole of a text is a sort of optical illusion or an illegitimate product of inference, is like supposing that the building materials in a house are real whereas the house itself is not, since the materials composing it can be conceived of as lending themselves equally well to a variety of different combinations or configurations. By the same token, although chemistry and physics might be employed to demonstrate that the building materials of a house are themselves composed of even smaller materials, it is not necessary to observe these smaller materials in order to observe the house. It would, in fact, be wrong to assume that an adequate explanation of the architecture of the house must wait upon an adequate explanation of the architecture of the atom, as though a new awareness of the complexity of the latter must necessarily require a change in one's attitude toward the former. Indeterminacy on the level of the atom does not translate into indeterminacy on the level of the house, in spite of the fact that the house seems to be composed entirely of atoms. Similarly, the ambiguity of a text's materials does not necessarily interfere with the determinate nature of a text's argument. Simplicity and complexity are, in this respect, correlative rather than mutually exclusive, because they have to do with different levels of analysis.

Another way of responding to deconstruction might be to remember that it is situated *inside* philosophy in the sense that it may be regarded as the consequence of a whole series of previous philosophical judgments. Thus, as Stanley Rosen demonstrates in his contribution to this volume, we may trace the sequence of arguments, in the philosophical tradition, which has led up to the adoption of the deconstructive reading strategy. To the extent that these arguments have constituted the strategy, they cannot themselves be cancelled by means of the strategy. If all the texts of philosophy in the world could be deconstructed, the reasoning that had prompted such a Herculean effort would not be confirmed. Nor, for that matter, would it be disconfirmed. It would simply be out of play, out of reach. The only way to encounter it would be to review the history of philosophy, and, if one were to do that, one might very well find that the deconstructive view of texts is not such a novelty as it is commonly supposed to be. In various ways, and at various times in the past, philosophers have addressed themselves to its governing principles, often enough rejecting them for reasons that still bear consideration.

Hobbes, for example, speaks out against deconstruction in *Leviathan,* when he asserts that "it is not the bare words, but the Scope of the writer that giveth the true light, by which any writing is to bee interpreted; and they that insist upon single Texts, without considering the main Designe, can derive no thing from them cleerly. . . ."[3] Hegel goes even further, maintaining that the whole of philosophy ought to be regarded as a single unfolding argument, the sense of which is unintelligible in its disconnected parts. His *Lectures on the History of Philosophy* open with a warning:

> [I]n thought, and particularly in speculative thought, comprehension means something quite different from understanding the grammatical sense of the words alone, and also from understanding them in the region of ordinary conception only. Hence we may possess a knowledge of the assertions, propositions, or of the opinions of philosophers; we may have occupied ourselves largely with the grounds of and deductions from these opinions, and the main point in all that we have done may be wanting— the comprehension of the propositions. There is no lack of voluminous and even learned histories of Philosophy in which the knowledge of the matter itself about which so much ado has been made, is absent. The authors of such histories may be compared to animals which have listened to all the tones in some music, but to whose senses the unison, the harmony of their tones, has not penetrated.[4]

It may be that Hobbes and Hegel are wrong about the way in which a whole is related to its parts, but, to the extent that it proceeds on the basis of a different view of this relationship, deconstruction in the course of its normal operations cannot determine whether or not this is so. By subjecting all texts whatsoever to its own peculiar mode of analysis, it automatically circumvents the task of attending to discussions of its own basic assumptions. Strictly speaking, it cannot even hear these discussions, for to hear them would be to know that deconstruction represents a philosophical position rather than a decisive analysis of the whole of philosophy.

It would be a pity not to attend to Hegel's critique of deconstruction, since, in the second and third editions of the *Encyclopedia,* it precedes the unfolding of Hegel's mature system and provides a sort of impetus which gets the system going by eliminating certain preliminary objections to it that had been raised against its very possibility. Once this is seen, it becomes clear that speculative philosophy may issue from a rejection of deconstruction every bit as much as deconstruction seeks to issue from a rejection of speculative philosophy. Each position takes its occasion from what it perceives to be the inadequacy of the other position, which means that it is wrong to suppose that there has been a necessary or an inevitable progress whereby thought has moved from speculation in the nineteenth century to deconstruction in our own century. Hegel's critique may be found in the *Encyclopedia Logic,* especially in the first part (§§1–83) which deals with the problems of prespeculative and antispeculative philosophy. Under the rubric of prespeculative thinking, Hegel includes both pre-Kantian metaphysics and empiricism, both of which he regards as being fatally dependent upon assumptions whose ultimate origin is popular conception and customary linguistic practice or usage. Philosophy, according to Hegel, cannot properly be based on such assumptions, because it is precisely the notions contained in these assumptions that require investigation. But, since the "process of investigation is itself a process of cognition," the notions employed by thinking, and the inspection or criticism of the notions contained in thinking, "must be united within the process of cognition." This can happen only when the process of cognition is the process of dialectic, for it is only within the process of dialectic that the forms or categories of thinking may be said to "determine their own limits and point out their own defects."[5] If the thinking that performs the investigation is extrinsic to the thinking (or the thought-materials) under investigation, the notions that the investigation itself depends on will themselves remain forever unexamined.

In Hegel's view, this is the essential weakness of both the old metaphysics and the new empiricism: they are compelled to launch their investigations on the basis of presuppositions or unexamined knowledge. Metaphysics takes its cue from hunches that have occurred to people concerning the nature of things, from religious experience or from what Lyotard refers to as "customary" or "traditional" knowledge. Thus, metaphysics takes its objects, says Hegel, "from *representation,*" and when it applies "the determinations-of-the-understanding to them," it grounds itself "upon them, as *ready-made or given subjects.*"[6] Consider, for example, ontology's effort to produce a description of the determinations or characteristics of Being:

> [I]n their manifoldness and finite validity, these determinations lack a principle; they must therefore be enumerated *empirically* and *contingently,* and their more precise *content* can only be based upon *representation,* [i.e.,] based upon the *assurance* that by one word one thinks precisely this, or perhaps upon the word's etymology. What can be at issue in this

context is merely the *correctness* of the analysis as it corresponds with the usage of language, and the empirical *exhaustiveness,* not the *truth* and *necessity* of these determinations in and for themselves.[7]

Empiricism seems equally uncritical, because, although it imagines itself to be antimetaphysical, actually it incorporates metaphysics without realizing that it has done so:

> The fundamental illusion in scientific empiricism is always that it uses the metaphysical categories of matter, force, as well as those of one, many, universality, and the infinite, etc., and it goes on to draw *conclusions,* guided by categories of this sort, presupposing and applying the forms of syllogising in the process. It does all this without knowing that it thereby contains a metaphysics and is engaged in it, and that it is using those categories and their connections in a totally uncritical and unconscious manner.[8]

Having recognized that the terms and methods employed by metaphysicians and empirical inquirers depend on unexamined presuppositions, Hegel supposes that the next step must be to think about these terms and methods. Instead of using them unconsciously or accepting them as given, he wants to examine the categories or concepts that inform them. It was Kant who opened up the path of "critical" thinking by making us realize the extent to which the objects of thought are themselves determined by thought. Now that we *have* become aware of this, we can begin to consider the dialectic or logic whereby thought can be said to determine itself. But just as we are about to begin our study of the logic inherent in the concepts employed by the various kinds of thinking and knowing, a crucial objection is raised by thinkers who imagine that the Kantian critique itself rules out such a study. To these antispeculative thinkers, it seems undeniable that all thinking, even speculative thinking, must be saddled with the presuppositions associated with popular conceptions and with historical and linguistic contingencies. Why should speculative thinking be any different in this respect from the thinking that goes into metaphysics or empirical inquiry? Don't speculative thinkers have to employ notions and expressions in order to carry out their own philosophizing without waiting for these things to be produced as a consequence or result of their own speculative activity? Are their own projects not captured by the vagaries of linguistic usage and by the subjectivity or relativity that afflicts all human endeavor, even that of philosophers?

Hegel's answer to these questions is clear and compelling. In the first place, he insists repeatedly that philosophical thinking is not an attitude or an orientation *toward* thinking that is applied to ideas from the outside, as though it were a doctrine or a method in its own right, detachable from the thinking it seeks to elucidate. As dialectic, "it is not brought to bear on the thought determinations from the outside; on the contrary, it must be considered as dwelling within them."[9] Further, it is not to be conceived as something instigated by gender, race, ethnicity, personal whim, or practical need, nor as something dependent upon particular verbal formulations, altering as they alter. The task of the philosopher is to expound objectively the immanent action of the concepts themselves as they explicate or unfold their own implications.

Hegel, of course, is well aware that the objectivity of philosophical cognition is denied by those who make it their business to study the contingencies of philosophical opinion, in the belief that objectivity can never be more than an unachievable goal. But he notes, in connection with this belief, that it rests on the assumption that an objective determination has been made concerning the subjectivity of thinking, a determination that is itself based on what is taken to be a genuine knowledge of the factors that rule out the possibility of genuine knowledge. To affect to know that thinking is always somehow deflected away from its object, one cannot regard one's own thinking as having been so deflected. In fact, the more we know about the conditioned nature of knowledge, the harder it is to be skeptical about the possibility of knowledge. Skepticism cannot detach itself from its own knowledge claims, and therefore it cannot pass a judgment against knowledge per se. Rather, by virtue of its own commitment to objectivity, it manifests its own involvement in the structure of knowledge and is therefore amenable to the dialectic, which embraces it.

Suppose, for example, that I add a set of figures together and arrive by mistake at an incorrect sum. Suppose I do this so often that it becomes reasonable to conclude that I can't work properly with the figures in my sums. It is certain that only a person who knew I was making mistakes would be in a position to arrive at this conclusion. If *I* can see that my sums are incorrect, it has to be because I *can* add correctly, since it is only by comparing my incorrect calculations with correct ones that I can know

I have been making mistakes. In the same way, inaccurate perceptions could not be perceived to be inaccurate if they were not succeeded by later perceptions, the accuracy of which becomes the basis for passing judgment against the earlier ones. It is along these lines that Hegel arrives at his distinction between the precritical thinking of the understanding and the rethinking of this thinking by means of the faculty of reason. Since it is reason that "sees what is conditioned in all this empirical awareness of things," Hegel deems it not inappropriate to refer to reason as "the faculty of the *unconditioned*."[10] The understanding produces an account of the world, an account of materials and processes, an account of objects and entities, on the basis of concepts. The kind of account it produces is conditioned by the concepts that organize and propel its investigations. The investigations of reason are not conditioned, because they are not launched on the basis of already existing concepts or an already established orientation toward the matters with which it deals. The task of reason is simply to show that concepts are systematically related according to an implicit or inherent logic. It is not to produce a rival account, or an alternative theory, concerning the matters with which the understanding deals. On the other hand, by rethinking the concepts of the understanding in terms of the logic that produces them and brings them into relation with each other, Reason, when it is made explicit by philosophy, *does* produce a massive reorientation toward the philosophical inferences that have been drawn on the basis of the understanding's conditioned awareness of things. By rethinking the concepts of the understanding in its own peculiar fashion, reason makes it possible to see the world of the understanding according to a new aspect that grasps, but is not in the grip, of the particular concepts that have produced that world.

Deconstruction is postcritical to the extent that it looks suspiciously at thoughts and expressions whereby philosophy itself proceeds (albeit on the imperfectly grasped basis of philosophical insight), but it is also precritical or incompletely critical to the extent that it disrupts philosophizing before the critical project can be fully carried out. Impressed (as Hegel himself is) by the discovery that the determinations of the understanding are riddled with self-contradictions, deconstruction assumes that the thinking that detects these self-contradictions, and describes them correctly, must be equally self-contradictory. Hence, it refuses to assemble or develop the implications that follow from a systematic inspection of the understanding's categories. But this means that its own analyses must repudiate the seeds of speculation they themselves contain and seek a basis instead in what it knows to be conditioned knowledge, paradoxically absolutizing such knowledge. Thus, if a rhetorical analysis of philosophical arguments is successful in deflecting philosophy away from its goal of grasping the true nature of knowing, it must be at the price of remaining permanently trapped within its own unanalyzable metaphysics. According to this metaphysics, what must be accepted is the paradoxical judgment that judgments cannot be made concerning the validity of such opinions as we already possess, because, in fact, it is these opinions that are necessarily employed in judging the judgments. Thought becomes a passive display of its own quirks and bents, with no hope of ever getting beyond quirks and bents. In view of what it takes to be the impossibility of achieving a synthetical grasp of its own constitutive phases or elements, thought subsides into a sort of "knowing" dogmatism, wherein every passing notion, every phenomenon, is granted equal validity or equal immunity from criticism. The result is that ideology, of one sort or another, may be deliberately embraced as such, after being pronounced unanalyzable and untranscendable. This, says Hegel, is "the more recent standpoint." Having "reached the result . . . that a cognition that proceeds by way of *finite* mediations is only cognizant of what is finite and contains no truth," this "modern standpoint changes nothing in the method of ordinary scientific cognition," but, at the same time, "it rejects this method, and hence *all* methods, since it does not know of any other method [appropriate] for the knowing of what is infinite in import":

> Therefore it surrenders itself to the untamed arbitrariness of imaginations and assurances, to moral conceit and haughtiness of feeling, or to opinions and arguments without norm or rule—all of which declare themselves to be most strongly opposed to philosophy and philosophical theses.[11]

There is, of course, another way of assimilating deconstruction to the philosophical traditions from which it emanates, besides encountering it through the hostile commentaries of philosophers like Hobbes and Hegel. In a friendlier way, we might be tempted to construe it as quintessentially philosophical because it is so obviously an offspring of the emancipation narrative and the speculative narrative. Surely, the first of these narratives, whether appealed to explicitly or not, has instigated the modern rebellion

against authorial intention, which, as we observed in chapter 1, characterizes not only deconstruction but also many other schools of criticism. The
notion that authors have authority over their own texts, and so by extension over the interpretations produced by readers of texts, is disturbing to
those of us who see in such authority an infringement of readers' rights.
Like kingly authority or priestly authority, the authority of mere author-
ship is an outrage, since it interferes with the intellectual autonomy of
readers. It is much more edifying to be told that a world of interpretive
possibilities is all before us as we read, beckoning to us and inviting us to
choose our place of rest or to take our pleasure as we will. That way we
can think of ourselves as constructors of meaning rather than as the slav-
ish recipients of meanings already constructed for us in advance by lordly
authors. Harry Berger, Jr., makes this point vividly, and with great subtlety,
in his deconstruction of Plato's *Ion,* when he declares his right as a reader
to interpret Socrates' "manhandling of Ion not as a victory for Socrates
but as a defeat" (*LQP,* 83). As Berger informs us, "textuality reverses the
chronological lines of force (or 'influence') that move from Socrates
through Plato to us, sending them back from readers through the Platonic
text to its representation of Socrates" (*LQP,* 83). Once we jettison the idea
that the meaning of a book is already constituted before we begin to interpret it and that this already-constituted meaning has some sort of claim
upon us that needs to be acknowledged as the starting point of our own
thinking about it, we can begin to regard the act of reading itself as that
which constitutes the meaning it arrives at, and we can begin to talk as
though this act were mainly an occasion for readers to make ethical or
political gestures.

   Of course, the idea that the meaning of a book is constituted by the act
of reading it makes sense only if one is prepared to embrace some form of
idealism, such as Arthur C. Danto embraces in his essay when he insists
that literature is "about each reader who experiences it," "each individual
that reads the text at the moment that individual reads it" (*LQP,* 18). The
degree of idealism present in reader-centered criticism can be measured
by the extent to which authorial intention is regarded either as an unknowable thing-in-itself outside the reader's circle of experience or else as a
readerly invention (there being, from the reader's point of view, nothing
outside the reader's circle of experience). Danto is no deconstructor, and
so he appeals openly to Hegel in support of his contention that a literary

work exists "only for the individual apprehending it, so that the apprehension completes the work and gives it final substance" (*LQP*, 18). But whether or not such an acknowledgment is made openly, every attempt to derive the objects of experience from within the field of experience itself (as we do when we say that the meaning of a book derives from the response made to it by a reader) depends upon a prior commitment to idealism. It stands or falls depending on the success or failure of the idealistic philosophy that informs it.

Mary Bittner Wiseman makes the emancipation narrative as explicit as possible in her essay on Roland Barthes ("Barthes and the Utopias of Language"). She makes it quite clear that the motive behind the performative gestures of Barthes's writing ("the pirouettes Barthes's texts make" [*LQP*, 300]) is a desire to "fulfill the utopic function of refusing language's referential and other semantic functions." Why do we want to refuse these functions? Because they have been imposed upon us from the outside by tyrannical social institutions, and thus they interfere with our own autonomy:

> The power of assertion is harnessed by social institutions that sanction both the ways of conceiving embedded in the languages and the truth-claims the languages are used to make. The different powers of language and of institutions reinforce each other so that a subset of all that is sayable in a given language is supposed by dint of repetition and institutional custom to be true. If one performs a Humean demystification of the effects of custom and repetition, however, and concludes that what is called natural and necessary are fictions created by the institutions in power, then one may wish neither to use nor to be used by the languages in place, which are, nonetheless, all the languages there are. Since the roster of institutions includes universities, academies, scholarly societies, publishing houses—in short, all the means of the dissemination of ideas, the question becomes one of how to speak against or outside of an intellectual tradition whose language one cannot help but speak. (*LQP*, 299)

This is such a clear explanation of the motive behind Barthes's interest in the possible deformations and reformations of language that it makes one see at once what is wrong with "the great refusal." It rests entirely on a prior analysis of "the institutions in power" with all their insidious effects—an analysis that could *not* be performed by language in any of its straining-toward-utopia postures but which, in fact, *was* performed before these postures were entered into by language not yet purified of its "referential and other semantic functions." If the thinking that has shown itself to be capable of carrying out such a powerful critique is itself scrapped on the grounds that it must be tainted by the effects upon it of precisely those elements it has itself analyzed *correctly,* the reason for straining toward utopia will have vanished, and we won't be able to answer the question, "Why are we doing this?" The passage from Professor Wiseman's own essay, which I have just quoted, would have to be rejected along with all the rest of the old-fashioned thinking it retails or depends upon concerning the relationships between social institutions and the thoughts and expressions of individuals. None of this old-fashioned thinking is compatible with the linguistic practices urged by Barthes, and yet it is appealed to at the very beginning as the indispensable ground of those practices. The home of this old kind of thinking is, of course, that collective body of texts which comprises the emancipation narrative, the same narrative that inspires J. Hillis Miller's assertion of the ethical and political implications of reading when reading is regarded as a fundamentally constitutive activity. In *The Ethics of Reading,* Miller writes:

> If there is to be such a thing as an ethical moment in the act of reading, teaching, or writing about literature, it must be sui generis, something individual and particular, itself a source of political or cognitive acts, not subordinated to them. The flow of power must not be all in one direction. There must be an influx of performative power from the linguistic transactions involved in the act of reading into the realms of knowledge, politics, and history. Literature must be in some way a cause and not merely an effect, if the study of literature is to be other than the relatively trivial study of one of the epiphenomena of society, part of the technological assimilation or assertion of mastery over all the features of human life which is called "the human sciences."[12]

Here we see the same desire to resist incorporation into already existing social structures, the desire of the individual to press back against these structures, that motivates Barthes's refusal of language's referential and other semantic functions. Here too a prior understanding of the situation of the individual is the condition or ground of a recommendation that the individual behave in such a way as to resist the idea that there can be such a thing as a prior understanding of his situation. To dispense with this prior understanding is to eliminate completely any possibility of assessing whether an individual's actions are relatively free or relatively conditioned, because a prior understanding is always the condition of the assessment. Any action that was truly sui generis, in the sense that it could be said *not* to depend in any way on a preliminary grasp of the situation wherein it occurs, could not aim to be sui generis, nor could it be accompanied by an awareness on the part of the individual that it was sui generis. The impulse to be free, since it depends on a prior contemplation of the prospect of freedom, cannot occur in a vacuum. A world from which to be free, or in which to be free, is its necessary presupposition. This world cannot be conceived as an effect of the effort that is made to *re*conceive it or evade it. Besides, the effort to think of the world as though its nature were given to it by the "performative power" of the individual mind has already been recommended by at least some of those philosophers who regard themselves as idealists. To recommend it again is to be caught up within the tradition of their thoughts and recommendations. Thus, it happens that the deconstructors (and the other insurgents against the authority of authors) may be regarded as latecomers to the emancipation narrative, which nevertheless remains alive and well in their literary-critical meditations, despite all efforts to be incredulous toward it.

The other narrative—the speculative narrative—is also, to a large extent, recapitulated in deconstruction. The tendency to suppose that there has been a progress in the history of thought from the relative blindness of philosophers (from Plato to Hegel) to the relative insightfulness of post-philosophers (from Nietzsche to Rorty) is perfectly in keeping with the speculative goal of arriving at a knowledge of knowledge. To assume that such a progress has been made is exactly to assume that later thought has the power to look back on earlier thought and to pronounce a valid judgment on it, even though later thought is necessarily an outgrowth of earlier thought. It might be said, in fact, that the detection of self-contradiction in the seemingly determinate descriptions of things that have been produced by naïve thought-projects is a type of analysis that deconstruction borrows directly from Hegel's critique of the understanding. Deconstruction feeds upon and consumes what it analyzes to the same degree that the Hegelian reason feeds upon and consumes the determinations arrived at by the understanding. In this sense, deconstruction represents a sort of continuation of Hegel whereby the extension of the Hegelian critique to philosophy itself is interpreted as a natural evolution of old-fashioned philosophy into grammatology or interpretation theory. Every attempt to construe deconstruction as a form of postphilosophy which is "higher" or "later" than the thinking it looks "down" on or "back" on, every attempt to construe it as the sign of an *event* in Western consciousness wherein consciousness has become more subtly aware of itself, is really an unwitting affirmation of the goal of speculative philosophy, which was (and is) to describe the unfolding of thought up to the point where thought finds itself able to embark on just such a description of itself. It is at this point that thought looks back on its old projects, not in terms of their original objects, but in terms of how those objects were constituted. When this happens, knowledge becomes the knowledge of knowledge, and consciousness becomes self-consciousness.

Even in the form of deconstruction, this knowledge of knowledge shows itself to be capable of synthesizing what it knows. Just as the postmodern scientist may be supposed to have a fuller, richer knowledge by virtue of his distinctive ability to know both the continuities *and* the discontinuities that characterize natural phenomena, so the deconstructionist is often supposed to possess a fuller, richer awareness of textual phenomena. Although she is not a contributor to Cascardi's essay collection, Barbara Johnson makes this point very nicely when she observes, in a piece called "Teaching Deconstructively," that "deconstruction is a reading strategy that carefully follows both the meanings and the suspensions and displacements of meaning in a text, while humanism is a strategy to stop reading when the text stops saying what it ought to have said."[13] Clearly, the implication here is that the deconstructive reader has seen the text as it really is, in its true complexity, whereas the ordinary reader—the humanizing reader—can see only those elements of it that fit neatly into reductive meaningful patterns. Humanists project into the act of reading their own sense of what a humanly designed work must be like, thereby ensuring that they will not be able to perceive elements that do not conform to this sense. Deconstructive readers (when they lean toward the speculative narrative rather than the emancipation narrative) pride themselves on not presupposing that texts are works, or products of human design, that mean to say things to us. Not being hampered by this presupposition, they are free—faint echoes here from the emancipation narrative?—to notice more than their humanist counterparts. Refractory elements, elements that somehow seem to be outside the patterns, can be held side by side *with* the patterns, so that the whole text comes into view as an irreducibly complex field of continuities and discontinuities. At first glance, it might appear that such a reading strategy expresses a willingness to accept the heterogeneousness of texts, but it also seems to indicate a desire not to leave anything out, not to leave anything unaccounted for, so that the totality of the text can be more completely registered. It is quite wrong, in any case, to suppose that texts presenting both meanings and suspensions of meaning have eluded determination and are thus a source of dismay to the thought that is trying to comprehend them. Just the opposite is true. For as soon as the multiplicity of a text has been detected, as soon as the discoordination of its elements has been determined, the despaired-of synthesis *has* been performed. Thought *has* worked out the relationship between meaning, on the one hand, and the suspensions and displacements of meaning, on the other. Reason has not been baffled at all; it grasps the object presented to it and describes it (correctly) as a combination of opposing or conflicting determinations. The tendency of language to baffle us when we look at a text is surmounted the moment we decide to look at a text in order to see in it "the tendency of language to baffle us." From that point on, it might be observed, the greater the bafflement, the merrier the critic. For, indeed, the bafflement has ceased to be baffling. Instead, it has become edifying. And that is because it has been comprehended or transcended. From this point of view, it certainly looks as though deconstruction *can* be assimilated into the philosophical tradition as a variant or hybrid of nineteenth-century German idealism. The only way to determine whether or not this is the case would be to compare Hegel's account of the understanding's self-contradictions with deconstruction's account of the self-contradictions within textual phenomena. Whatever the outcome of such a comparison, the real result would be that the underlying philosophy of deconstruction would come into view, and the illusion that it was beyond philosophy, or postphilosophical, would be dispelled. Reason, called upon to determine which is the more reasonable view of self-contradiction, would give no evidence of being in a state of crisis.

Not all the essays in *Literature and the Question of Philosophy* are deconstructions, however. A number of the essayists take it for granted that philosophy's impotence has been sufficiently exposed already, so that now the time has come to show what thought can be, what thought can accomplish, after philosophy. Is it not possible to adopt ways of thinking and being in the world that are philosophy-free or philosophy-proof? Are not growth experiences, particularly those associated with art and literature, properly constitutive, rather than reflective, of moral awareness? Charles Altieri and Martha Craven Nussbaum are concerned to show in their essays that the arts (to use Altieri's phrasing) "help us understand ourselves as value-creating agents and make possible communities who can assess those creations without relying on the categorical terms traditional to moral philosophy" (*LQP*, 135). Philosophy imposes its terms upon us from above, without regard to the "actual nature" or "moral priorities" of the individual. It seeks to coerce the individual into conforming to general principles, whereas a proper morality would "derive its third-person principles from first-person commitments" (*LQP*, 136). These commitments are displayed to us best of all, in their full complexity and concreteness, in the pages of literature, which is why the cultivation of aesthetic sensitivity suggests itself as the means whereby we can come into contact with the "most fully articulated models" of our own possible commitments. Those who are most familiar with the importance of cultivating aesthetic sensitivity, such as art critics and art theorists, have a greater importance than ever, since they are the ones who know best how it is that "the claims one must make about human powers and concerns have a substantial basis in the experience of those responsive to the arts" (*LQP*, 138).

In her essay on Henry James's novel *The Golden Bowl*, Nussbaum argues that moral awareness grows out of an aesthetic grasp of concrete situations with everything depending on what she calls "the fine-tuned perception of particulars" (*LQP*, 181). The best of James's characters have wonderfully refined sensibilities rather like James's own sensibility, and, if we wish to be like them, we shall have to become (or try to become) people on whom nothing is ever lost. For help, "we will need to turn to texts no less elaborate, no less linguistically fine-tuned, concrete, and intensely focused, no less metaphorically resourceful than this novel [*The Golden Bowl*]" (*LQP*, 180). As Nussbaum phrases it, the ultimate moral model is "the fine Jamesian perceiver," the man or woman who "employs general terms and conceptions in an open-ended, evolving way, prepared to see and respond to any new feature that the scene brings forward" (*LQP*, 180). For such a perceiver, the universals of experience must be constantly changing in accordance with changes in the particulars. Otherwise, the particulars themselves threaten to disappear from view, being replaced by stereotypes and caricatures.

But is it really possible to make a philosophy-free aesthetics the basis of moral values or moral awareness? Is philosophy so easily eluded or bypassed that it does not make an appearance in the thinking that urges such a pure commitment to the particulars of experience? Surely, the turn toward literature and the arts is grounded in an evaluation of what are perceived to be the relative inadequacies of philosophy. This evaluation must know in advance what counts in the building up of a proper moral life and what does not. It must know already that the right way to live consists of certain kinds of activity, whereas the wrong way consists of other kinds of activity. This is a very big thing to know, and to the extent that, being known, it becomes the impetus to live in a certain way, or the principle by which we live, it cannot be said to be a result, or a thing discovered along the way. To place a high value on experience because experience is the method whereby one hopes to arrive some day at a conception of what deserves to be highly valued is to have a moral philosophy already in place, benignly presiding over the developments whereby one intends to arrive at one's moral philosophy. If experience alone could be trusted to produce large quantities of fine Jamesian perceivers, there would be little need to argue vigorously in behalf of such. Evidently, experience can go wrong and be less than it should be. The more anxious we are to see that it goes right, the clearer it is that we are operating with a philosophy of experience that cannot be supposed to have emerged from the experience being contemplated as a future prospect. On the other hand, if past experience is appealed to as the basis of this philosophy, then past experience has become the source of norms, rules, or principles, designed to ensure that future experience will conform to a certain character. In short, past experience has assumed the shape of a philosophy, albeit a very strange one if it presumes to advise us not to accept philosophical advice.

The paradoxes of aestheticism are perhaps best seen in the classic formulations of Walter Pater's conclusion to *The Renaissance.* With masterful economy, Pater describes the deconstructions that the most sophisticated thought has performed on both the outer world of nature and the inner world of mind. As a result of these deconstructions, it is now known (says Pater) that the "realities" of mind and nature are really illusions or caricatures. The stability of the external world disappears when seemingly simple objects are reduced to an infinite flux of elements and processes, and the inner world, too, loses its coherence when reflection reduces it to its ultimate elements, namely, momentary, evanescent impressions. Since impressions alone are what we really have to work with, the things that appear to a cruder thought to be the causes of these impressions are really chimeras or phantasms. The positive sciences, because they concern themselves with what they wrongly take to be objective entities, are deluded. So are religion and philosophy deluded. Since impressions alone are real, only the discrimination of impressions really matters. Anything at all that diverts us from what Nussbaum has termed "the fine-tuned perception of particulars" is a gross imposition on us. Pater knows that the upshot of all this is the decision to live aesthetically:

> With this sense of the splendor of our experience and of its awful brevity, gathering all we are into one desperate effort to see and touch, we shall hardly have time to make theories about the things we see and touch. What we have to do is to be forever curiously testing new opinions and courting new impression never acquiescing in a facile orthodoxy of Comte, or of Hegel, or of our own.[14]

Pater's statement is the classic one, and it allows us to see what the philosophy of living aesthetically can look like when it attempts to formulate itself in its most extreme terms. The first thing we notice about it is that it is a deduction, a conclusion, something that follows from a whole series of skeptical deconstructions. It defines itself as the only thing left to do *after* the naïve illusions of Western thought have been fully exposed for what they are. Aestheticism must begin with, and hold onto throughout its career, a single moral principle, according to which the highest thing of all may be said to be the exercise of a "quickened, multiplied consciousness." And this means that it can't really learn anything, it can't be a means to an end. It already knows the end: "Not the fruit of experience, but experience itself, is the end." Indeed, what aestheticism guarantees is an endless stream of experiences that do not matter because they cannot alter, in any important way, the attitude of the mind that is having them. Nothing can come up against such a mind that can lay a claim upon it, since it already knows the vanity and inconstancy (i.e., the deconstructibility) of everything it encounters *before* it encounters it. The exercise of quickened, multiplied consciousness is what comes *after* the exposé of values and principles. It cannot lead to the discovery of these things except insofar as they can be identified as grist for the mill of exquisite experience. To this extent, the aesthetic attitude represents a final position rather than a means to attain new ones. It is the attitude, not of an "open" sensibility, but of a "closed" one. In reading Pater's tiny essay, one notices almost immediately that it presents a view of things that is profoundly philosophical, in the sense that it draws a big conclusion which could only result from a massive exercise of the powers of synthesis and analysis, which exercise constitutes a massive violation of its own prohibition against drawing conclusions or even theorizing about things. Apparently, even the purest of aesthetes must be constantly on guard against turning into a philosopher. But to be always "on guard" against the natural tendency to draw big conclusions from our experiences, to proceed always with Pater's maxims in mind about the danger of adding things up, is precisely to have a philosophy locked in that could never have been produced by the experiences it approves of. That is why a thoroughgoing aestheticism, such as Pater tries to propound, cannot be construed as a basis for the discovery of ethical or moral principles. The highest values of all, indeed the only ones possible, are already invisibly in place before the mock search for them, through having the "right" kind of experiences, can begin.

In fairness to Altieri and Nussbaum, however, it must be said that they do not embrace the extreme form of aestheticism that Pater describes. Neither of them wishes to deconstruct persons, and both state clearly that a concern for persons is fundamental to the very idea of ethics or moral awareness. Altieri's belief that the structure of "first-person commitments" needs to be studied sympathetically is surely the sign of a modified aestheticism, as is his respect for the "moral priorities" and "actual natures" of individuals. Nussbaum's aestheticism is similarly modified to the extent that she emphasizes, in discussing *The Golden Bowl,* that even perception itself must be rooted in affection if it is to have a moral aspect: "James suggests that if, as members of moral communities, we are to achieve shared perceptions of the actual, we had better love one another first, in all our disagreements and our qualitative differences" (*LQP,* 184). With respect to these modified aestheticisms, the whole issue turns, I think, on whether concern for persons is an effect of perceptiveness or a cause of perceptiveness. Once in place, there is no doubt that it can stimulate a more sensitive or perceptive awareness of the situations in which persons are involved. A flexible, open-ended expression of this concern will not be hard to register, if the concern is already present as a dominant factor in our lives. The question is, can this concern be arrived at on the basis of a distinctly aesthetic perception of particulars, which is in itself already informed morally or ethically? The answer, I think, is that it cannot. Even in a modified aestheticism, the fine-tuned perception of particulars is a consequence of already valuing something; it is a way of applying or refining upon "moral priorities" that are already constituted. Perceptiveness is, in itself, an expression of concern, not a strategy for determining something to care about. Fundamental principles are not the fruit of experience, although it may take a lifetime to recognize them fully as such. As "members of moral communities" (to use Nussbaum's phrase), we are immersed in them from the beginning, and we carry them with us as we go, cognizing the moral character of events and situations by means of them. If this is so, we can't suppose that experiences of art and literature can generate their own moral intelligibility in perceivers who are not already morally informed, as to the reality of moral collisions and the importance of moral judgments.

Evidently, the object of aestheticism, posed as a doctrine, is to prevent speculation (of which it is a specimen) from interrupting our own prereflective, subphilosophical estimates of things. But it can only do this by erecting a defensive rationalization of the processes whereby such estimates occur. A formal ethics is just as necessary as ever, if only to ensure that experiences of the right sort are entertained and experiences of the wrong sort avoided. Rules and principles having to do with the right interpretation or the right appropriation of experience are no less important here than in any other ethical doctrine. Thus, it is clear that aestheticism (modified or pure) cannot avoid having the character of a philosophy, despite its own good intentions to be postphilosophical.

Indeed, as we have seen, the entire postmodern effort to transcend philosophy is inescapably philosophical in its motives and procedures. This should not be passed off as a superficial appearance owing to the conditions of discourse and, therefore, as a subtractable nuisance. Every contributor to Cascardi's book is essentially engaged in drawing inferences from "the crisis of reason" narrative, and this means that every essay is, to a greater or lesser degree, an example of the kind of thinking that many of the contributors seem to regard as obsolete or illegitimate. No

amount of hand-wringing about the insidiousness of the Western onto-
theological tradition can do anything but confirm the fact that we keep
running into, which is that "there are certain modes of activity, certain
laws of the rational will, which we reinstate and verify, through the very
act of attempting to presuppose that these modes of activity do not exist,
or that these laws are not valid."[15] What am I to do, after all, when philosophers urge me to abandon philosophy and take up literature instead? Should
I follow their advice and take up literature, for the very good reasons they
have brought to my attention? Or should I ignore this advice, having noticed that it constitutes a sort of philosophy and is being promulgated by
philosophers? If I accept what they have to tell me, I shall have to reject
what they have to tell me. But if I reject what they have to tell me, on the
strength of their own good arguments concerning the limitations of philosophy, I shall really be accepting philosophy after all. What I would
prefer to do would be to accept some of what has been said against philosophy with the immediate proviso that, of course, this must mean that
philosophy has thereby eluded or exceeded its supposed limitations. To
the extent that it presents us with such a fruitful self-contradiction wherein
it affirms the power of that which it declares to be powerless, *Literature
and the Question of Philosophy* may be compared to the other book we
have examined, *The Postmodern Condition*. Both books are to be prized
for offering exemplary illustrations of the difficulty that so often attends
upon discussions of the incapacity of reason.

CHAPTER 9

CONCRETE HISTORY OR MERE HOLOGRAM?
Hegel versus the New Historicism

In what follows, I propose to compare Hegel's idea of history with certain ideas that have come to be associated with the New Historicism. My object in making this comparison is to suggest, first, that Hegel's idea of history is less naïve than might be imagined, and, second, that it takes into account the New Historicist view of history and rejects it for reasons that remain pertinent today. At first glance, this might seem impossible. Hegel, after all, comes before that great wave of postphilosophical, postmodernist thinking that seems to have been ushered in by the likes of Marx and Nietzsche. He could not possibly be aware of the subtle considerations that now occupy the minds of the poststructuralists, who take their cue from Derrida and Foucault. Hegel was notoriously a champion of modernity, who appears to have regarded the modern nation-state as the rational culmination of all previous history, by means of whose institutions the content of history could at last be understood and correctly described. Indeed, because of what appears to be its hubris, Hegel's philosophy is often described as though it were something like the Pickett's Charge of Western thought—the last great effort on the part of philosophy to grasp the whole of reality correctly and completely. After Hegel, supposedly, comes the deluge, the breakup, philosophy with a lowercase "p." The modern world starts turning into the postmodern world, not all at once, but gradually and irresistibly. Even now, the import of this transition is still being debated, since the new episteme, as some have termed it, is still in the process of emerging. How, then, could Hegel possibly be in a position to pass judgment on critics and historians who in the 1980s and 1990s are still struggling to express the great paradigm shift that seems to have occurred since Hegel's death? To answer this question, I should like to begin by giving an account of the approach to history taken by the New Historicists.

An excellent brief characterization of the New Historicism has been formulated by Richard Wilson in his introduction to an essay collection entitled *New Historicism and Renaissance Drama* (1992). According to Wilson, the New Historicism "is best seen as an annexation of history by linguistics."[1] He means by this, I think, that the New Historicism should be regarded as an effort to apply the insights of poststructuralism to the phenomena of history on the assumption that history ought properly to be conceived as a sort of gigantic text, whose actual component elements are, quite literally, texts or verbal documents. The great mistake all along has been to reify or hypostatize the contents of these texts and thus to think of history as though it were composed of actual persons or actual events, capable of being accurately or inaccurately reflected in the verbal documents wherein they have been reported. This mistake springs, naturally, from the logocentrism of Western thought or from a naïve confidence in the transparency of signs. The truth is that history cannot be seen as something independently real which is the cause or ground of the various efforts that have been made to reflect it or report it. Instead, all of these efforts *can* be seen to be textual or linguistic in their very nature, which means that they have been constituted and appropriated by means of processes known especially well to poststructuralists. From them, we know that there is no going around such processes, no independent access to the truth of things. The truth *is* the truth of these processes; it is the dynamics of semiosis itself.

Once this has been grasped, it becomes possible to interpret everything as though it were equally problematic because equally textual. There is no such thing as an unproblematic historical context that can be taken as a background or setting for masterpieces or canonical texts that deserve to be foregrounded as works of literature. Thus, for example, it is wrong to think of Renaissance England as the unproblematic, actually existing background against which to see the works of Spenser or Shakespeare. "Renaissance England" is itself a literary or textual phenomenon, a fabrication that is demonstrably the effect of the processes of semiosis and interpretation. It is decomposable into a vast array of so-called primary and secondary documents, each of which poses its own interpretive and historical problems. Furthermore, any effort to arrange these documents in such a way as to produce larger patterns of one sort or another is an exercise in fiction-making or literature. For this reason, there is no such thing as "the Elizabethan world picture," or "the Protestant ethic," or "medieval Catholicism," strictly speaking. These things are, to use one critic's phrase, "mere holograms,"[2] mere optical illusions. At the drop of a hat, each one of them could be dissolved into a multitude of component texts, which are themselves conglomerates or constructions bearing the traces of previous semiotic and interpretive activity and therefore infinitely various in implication.

Certainly, it is a heady thing to discover that any part of our historical knowledge (including the parts we most rely on or most take for granted) can suddenly be foregrounded and textualized. It means, among other things, that there will always be work for critics. Every act of interpretation, no matter how skillful it is in exposing the holograms of some other interpretive act, must needs carry its own burden of holograms, like a cross. Each new arrangement of holograms provides the occasion for yet another act of interpretation. And so the work of interpretation may go on forever. An immense body of critical historiography can thus he substituted for every historical fact that has ever been relied upon, since "facts" are really textual constructs.

Important as it is, however, the emphasis placed by the New Historicists on *the textuality of history* represents only one side or one aspect of the New Historicist project. An equal emphasis is placed also on the *historicity of texts,* which means simply that texts ought not to be focused on as independent or free-standing entities but ought rather to be recognized as spin-offs or by-products of social and historical processes. From this point of view, texts are like the tips of icebergs. When we look at them, we tend to forget that they have been produced under conditions we cannot see and that they are really the visible projections of larger structures associated with these conditions. We also tend to forget that texts are disseminated, interpreted, and (as sometimes happens) canonized in ways that are similarly conditioned. The notion that a classic text, for example, is produced as a consequence of a free, disinterested act of genius needs to be abandoned, as does the corresponding notion that it is possible to read such a text by engaging in a similarly free, disinterested action of pure intellect. Neither a reader nor a writer can rise up out of his or her particular situation in history; each is located somewhere in time and space and is necessarily responsive to the forces at work then and there. Thus, one of the goals of the New Historicism is to reconstruct the dramas having to do with the operation of these forces in order to show the way in which acts of reading and writing have been socially or culturally determined.

At first glance, it must appear that the textuality of history cannot be reconciled with the historicity of texts. Either textuality is the real substance of that which presents itself to us as the phenomenon of history, or else perhaps history is the real substance of that which presents itself to us as textual phenomenon, but how can we have it both ways at once? Which is to have the upper hand, finally—history or textuality? If it be suggested that these two things are related to each other after the fashion of a chemical solution, which is the solvent and which is the solute? The answer to this question is, in fact, rather tricky. Somehow an effort has to be made to collapse the distinction between worldly process and semiotic process, so that the whole of what happens can be conceived as a single, unified process involving real people whose heads are stuffed with fictions or holograms. These holograms cause the people who entertain them to read and write and generally behave according to certain patterns which it is the object of the New Historicism to trace. In simpler terms, this means that ideology of one sort or another is the cause of cultural practice, or that cultural practice may be explained as the expression of ideological commitment. Thus, whenever we look at a cultural artifact such as a text, what we are looking at is a real gesture made by a real person whose intelligence has been bewitched by holograms. If one were to study the holograms separately by themselves, out of the context of the forms of life wherein they have flourished, their occasions and functions would be missed entirely. (This is what happens, in fact, when a so-called classic text of literature or philosophy is read for its own intrinsic interest or when it is treated as though it existed alongside other such texts, composing with them a sort of ideal order having its own intrinsic character.) By the same token, if one were to study the events of the past apart from the holograms in the heads of those who participated in the events, recording them and interpreting them for posterity, everything historical, including the events themselves, would disappear. There is no such thing as the events themselves, just as there is no such thing as the holograms themselves. That, in a word, is the key insight of the New Historicism.

Whenever a New Historicist sees a piece of stray textuality (which can be anything from the merest jotting to a canonized masterpiece), what he or she starts looking for is the context, the actual form of life in which the text in question was a gesture or an event. On the other hand, when it is a question of what is supposed to have been happening at a certain time and place, what he or she starts looking for are the holograms that are responsible for making the past appear as though it had this or that particular character. What were the fictions at work in the heads of those who participated in the action, and, most importantly, what are the fictions at work in the heads of those who have offered to say what the action was or means? The past for us now must always be an imaginative construct, but even when it was present it was being constructed according to the interpretive activity or semiotic behavior of those who were engaged in it. To the extent that there is a dominant form of this behavior going on at any given time, it may be said that a whole group or even a whole culture is in the grip of an unconsciously maintained poem. If this is the case, the actual structure of economic and social practices (including those having to do with the production and dissemination of verbal texts) may well be obscure to all but the New Historicist, whose task it is to read the poem that is being articulated by all these various practices. Perhaps this is why Stephen Greenblatt, who coined the term "New Historicism," now prefers to use the term "Cultural Poetics" to designate more precisely the focus of his own critical activity. It is a poetics of culture that he wishes to formulate, a description of the system of meanings or evaluations whereby a culture imagines and expresses itself.

In Britain, there is a version of what I have been calling New Historicism which goes by the name of Cultural Materialism. Cultural Materialism tends to focus less on the poem that a society unwittingly articulates and more on the rootedness of holograms in political and economic power struggles. If Cultural Poetics can be said to give a slight edge to the textuality of history, Cultural Materialism seems to favor the opposite emphasis on the historicity of texts. Among other things, it makes the point that real people can resist the dominant cultural poem, the privileged holograms some people maintain in order to exercise power over others. With this object in mind, the Cultural Materialist believes that the important thing is not to be mesmerized by the holograms themselves, but instead to collapse them quickly down to the level of actual cultural practice, the material level of the actual people who are affected by them, one way or another. Thus, in contemplating the so-called masterpieces of a culture, we must not be like Dorothy, gazing with awe at the projected image of Oz the Wizard. Rather we must always be looking for the man behind the curtain, or whoever it may be that is running the projector. This is the only way to keep from being imposed upon or duped.

One problem with this whole approach, whether it takes the form of

Cultural Poetics or Cultural Materialism, is that the critic who adopts it is forced to admit, sooner or later, that his own analysis must necessarily be an exhibition of the same kinds of error or illusion that he has made it his business to expose in others. To the New Historicist himself, this is not a problem. Instead, it is a virtue. Stephen Greenblatt calls it "methodological self-consciousness," which he says is "one of the distinguishing marks of the new historicism in cultural studies as opposed to a historicism based upon faith in the transparency of signs and interpretive procedures. . . ."[3] In effect, to be methodologically self-conscious, one has to confess that one's own head cannot help but be stuffed with fictions and holograms in the same way that other heads are. As Richard Wilson puts it, "no author is the origin or owner of his/her meaning, but . . . all statements are written through pre-existing texts, which have intersected then disperse."[4] In part, this means that all users of language are necessarily complicitous with the judgments and assumptions imbedded in language. It also means that, in writing one's own text, one has to employ, at least to some extent, concepts and fictions that are the mark of some previous writer's (or culture's) bemusement. Thus, whenever a New Historicist offers to explain the dramas in which verbal texts are merely factors or moments, a reified history, history with a capital "H," threatens to rise up and offer itself as "the truth of things," and so must be apologized for. In fact, each new interpretation must honestly declare itself to be a new hologram, composed of bits and pieces of old holograms, no nearer the truth than they (since there is no truth), and valuable mainly as a gesture of self-expression or of solidarity with others. But here too there must be apologies. There must be an acknowledgment that such gestures emanate from a person whose thinking is caught up in a variety of practices and situations that have the effect of putting a particular spin on it.

In the following remark, Louis A. Montrose gives an example of the typical apology. "Like any others," says Montrose,

> my own readings of Elizabethan cultural texts cannot but be partial—by which I mean incapable of offering an exhaustive description, a complete explanation; but also, incapable of offering any description or explanation that is located at some Archimedean point outside the history I study, in some ideal space that transcends the coordinates of gender, ethnicity, class, age, and profession that plot my own shifting and potentially contradictory subject positions.[5]

But what is the good, finally, of this kind of confession? It sits like a crown of thorns on the head of learning and scholarship. How can Professor Montrose know so well the factors conspiring to prevent him from knowing things well? If, in fact, his own point of view is so thoroughly hedged about, so thoroughly unable to transcend the coordinates of gender, ethnicity, class, age, and profession, where can the knowledge possibly come from that enables him to think so? Is he indeed able to see himself in the act of failing to overcome the limitations of his own bad vision? Where is the Archimedean point that accounts for *that* description, *that* explanation? In short, how can anyone know, with such nimbleness and subtlety, that his own acts of knowing are so gross and fumbling, unless in knowing that such is the case, he has escaped the limitations which (according to his own doctrine) he is not supposed to be able to escape?

We have, of course, stumbled upon one of the great paradoxes of poststructuralist metathinking: in scrutinizing the conditions that govern the formation of perceptions, this metathinking perceives that perception itself is an illusion. Then, suddenly, it realizes that its own insights must give the appearance of being perceptions (must indeed *be* perceptions), and for this it must apologize. Surely, like all other perceptions, its own insights must be accepted as political gestures or poetic figments ("mere holograms"). And so, in a sense, we are both invited *and not invited* to regard the demonstration that this is the case as a demonstration that this is the case. It shimmers when we look at it. It wobbles back and forth, positing itself and canceling itself, positing itself and canceling itself, thereby creating what is sometimes called the moment of the uncanny.

Essentially, then, the New Historicism presents itself according to two different aspects. On the one hand, it may be seen as a meditation on the ways in which concepts and ideologies have emerged and prospered according to certain specifiable conditions or under certain specifiable circumstances—as a history of the formation of mentality, or of the conflicts within mentality, or of the conflicts between different mentalities. Whenever it assumes this aspect, it is recognizable as a work of historical scholarship, and it can be judged in exactly the same way that any such scholarship can be judged. As such, it shows itself to be an edifice of knowledge. But when it becomes methodologically self-conscious and starts apologizing, it cancels itself as this edifice and becomes instead just a few personal remarks by an author candid enough to admit that the whole thing can be regarded as an episode within his or her own mentality. The world as such disappears, the history of mentality as such disappears or reverts back to the status of a hologram, and we are left staring at an author who has been making a poetical figment or else a political ploy, or both at the same time. In order to get the full shimmering effect or wobbling effect, all we have to do is to imagine that we have arrived at last at *the truth* about mentality, that this is what the history of mentality has revealed to us, namely, that mentality has been nothing more than a series of aesthetic and/or political gestures, so that the author's own mentality cannot help but be part of the series. In a flash, it will dawn on us that we could not possibly know all this unless we were somewhere outside the whole situation, looking at it from the Archimedean point. After all, this is the vision that seems to demand from us a confession, but the substance of the confession is that there cannot be such a vision. Our heads begin to ache, as though from an overdose of holograms, and we begin to yearn for some simple task to perform, anything that will allow us to remain less enlightened about the fact that we can never really hope to attain a state of enlightenment.

The relevance of Hegel comes in just here, and it has to do with the fact that the New Historicism, as I have been describing it, is yet another form of what Hegel would call irony. This is because, in Hegel's time, intellectuals had already made the discovery that the world can be reduced to representations of the world presided over by conflicting or competing egos who have learned how to adopt an ironical stance toward the phenomenon of representation itself. The essence of irony, according to Hegel's notion of irony, is that it expresses both the delight and the dismay of the self-conscious ego as it contemplates the dependency upon itself of all things previously thought to be independently real. Originating in the aesthetic theories of Friedrich von Schlegel and derived, in part, from the philosophy of Fichte, Romantic irony has become, according to Hegel, the operative principle of all those intellectuals (not just poets) who have taken it upon themselves to contemplate the hologram nature of things. In Hegel's words, when the ego is set up as "the absolute principle of all knowing, reason, and cognition," the result is bizarre:

> [N]othing is treated *in and for itself* and as valuable in itself, but only as produced by the subjectivity of the *ego*. But in that case the *ego* can remain lord and master of everything, and in no sphere of morals, law, things human and divine, profane and sacred, is there anything that would

not first have to be laid down by the *ego,* and that therefore could not equally well be destroyed by it. Consequently everything genuinely and independently real becomes only a show, not true and genuine on its own account or through itself, but a mere appearance due to the *ego* in whose power and caprice and at whose free disposal it remains. To admit or cancel it depends wholly on the pleasure of the *ego,* already absolute in itself simply as *ego.*[6]

With respect to the New Historicism, this means that the past is not something that confronts an interpreter with a definite content of its own, to be acknowledged as such. Instead, it is to be regarded as something produced by interpretive activity. Although it may look as though we have an unimpeded access to the past from the literature that comes down to us from the past, in fact all this literature is flawed to the extent that it could not possibly be aware of the processes governing its own constitution. Therefore, it falls to us to bring forth the real content of this literature (bypassing the ostensible content) according to our own insight into these processes. No cultural artifact, no text *about* the past or *from* the past, can be an object that has a claim on the interpreter; instead, each of these things presents itself as an occasion for analysis, as a pretext for the interpreter's new construction. By being methodologically self-conscious, the New Historicist can pick and choose among various methods of interpretation, like those associated with Marxism, or Feminism, or Psychoanalysis. Each method will give the materials to which it is applied a certain character, which poses no problem for the interpreter, so long as he never forgets that it is not the true character of the materials that is being displayed but rather the effect of viewing them either this way or that way. A different interpretation of the same set of materials, using a different method, will give them a different character. This, I think, is what Hegel means when he says that cultural materials of every sort are at the "free disposal" of the Romantic ironist, who may shape them as he pleases, according to principles they themselves are powerless to constrain.

The power felt by the Romantic ironist in relation to the past is well expressed by Professor Montrose when he speaks of "producing" the Renaissance or "re-inventing" Elizabethan culture. "By choosing," he says, "to foreground in my readings of Shakespeare or Spenser such issues as the politics of gender, the contestation of cultural constraints, the social instrumentality of writing and playing, I am not only engaged in our necessary and continuous re-invention of Elizabethan culture but I am also endeavoring to make that engagement participate in the re-formation of our own."[7] Here, we see the drama of an ego that has become conscious of itself as an artist, shaping and configuring the materials of history so as to make them conform better to its own felt needs and interests. For the most part, this feeling of power is accompanied by the sensation of being freshly liberated from the ostensible themes and purposes of the works under analysis. Having broken free from the influence of these things, the New Historicist is in a position to impose upon them what Hegel calls a "formal and abstract thinking,"[8] which, in his own time, Hegel associated with the categories of Enlightenment rationalism, and which, in our time, we can associate with the extension of such categories in the abstractions of linguistics or in the abstractions appropriate to psychology or economics. In this way, no one has to strain to grasp what might have been meant by the obscure and mystified notions of the past, but instead one can enjoy these notions in a safely rationalized form wherein one's own demystified understanding can be reflected back to oneself.

However, this is only one of the ways in which the egotism of Romantic irony manifests itself. It wouldn't be ironical at all if it didn't, at suitable moments, cancel its own constructions and pronounce them to be no less mystified than the others (with the possible exception of their palinode parts). With an apologetic gesture, the critic confesses that his own ideas are necessarily contaminated by the cultural contents they would presume to analyze—by the fictions of language, by the politics of race or class or gender. After all, the critic cannot be expected to leap up out of his own beleaguered subjectivity in order to give an objective account of these things. That would be unthinkable. And so, in lieu of that, he repels away from the content of his own descriptions and theories, preferring to regard them as acts of contestation or as gestures of solidarity or opposition. By knowing and confessing that even his own scholarship must be, to some indeterminate degree, determined by structures pertaining to the semiotic or social process, the critic paradoxically wrenches free, or at least wills his freedom, from just this determination. Certainly, it is an act of ego-saving irony to lament the co-optation of one's own thought by systems that are helping to shape the lamentation itself, just as it is an act of similar irony to engage in deliberately smallish gestures of critical intervention (hoping thereby to distance oneself from theory), when it is clear that only theory itself is in a position to assess the differences between theory and praxis and thus theory itself has to be that which has motivated the smallish gestures.

Irony in this phase of its self-consciousness has shifted from delight to dismay. No longer does it seek to master the contents of culture by understanding them and accounting for them through its own superior categories. Instead, it withdraws into itself in order to deplore those contents as a whole, or else to prepare disruptions of them that will expose them in their hologram nature. Some New Historicists tend to be rather pessimistic about the possibility of resisting the illusions of culture. According to Professor Greenblatt, "the modern state is based on deceit, calculation and hypocrisy," and even "ludic self-improvisation" is constrained by the fact that there are "no moments of pure unfettered subjectivity."[9] Professor Montrose basically concurs, although his pessimism is somewhat mitigated:

> The possibility of political and institutional agency cannot be based upon the illusion of an escape from ideology. However, the very process of subjectively *living* the confrontations or contradictions within or among ideologies makes it possible to experience facets of our own subjection at shifting internal distances—to read, as in a refracted light, one fragment of our ideological inscription by means of another. A reflexive knowledge so partial and unstable may, nevertheless, provide subjects with a means of empowerment as agents.[10]

Some critics talk about the value of adopting an "oppositional" attitude based on "indeterminant negativity,"[11] which can be employed as necessary on an ad hoc basis against whatever is perceived to be "the dominant socio-cultural order."[12] Such an attitude prides itself on its ability to resist being grounded in anything at all other than the will to resist. In this way, it hopes to demonstrate that power struggles are themselves more fundamentally real than the interpretations that appear to have fostered them or that seek to account for them and thereby contain them in thought or discourse.

In trying to show the similarity between what Hegel saw as a new kind of irony and what presents itself today as a new kind of historicism, I am suggesting that, in principle, Hegel's philosophy already comprehends the latter. Hegel was familiar with the attitudes and postures we have been considering, not only because they had been gathered together in Schlegel's Romantic aesthetics, but because they had already begun to dominate the various forms of antiphilosophy which Hegel hoped to challenge. One has only to look at the prefaces and opening parts of practically any of Hegel's expositions to see that Hegel is attempting to refute the views of intellectuals who imagine that philosophy has become passé. In general, these intellectuals fall into two basic groups. First, there are those who seem unduly impressed by the results of one or another of the modern empirical sciences, such as psychology or philology. Being familiar with the "enlightened" thought-categories of these sciences, this group supposes that the philosophical quest for truth can be explained adequately by the application of them to the results of all previous reflection. The second group contains those who seem unduly impressed by what they take to be the negative result of the Kantian critical philosophy. This group supposes that reason has been broken down into contradictions and irresolvable antinomies, so that the truth of things cannot be known but must remain, as it were, out of thought's reach. Both groups—the first with its positivistic self-confidence and the second with its despair concerning the possibility of attaining genuine knowledge—have contributed, in Hegel's view, to the feeling that philosophy has at last been exposed as impotent. "The consequence," he says,

> has been indifference, and even such an outright contempt for philosophy as a science, that nowadays a self-styled modesty even imagines it can join in the discussion of the deepest problems of philosophy, that it may presume to pass judgment about them, and deny to philosophy rational cognition that used to be comprehended under the form of "proof."[13]

Indeed, because of the way in which they assume they have gone beyond philosophy or seen through it, Hegel, in effect, accuses both groups of exhibiting what he refers to as "the conceit of a schoolmaster thinking to give lessons to the philosophical spirits of all the centuries, mistaking what they are, and most of all what it is itself."[14]

Philosophy is not, according to Hegel, some sort of magisterial thing that is sweeping over everybody with the irresistible finality of its conclusions; rather, it is already being pretty much dismissed by those who are in the know. Indeed, Hegel almost always gives the impression that he is having to make a case for it, as though it had yet to be given a fair test.

Still, he never presents it as the only thing to do or as an authority over other disciplines with which it may interfere. Anyone who wants to can textualize history or historicize textuality to his heart's content, and those who do will presumably receive the information that their inquiries make it possible for them to receive. On the other hand, those who want to know the truth of things from a philosophical point of view will have to be curious about the truth and willing to engage in the pursuit of it. Those who know in advance that truth is a vain thing or a chimera will, of course, not make the effort to pursue it, and, as far as I can tell, Hegel never speaks a word against them, except to say that their opinions of what the pursuit is like (or of what is to be found along the way of it) are of no consequence.

As much as any ancient or modern thinker—as much as Socrates or Wittgenstein—Hegel realizes that philosophy is an activity or a way of life—not *for* everybody and with no prejudice *to* anybody. In the preface to the first edition of his *Encyclopedia of the Philosophical Sciences,* he speaks of the fact that, in some, there is felt a "need" for philosophical knowledge, a "concern with *cognition of the truth,*" an "earnest love" of cognition which attests to "the continuing inner drive of rational insight."[15] These things are the human precondition of doing philosophy, without which the project simply will not be embarked on. Thirteen years later, in the foreword to the third edition of the *Encyclopedia,* Hegel refuses to lament the fact that philosophy has fallen so badly out of intellectual favor. Without the encouragement of any authority, he says, "our occupation with this science stands all the more freely upon our concern with the matter and with the truth alone." In fact, philosophy "is left altogether to the freely-felt need of the subject," which must remain "steadfast against insinuations and dire warnings" if it wants to attain "the gratification that the impulse of reason deserves":

> The deeper and more serious participation is lonelier at home, and more silent abroad. Vanity and superficiality is quickly ready, and feels driven to a hasty meddling; but serious concern about an inwardly great matter—one for which only the long and difficult labour of a complete development suffices—submerges itself in it in quiet pursuit for a long time.[16]

It is crucial, I think, to consider what Hegel means by "the long and difficult labour of a complete development." Philosophy, for Hegel, is not a set of right conclusions or right doctrines about the nature of things. Nor is it a set of arguments or theories about the nature of knowledge or the methods of inquiry. Instead, it is an immersion in what there is to be known, which has for its ambition the achievement of what Hegel regards as an absolute knowing or a concrete knowing. The quick assimilation of what there is to be known in terms of the imposition on it of schemes and notions abstracted from tiny portions of it cannot be anything other than a perversion of this goal. Far better it were to submit to the complexities of the knowable as they present themselves to the knowing mind. The natural world must be allowed to present itself to us so that our notions of it may conform with its complexities. In a similar way, the world of human endeavor, the world of culture and of social institutions, must be permitted to appear in a way that will allow its complexities to be noted. This means that history must be attended to if there is to be a concrete knowing of the arts and sciences, of political life, of economic and social processes, of religion and philosophy. The persistence and development of all these things over the course of time constitute what there is to be known about them, and a truly philosophical knowledge must, in Hegel's view, incorporate within itself a patient examination of the productions of culture and the events of history. Indeed, a truly philosophical knowledge must be aware of its own historical and cultural ramifications. To the extent that it includes philosophical reflection, as well as the arts and sciences that mediate to us our knowledge of the natural world, history is, for Hegel, very nearly the whole of what there is to know. Thus "the long and difficult labour of a complete development" of philosophy would include the long and difficult labor of tracing that which is presented to us by history.

In *The Philosophy of Right,* Hegel makes the important point that his own philosophical exposition of the concept of Right ought to be regarded as a thinking through of matters already exhibited implicitly in the productions of actual historical institutions. "After all," he says, "the truth about Right, Ethics, and the state is as old as its public recognition and formulation in the law of the land, in the morality of everyday life, and in religion."[17] All that is required is to show that the truth in its concrete historical actuality is compatible with, or comprehensible to, philosophical reflection. In the preface to the second edition of the *Encyclopedia,* he insists that there is no reason to suspect otherwise:

> It is only an ill-minded prejudice to assume that philosophy stands antithetically opposed to any sensible appreciation of experience, or to the

rational actuality of legal right and to simple-hearted religion and piety. These shapes [of consciousness] are themselves recognized by philosophy, and even justified by it. Rather than opposing them, the thinking mind steeps itself in their basic import; it learns from them and grows strong, just as it does from the great intuitions of nature, history, and art; for this solid content, once it has been thought, is the speculative Idea itself.[18]

It follows, according to this same preface, that "what lies before science is the rich content that hundreds and thousands of years of cognitive activity have brought forth for itself":

[T]his content does not lie before it as historical information that only *others* possess. Then it would be something-dead-and-gone for us, just an occupation to exercise our memories and our acuteness in the critical evaluation of reports, not [a topic] for the cognition of the spirit and the [rational] concern with truth. What is most sublime, most profound, and most inward has been called forth into the light of day in the religions, philosophies, and works of art, in more or less pure, in clearer or more obscure shapes, often in very repulsive ones.[19]

In order to proceed with the investigation of this content, all that is necessary is that thought should have come to regard itself as "free" and "untrammeled" and, therefore, as able to know. If it does not approach its task in this particular attitude, if it has already an agenda of special interests or if it preknows already that it cannot really know anything, the investigation cannot begin, or, if it does, it will take on a sort of freakish character and reflect back to itself its own prejudices concerning what there is to find.

Much of Hegel's writing is concerned to show that skeptical, as well as dogmatic, preknowing is already on the board, preventing inquiry. In opposition to such preknowing, there stands "the rich content that hundreds and thousands of years of cognitive activity have brought forth for itself." Whether or not Hegel is right in his assessment of the meaning of this opposition, it is at least an invitation to look and see for ourselves. But how can one see anything at all if one lacks confidence in one's ability to see? To know in advance that one is blind or that, in fact, there is nothing there to be seen is to abort in advance the whole project of looking and seeing. Thus, we arrive at the impasse between philosophers and antiphilosophers. Philosophers are persons who see no reason to believe that knowledge is impossible, and on the basis of their hunger for it ("the continuing inner drive of rational insight") they proceed to acquire it by inspecting "the rich content." Antiphilosophers are persons who *do* see a reason why knowledge must be impossible, and on the basis of this insight, they proceed to demonstrate the verbal and psychological mechanisms that account for the illusion that there can be such a thing as insight or demonstration.

In view of his awareness of this impasse, it seems to me that Hegel has already considered and rejected the assumptions and practices of the New Historicism. He is not unaware, for example, that language, which constitutes the textual substance of all historical consciousness, is itself a residue or by-product of social and intellectual processes which are now obscure to us. Thus it might be possible, at least theoretically, to sidestep the superficial "content" of a text in order to consider what might be inferred concerning the formation of the verbal substratum. Hegel never denies this possibility, but he does deny that the dramas that might be hypothesized as an explanation of the substratum are more accessible than the dramas that are the focus of historical reflection. For him, there can be no such thing as "an annexation of history by linguistics." As he explains in the Introduction to his lectures on world history:

> Language is the *activity* of the theoretical *intelligence* in the proper sense, for it is through language that it receives its external expression. . . . But this whole theoretical activity, together with its further development and the more concrete process which accompanies it—i.e., the dissemination of peoples, their separation from one another, their interminglings and their migrations—remains buried in the obscurity of the voiceless past; these are not acts of a will becoming conscious of itself, of freedom giving itself an external embodiment and a proper reality. Since they do not partake of this true substance, all such changes—regardless of the linguistic advances that accompany them—have not attained the status of history.[20]

To the extent that we can, in part, reconstruct "the voiceless past" of peoples or nations or even individuals in order to show the dramas whereby language itself has been constituted, the result might well be termed "an annexation of linguistics by history." Nevertheless, from Hegel's point of view history is primarily concerned with the consequences of purposive activity, or, in other words, with the projects and fortunes of consciousness. Even if it were possible to give an account of factors or forces or conditions that might be said to have affected consciousness surreptitiously, the patterns having to do with the consequences of purposive activity would still be what they are. They could not be made to disappear simply because one wished to turn one's attention to other phenomena. Of course, it is always possible to indulge in what might be called the natural history of man, and in such a history the projects of consciousness might seem to be a very small thing, in themselves absurdly inconsequential, being helplessly buffeted by all sorts of things beyond our ken. But, on the other hand, one can always revert back to consciousness as to something that is all-inclusive and whose career or development can be found in the transformations of culture. In the context of a history of consciousness in this sense of the term, of a history of spirit (as Hegel sometimes calls it), the sciences that treat of factors or forces or conditions beyond our ken must themselves necessarily appear as episodes or moments *inside* this very history. Such a history is irreducible; it must remain what it is, regardless of the standpoint that might adopted if one were suddenly to take up the abstract position occupied by one of these sciences, and regardless of how the world might appear from this particular standpoint.

To Hegel's mind, the history of what he means by spirit is the most concrete of all the possible kinds of history, whereas history as seen from any one particular point of view can only be an abstraction. Thus, he claims:

> The perspective adopted by the philosophical history of the world is
> . . . not just one among many general perspectives, an isolated abstraction
> singled out at the expense of the rest. Its spiritual principle is the sum
> total of all possible perspectives. It concentrates its attention on the con-
> crete spiritual principle in the life of nations, and deals not with indi-
> vidual situations but with a universal thought which runs throughout the
> whole. This universal element is not to be found in the world of contin-
> gent phenomena; it is the unity behind the multitude of particulars. The
> object of history is the most concrete of all, for it comprehends every
> aspect of existence; the world spirit is its individuality. What philosophy
> is therefore concerned with in its treatment of history is the concrete ob-
> ject in its concrete form, and it traces the necessary development of this
> object.[21]

It is clear from this passage, I think, that Hegel is here attempting to take what we might call an ecological view of history, the goal of which is to form an estimate of the various cultures or societies that have evolved over time, with special reference to the patterns exhibited by their achievements and limitations, by their growth and decay. His contention that history presents us with an intelligible series of social and cultural ecosystems seems, on the face of it, no less reasonable than the contention that nature, over the course of time, presents us with a similar series of such systems. Indeed, the difficulty involved in perceiving large-scale patterns in the political and cultural history of the planet is probably no greater than the difficulty involved in perceiving such patterns in the planet's natural history. If our immersion in history prevents us from knowing the broad outlines of history, then it would seem our immersion in nature ought to prevent us from grasping the comparable outlines of nature. On the other hand, if belonging to the tangled bank does not keep us from having an awareness of ecology, then perhaps living in a particular society at a particular time need not keep us from developing an awareness of history in what Hegel takes to be its ecological aspect.

In opposition to Hegel's view of history as an ecosystem or as an evolving series of ecosystems, the New Historicist seeks to raise the noise level as much as possible by calling attention to the fact (which is undoubtedly true) that within these systems there are always millions of impressions as to what is going on, or has gone on, at any given moment. If the incommensurability of these impressions can be made to be the dominant consideration whenever history is being thought of, then the effort to show that they are the component elements of an objective system can be frustrated. As Jonathan Dollimore would have it, "it is the task of the oppositional critic to re-read culture so as to amplify the voices of the ruled, exploited, oppressed, and excluded."[22] This might be called an anti-ecological approach, though it leans, in the usual self-contradictory way, toward the view it opposes. Whereas Hegel takes it for granted that "the sum total of all possible perspectives" is precisely the phenomenon that presents itself to us as the tangled bank, the New Historicist assumes that the conflicting testimonies of the bank's denizens are such that none of them really justifies the hypothesis that there is any such thing as a tangled bank at all (which assumption immediately cancels out the possibility of an ecological view of history, albeit on the basis of the very ecology it disallows).

For a man who has the reputation of having made too much out of his own knowledge of the past, Hegel is extremely restrained when it comes to stating what lessons there are to be learned from history. For example, he never claims that it can teach us what to do in the present or what will happen in the future. If history teaches us anything, he says, it teaches us "that nations and governments have never learned anything from history or acted upon any lessons they might have drawn from it," nor could they have done so with profit, since "each age and each nation finds itself in such peculiar circumstances, in such a unique situation, that it can and must make decisions with reference to itself alone."[23] It is largely for this reason that, as Hegel remarks, "prophecy is not the business of the philosopher."[24] Still, in spite of these warnings, it is tempting to consider Hegel's description of the assault on philosophy with which he was familiar in terms of its relevance to the work of today's antiphilosophers. To the extent that his analysis of irony as "the self-conscious frustration of the objective"[25] remains applicable to the New Historicism, it may be said that he presents us with a prophetic comprehension of the new episteme that is commonly supposed to be just now forming on the basis of post-Hegelian reflections.

CHAPTER 10

SANTAYANA'S CRITIQUE OF TRANSCENDENTALISM

> The British and German philosophies belong to an analytic
> phase of reflection, without spiritual discipline, and their value is
> merely psychological. Their subject matter is human knowledge;
> and the titles of many of the chief works of this school confess that
> this is their only theme. Not moral life, much less the natural world,
> but simply the articulation of knowledge occupies them; and yet, by
> the hocus-pocus of metaphysics, they substitute this human experi-
> ence for the whole universe in which it arises.
>
> —Santayana, "The Progress of Philosophy"

If Richard Rorty is correct about the fact that we are currently going through
the process of becoming a postphilosophical culture, it may be that he is
also right when he tells us that in our new culture we won't be wasting our
time considering the arguments and opinions of philosophers. In the meantime, he certainly urges us not to consider them. Lyotard gives, I think, the
same bad advice in *The Postmodern Condition* when he urges us to consider the collapse of speculative philosophy as something already accomplished and not to be lingered over. The implications of this collapse were
keenly felt in the earlier part of our century, says Lyotard. There's no need
to mull it over again or to remain wistful about it: "We can say today that
the mourning process has been completed. There is no need to start all
over again."[1]

But suppose we have no intention of mourning. Suppose we just want
to see how it all happened. It may be that the limits of reason *were* exposed
and that philosophy *did* collapse, as the Enlightenment critique of reason
was extended throughout the nineteenth century and into the twentieth.
Postmodern intellectuals are supposed to be suspicious with regard to large-
scale narratives—narratives that affect to explain the trajectory of Western culture—but with regard to this narrative, suspicion seems lacking.
Can it be true that, after two thousand years of self-deception, the West
has undergone a crisis of self-scrutiny from which we, at the end of the
twentieth century, are only just now emerging? If it is true, can we be
certain that we have understood the crisis and its aftermath correctly, if we
follow the advice of Lyotard and Rorty not to look back for fear of being

disoriented or corrupted? What would we see if we did look back? One of things we'd see would be the philosophy of Santayana, which explores at length precisely the thesis that is now being offered to us as a *mere* thesis, merely to be accepted.

Santayana was, above all, a speculative thinker (a beholder or watcher), whose long life coincided almost perfectly with what many have taken to be the period of transition from modernity to postmodernity, the period during which the speculative pretensions of reason itself are supposed to have been abandoned. Santayana saw what was happening firsthand, and he acknowledged that traditional culture *was* breaking up and that, in some sense, traditional philosophy *was* being attacked or ignored by philosophers who were trying to establish a new approach to knowledge. What makes him especially valuable to us is that he insisted on viewing the entire process speculatively, refusing to take sides in a partisan fashion either as a progressive or as a reactionary. He wished to do justice to all the forms of human experience, to all the varieties of thought and endeavor that might be said to constitute the life of reason. He deplored reductive systems, which tried to explain the whole of things in terms of particular metaphysical principles or substances established by particular lines of inquiry that had come to regard themselves as absolute. But, at the same time, he also deplored the complete neutrality of Rorty's "all-purpose intellectual," with whom he might easily be confused. He was not a pragmatist or a relativist in the way that Rorty was, believing that all thought and endeavor was on an equal footing since all of it was necessarily an expression of some aspect of human nature or human interest. If he had been such a pragmatist or such a relativist, he could not have written the following:

> In saying that a man's *nature* is, for him, the arbiter of values, we may understand that nothing is good or bad but thinking makes it so. We shall then have confused what a man is with what he thinks he is, and identified his interests with his wishes. Under cover of freedom to be ourselves we shall be denying that we have any true nature; and under cover of asserting our native rights we shall be denying that we have any ultimate interests. Humanism, so understood, will have disintegrated humanity, declared all passions equally good and proclaimed moral anarchy.[2]

Perhaps the simplest way to characterize Santayana would be to say that he wished to be cognizant of the strengths and weaknesses of all systems of thought, in the belief that a philosophical grasp of the whole array of systems was both possible and desirable. Thus, he refused to accept the idea that a choice must be made between thinking narrowly inside a particular system or accepting the prospect of a loose plurality of systems that are nonrectifiable and, taken as an aggregate, patternless. With regard to ancient thought, modern thought, and the latest currents of postmodern thought, he insisted on being both generous and critical, practicing in just about equal measure a hermeneutics of suspicion and a hermeneutics of sympathy, to the great dismay of both the reactionaries and the progressives. Half of the time, he seemed to be what William James termed him, "a representative of moribund Latinity," whose object was to defend the deep rationality of just those remnants of the past that appeared least likely to survive the onslaught of modern (or postmodern) criticism, such as the doctrines and institutions of Catholic Christianity. To those who greeted with enthusiasm the cultural transformations of the nineteenth and twentieth centuries, a book like *Interpretations of Poetry and Religion* seemed perverse and backward-looking, the production of a man who took a malicious delight in demonstrating that contemporary innovations were really barbarous. On the other hand, it seemed equally clear that Santayana was not unaware that the intellectual underpinnings of traditional culture had not emerged unscathed from the criticisms of the moderns and the postmoderns. For all their intuitive sympathy, his own cultural studies were themselves "critical" in spirit and thoroughly disillusioned. They seemed to acknowledge (perversely, from the point of view of the traditionalist) that all cultural formations are based on idealizations or rationalizations of experience, rather than on immediate contact with reality, with the result that the chief differences between them are aesthetic and moral, rather than cognitive or epistemological. To the exposers of rationalization, he looked liked a defender of rationalization, while to the defenders, he looked like an exposer. In the end, almost nobody was satisfied, and he was written off as a mere stylist or as an "edifying" philosopher.

Santayana's peculiar position may be attributed directly to his insistence on viewing speculatively, not only what he took to be the dying culture of Christendom, but also the critique that was being administered to the same. Ultimately, the result was that he produced what might be called a critique of this critique, the implications of which are strikingly pertinent to our own theoretical discussions. Thus, his criticisms of the transcendentalist impulse in British and German philosophy of the eighteenth and nineteenth centuries, which seemed to him the dominant impulse of modern philosophy generally (plainly evident in American philosophy from Emerson to Dewey, and equally evident in the so-called philosophical revolution of the twentieth century), reach forward into our own time and remain relevant with respect to the methods and assumptions of recent critical theory and practice. These methods and assumptions were not unknown to him, because they were already clearly implicit, and often explicit, in the efforts he observed to expose or to bypass the shaky foundations (indeed, the whole edifice) of Western thought. Two themes continually ran through his observations of these efforts: one had to do with the fact that the critique of knowledge could always be shown to have incorporated within itself, or to be founded upon, the very knowledge it imagined itself to be undermining; the other had to do with the fact that the idealism or subjectivism that had been developed by the British empiricists and the German idealists had *not* been superseded but had gone on developing in the later forms of philosophy and continued to be a force even in the ruminations of those who imagined they had eluded philosophy or else gone beyond it. Santayana's pursuit of these themes in relation to the intellectual projects of his own contemporaries may easily be extended to the projects of post-rational criticism in the late twentieth century.

Santayana would occasionally lament that it had been his fate to be educated in the British and German schools of philosophy, which had privileged investigations into the origins and conditions of knowledge and, as a consequence, "for three hundred years . . . had hardly been able to distinguish the universe or the realm of essence from the vapours of animal feeling."[3] And yet, because of his education, it was natural for him to begin philosophizing on the basis of epistemological considerations. The starting point of his early books—*The Sense of Beauty, Interpretations of Poetry and Religion,* and *The Life of Reason*—is, in fact, the very simple (or at least simple-seeming) idea that our conceptions of things are determined by experience, or by the processes of experience. Although he believed that a sound philosophy must concur with common sense in regarding the world as the *cause* of our experiences of it, he also believed that such a philosophy would have to include, or indeed begin with, an account of how the idea of a world is itself arrived at by the mind that thinks it. Thus, a sound philosophy would have to acknowledge the active process of cognition, which it had been the genius of British and German philosophy to call our attention to. Here, for example, is a typical passage from *The Sense of Beauty,* in which Santayana speaks of "certain . . . fields where the human mind gives a series of unstable forms to objects in themselves indeterminate":

> History, philosophy, natural as well as moral, and religion are evidently such fields. All theory is a subjective form given to an indeterminate material. The material is experience; and although each part of experience is, of course, perfectly definite in itself, and just that experience which it is, yet the recollection and relating together of the successive experiences is a function of the theoretical faculty. The systematic relations of things in time and space, and their dependence upon one another, are the work of our imagination.[4]

A bit later in the same book, this crucial point is reiterated. "From the beginning to the end of our perceptive and imaginative activity," says Santayana, "we are synthesising the material of experience into unities the independent of reality of which is beyond proof, nay, beyond the possibility of a shadow of evidence."[5] But the consequence of this discovery is not skepticism. Rather, what follows is that the mind's constructive activities are acknowledged and accepted as both necessary and appropriate. If it is true that the world as we apprehend it is made up of "synthetic unities" we ourselves have created, "yet the life of intelligence, like the joy of contemplation, lies entirely in the formation and inter-relation of these unities."[6]

To put it simply, Santayana regards the tendency of the mind to arrive at its various determinations of the world as a good tendency, and he calls the resulting determinations rational because they are the work of "reason." He is quite prepared to admit that there is no way to compare the productions of reason with anything that might be imagined to exist beyond reason's scope, but he does not construe this as a limitation of reason, for the simple reason that, if he did so, he *would* be comparing reason's productions to something imagined to be unreachable for comparisons. Epistemology itself would seem to be an expression of "the life of intelligence," somewhat late in coming, rather than a foundation for this life or a momentous disruption of it. Since the materials of experience (themselves known to be such through the operations of reason) are what we have to work with, Santayana's attitude is, let the work proceed as it may. Let the mind follow its own course, developing such notions as it can, all the while subjecting them to its own adjustments and revisions. The result can hardly be anything less than "the spectacle which science and history now spread before us," as Santayana puts it in his next book, *Interpretations of Poetry and Religion*.[7] To apprehend this spectacle in detail, we have the whole array of intellectual disciplines, each with its own particular scope and powers. And the key thing to notice is this: every doubt or skepticism that can possibly arise can only arise *within* this mental framework and as a function of the operations of reason. Total or fundamental criticisms of what Santayana means by "the life of intelligence" or "the life of reason" simply cannot occur, for when they *seem* to occur, they can always be shown to be expressions of this life that are dependent upon the reliability of its productions. Santayana thus affirms the progress of reason in such a way as to deny that reason can be radically repudiated or narrowly circumscribed according to what might be imagined to be its boundaries or limits. From this point of view, the criticism of knowledge is dependent upon the knowledge it examines. It cannot subvert it or dismantle it or concern itself with something that might be imagined to be anterior to it, something that explains its operations without being itself explained by them. Accordingly, in *Reason in Science,* Santayana writes the following rebuke of epistemological skepticism:

> The sciences have nothing to supply more fundamental than vulgar thinking or, as it were, preliminary to it. They are simply elaborations of it; they accept its presuppositions and carry on its ordinary processes. A pretence on the philosopher's part that he could get behind or below human thinking, that he could underpin, so to speak, his own childhood and the inherent conventions of daily thought, would be pure imposture. A philosopher can of course investigate the history of knowledge, he can analyse its method and point out its assumptions; but he cannot know by other authority than that which the vulgar know by, nor can his knowledge begin with other unheard-of objects or deploy itself in advance over an esoteric field. Every deeper investigation presupposes ordinary perception and uses some at least of its data. Every possible discovery *extends* human knowledge. None can base human knowledge anew on a deeper foundation or prefix an ante-experimental episode to experience. We may construct a theory as disintegrating as we please about the dialectical or empirical conditions of the experience given; we may disclose its logical stratification or physical antecedents; but every idea and prin-

ciple used in such a theory must be borrowed from current knowledge as it happens to lie in the philosopher's mind.[8]

Now, from Santayana's point of view, the peculiarity of modern philosophy was that it had become too much impressed by the discovery that thinking is involved in our conceptions of reality. By suspending or bracketing already existing knowledge, philosophers since Hume and Kant had endeavored to examine the processes or mechanisms that might be supposed to constitute the prior condition or the inherent substance of what later appeared as knowledge. In Santayana's opinion, the crucial questions were always begged, because the suspending or bracketing process itself could not be carried out consistently or completely. But still the project was attempted, again and again, by philosophers whose wariness concerning conceptions of reality had instigated what they hoped would be a deeper investigation into the reality of conceptions. Instead of regarding the conceptions themselves as an adequate justification of the processes that produced them, these philosophers reached almost the opposite conclusion, which was that the conceptions ought to be regarded as needing to be justified by an independent investigation of that which had spawned them. The objects of thought, established as such *by* thought and formerly supposed to be real, were to be deemed fictions, whereas the conditions or mechanisms of thought were to be deemed alone worthy of attention. The result was transcendentalism, which either lamented or forgot its own thoughtful origins.

Santayana's criticism of his own contemporaries and immediate predecessors is firmly rooted in his analysis of this fundamental shift of focus. Instead of pursuing the themes and considerations suggested by science and common sense, the thinkers whom he criticizes sought to undermine such themes and considerations by investigating the deeper reality of "pure" or "immediate" experience, or by studying discourse or language as the all-determining basis of the world's appearances. In *The German Mind* (originally published as *Egotism in German Philosophy*), Santayana claims that the consequence of transcendentalism is that "views, and the history and logic of views" have come to be regarded as "more primitive and important than the objects which these views have in common."[9] That is to say, we find ourselves in the situation called pluralism, wherein the perspectives of interpreters (or interpretive communities) have become more real than the objects ostensibly being interpreted. The feeling that a common object must be the basis of the various interpretations that are made of it has been superseded by the conviction that, since no object can be conceived apart from an interpretation of it, each distinctive interpretation must have its own distinctive object. Thus, we have, in principle, already arrived at the incommensurable language games hypothesized by Lyotard or the "historically contingent final vocabularies" hypothesized by Rorty, without having to depend on the midwifery of Wittgenstein.

Santayana was perfectly aware that the study of "views" or (as we now sometimes term them) "discursive practices" might be given two different emphases: one in favor of the selfhood or subjectivity of interpreters considered as persons, and the other in favor of the modality or instrumentality of discourse itself as the post-humanistic truth of interpretation. We might, for example, seek to maintain at all times a transcendental awareness of ourselves as producers and consumers of interpretation activity, taking, as Santayana describes it, "what views we will of things," and then declaring "that the things are mere terms in the views we take of them."[10] Though Santayana did not live long enough to observe the criticism of Derrida or Rorty or any other of the self-conscious exercises in "reading" that rose to prominence in the late twentieth century, he was aware of Emerson, whom he describes thus in *Winds of Doctrine:*

> More, perhaps, than anybody that has ever lived, he practised the transcendental method in all its purity. He had no system. He opened his eyes on the world every morning with a fresh sincerity, marking how things seemed to him then, or what they suggested to his spontaneous fancy. . . . [H]e never insisted on his notions so as to turn them into settled dogmas; he felt in his bones that they were myths. . . . Had he made a system out of his notion of compensation, or the over-soul, or spiritual laws, the result would have been as thin and forced as it is in other transcendental systems. But he coveted truth; and he returned to experience, to history, to poetry, to the natural science of his day, for new starting-points and hints toward fresh transcendental musings.[11]

The point, of course, is that Emerson's thinking, in becoming self-conscious and in seeking to maintain itself as such, became indifferent to anything that might be supposed to exist beyond its own immediate field of activity. To be sure, says Santayana, Emerson "fed on books":

There was a great catholicity in his reading; and he showed a fine tact in his comments, and in his way of appropriating what he read. But he read transcendentally, not historically, to learn what he himself felt, not what others might have felt before him.[12]

Therefore, his genius "was employed on a sort of inner play, or digestion of vacancy": "It was a refined labour, but it was in danger of being morbid, or tinkling, or self-indulgent. It was a play of intra-mental rhymes."[13]

The alternative to interpretive self-consciousness was to allow everything to be swallowed up by discourse itself, although, as Santayana remarks wryly in *Scepticism and Animal Faith*, "discourse, no less than the existence of a self, needs to be posited, and the readiness with which a philosopher may do so yields only a candid confession of personal credulity, not a proof of anything."[14] According to this option, instead of focusing on his own activity of self-elaboration or self-creation, a rigorous thinker might come to regard himself as an inference no more legitimate than that of the external world. The study of experience might then proceed on the condition that the *subject* of experience (no less than the *objects* of experience) be regarded as a fiction. Each "item" of experience, each "element" of it, would acquire its intelligibility, not by reference to an intending mind or an intended object, but only by reference to some other "item" or "element" existing with it in a unified field. Not requiring the midwifery of Saussure, Santayana understood that this was the transformation of transcendentalism into "a direct materialistic sort of realism," which, he thought, promised to be "the ultimate result of pragmatism":

> Nor is the transformation very hard to effect. The world of solipsistic practice, if you remove the romantic self that was supposed to evoke it, becomes at once the sensible world; and the problem is only to find a place for those cognitive and moral functions which the soul was once supposed to exercise in the presence of an independent reality. But this problem is precisely the one that pragmatists boast they have already solved; for they have declared that consciousness does not exist, and that objects of sensation (which at first were called feelings, experiences, or "truths") know or mean one another when they lead to one another, when they are poles, so to speak, in the same vital circuit. The spiritual act which was supposed to take things for its object is to be turned into "objective spirit," that is, into dynamic relations between things. The philosopher will deny that he has any other sort of mind himself, lest he be shut up in it again, like a sceptical and disconsolate child. . . .[15]

In this conception of a unified field consisting only of "dynamic relations between things," discourse is not *about* reality, nor is reality *independent* of discourse. Instead, reality is a matter of discourse, and discourse is the structure of reality. To apprehend one or the other as merely objective or merely subjective is to misapprehend the unity of the field. Thus, as Santayana observes in his chapter on Royce in *Character and Opinion in the United States,* the ultimate tendency of idealism, when carried forward to its inevitable conclusion, was to focus not on minds or selves as generators or beholders of ideas but on "the qualities and divisions" found *in* the world of appearance, conceived not as "a concourse of existences" but rather as "a web of themes":

> This is the very essence and pride of idealism, that knowledge is not knowledge of the world but is the world itself, and that the units of discourse which are interwoven and crossed units, are the only individuals in being.[16]

The question of whether discourse was to be understood as emanating from persons or spirits, or whether persons or spirits were to be understood figments of discourse, was perhaps a matter of indifference, since, in Santayana's analysis, "the assumption that spirit discoursing [Descartes's thinking] exists, and is more evident than any other existence, leads by a slightly different path to the same conclusion as the assumption of the self as the fundamental fact": "In the one case discourse will soon swallow up all existence, and in the other this chosen existence, myself, will evaporate into discourse."[17] Nevertheless, for the transcendentalists at the end of the twentieth century, it remained a matter of dispute whether "views" were to be explained by referring to persons (or groups of persons) or whether persons and groups themselves became intelligible by referring to "the history and logic of views."

Santayana's critique of transcendentalism was itself partly a criticism of the logic of transcendentalist arguments and partly an account of the motives behind these arguments. In the last chapter of *Reason in Science,* he epitomizes the entire transcendentalist project, together with its inevitable outcome, in these words:

> The dethronement of empirical knowledge which [the transcendentalists] announced was occasioned by the discovery that empirical knowl-

edge was ideal and hypothetical; that its terms, like all terms in thought, were thrown out during the fission or crystallisation of a growing experience. Science accordingly was merely a set of ideas; its subject-matter seemed to be sucked in and absorbed by the theory that presented it, so that when the history of science was written the whole substance and meaning of science was exhausted. This damaging implication that what is ideal is imaginary and that what is inferred exists only in the fooled mind that infers it, would, if it were allowed, make short work of all philosophy. Theology would fare no better than science, and it is hard to see how transcendental idealism itself could stand, if it pretended to constitute an articulate theory of reality. All faith would be invalidated, since it would be proved to be faith only [or, as we now say, mere ideology], having no real object. But then history itself is a science; and to represent a series of events or related phenomena in time would be to pretend to impossible knowledge. It would become necessary to retract and withdraw the alleged evolution of thought itself, in which science was to figure as an imaginative device and a passing episode. History and experience would be nothing but the idea of them; and the Absolute Ego or Absolute Life also, in so far as anything could be said of it, would be simply an integral term in the discourse that described it. And this discourse, this sad residuum of reality, would remain an absolute datum without a ground, without a subject-matter, without a past, and without a future.[18]

Or, to borrow a phrase used much later to describe the logical realism of Bertrand Russell, the universe would at last become "a dictionary of the terms in which we apprehend it."[19] In *Scepticism and Animal Faith,* Santayana makes reference to Hume's "analyses of our notions of material things, of the soul, and of cause," and he calls these analyses "bits of plausible literary psychology, essays on the origin of common sense," which paved the way for subsequent versions of transcendentalist criticism:

They are supposed . . . by Hume and by the whole modern school of idealists, to destroy both the meaning of these notions and the existence of their intended objects. Having explained how, perhaps, early man, or a hypothetical infant, might have reached his first glimmerings of knowledge that material things exist, or souls, or causes, we are supposed to have proved that no causes, no souls, and no material things can exist at all. We are not allowed to ask how, in that case, we have any evidence for the existence of early man, or of the hypothetical infant, or of any general characteristics of the human mind, and its tendencies to feign. The world of literature is sacred to these bookish minds; only the world of nature and science arouses their suspicion and their dislike. They think that "experience," with the habits of thought and language prevalent in all nations, from Adam down, needs only to be imagined in order to be known truly. All but this imagined experience seems to them the work of imagination. While their method of criticism ought evidently to establish not merely solipsism, but a sort of solipsism of the present datum, yet they never stop to doubt the whole comedy of human intercourse, just as the most uncritical instinct and the most fanciful history represent it to be. How can such a mass of ill-attested and boldly dogmatic assumptions fail to make the critics of science uncomfortable in their own house? Is it because the criticism of dogma in physics, without this dogma in psychology, could never so much as begin? Is not their criticism at bottom a work of edification or of malice, not of philosophic sincerity, so that they reject the claim to knowledge only in respect to certain physical, metaphysical, or religious objects which the modern mind has become suspicious of, and hopes to feel freer without? Meantime, they keep their conventional social assumptions without a qualm, because they need them to justify their moral precepts and to lend a false air of adequacy to their view of the world. . . . This whole school criticises knowledge, not by extending knowledge and testing it further, but by reviewing it maliciously, on the tacit assumption that knowledge is impossible. But in that case this review of knowledge and all this shrewd psychology are themselves worthless. . . .[20]

It should be obvious that Santayana's strictures against what he took to be the transcendentalist bias of modern philosophy are still applicable to our own most recent thinking. The new pragmatists, the new historicists, and the deconstructionists have all, in their different ways, made views and perspectives, or the instrumentalities of views and perspectives, the paramount focus of their investigations, in the belief that reality is a social or linguistic construction that is ultimately reducible to a variety of discursive practices or to a variety of interpretive communities. The implication seems to be that there is no way to coordinate the variety of practices or the plurality of views so as to arrive at a comprehensive view of them in relation to their objects. Practices and views are taken to be multiple, discontinuous, and nonrectifiable, and the eclipse of reason is taken to be precisely the discovery that no synthesis of them is possible. To make this discovery is to enter what Lyotard, Rorty, and by now countless others have described as the postmodern condition. The value of Santayana's philosophy is that it enables one to see how this whole situation is, in fact, a sort of optical illusion. For if the postmodern thinker invites one to contemplate a plurality of views or a variety of discursive practices, this very plurality or variety must become in itself an object of knowledge, not to be confused with any of the views or practices that are thus comprehended. And this, in turn, means that the condition or situation of pluralism must be regarded as having the status of a reality, which can either be conceived correctly or else be misconceived. Indeed, the ability to pass in review a variety of language games or a variety of ideological perspectives, and to see, by means of this review, not only that they are different but also how they are different from each other, is exactly the ability to coordinate them. This in itself constitutes a synthetic act of reason, which is identical with the gesture of speculative philosophy, as Santayana understands it. It cannot be an occasion for the abdication of reason.

CHAPTER 11

HEGEL AND SANTAYANA ON
THE NATURE OF PHILOSOPHY

> ... science is nothing but developed perception, interpreted intent,
> common sense rounded out and minutely articulated. . . . [I]t is alto-
> gether autonomous and unjustifiable from the outside. It must lean
> on its own vitality. . . . . The panic came from the assumption (a
> wholly gratuitous one) that a spontaneous constructive intellect can-
> not be a trustworthy instrument. . . .
>
> —Santayana, *Reason in Science*

> It is only an ill-minded prejudice to assume that philosophy stands
> antithetically opposed to any sensible appreciation of experience. . . .
> the *factum* of philosophy is cognition already elaborated; so the in-
> terpreting can only be a "thinking-over" in the sense that it is a *fur-
> ther* thinking that *comes later.*
>
> —Hegel, Preface to the Second Edition of *The Encyclopedia*

Perhaps the most curious thing about the postphilosophical positions that
came to be adopted by intellectuals at the end of the twentieth century was
that they had already been clearly envisaged and described, first by Hegel
at the beginning of the nineteenth century and then by Santayana at the
beginning of the twentieth century. These two philosophers not only rejected postphilosophy on the basis of what they took to be its weaknesses
and internal contradictions; they went so far as to declare that postphilosophy is precisely that which gives philosophy itself its true occasion or
impetus. For both Hegel and Santayana, the crisis that precipitates philosophy is the false supposition that post-rational thinkers have somehow
managed to construct "a formidable indictment of physical and moral science,"[1] through the effort "to base science on a deeper foundation or to
override it by a higher knowledge."[2] As Hegel put it in one of his lectures,
the result, for many of his contemporaries, of investigating the claims of
cognition more closely was that they "professed to have discovered that
[thinking] was presumptuous and could not accomplish what it had undertaken."[3] Thus, it is the subsequent search for supplements or alternatives
to rational cognition that provokes the philosophical justification of cognition. In Hegel's view, it was not philosophy that sought to go beyond the
"absolute import" of cognition; it was postphilosophy that sought to do

this. "The scientific cognition of truth," which, as Hegel says, "is what I have laboured upon, and still do labour upon always, in all of my philosophical endeavors," was, after all, "nothing else but the reestablishing of that absolute import beyond which thought initially strove to go, and above which it posited itself."[4] In strikingly similar terms, Santayana, in *Reason in Science,* describes the vanity attached to the post-rational conclusion that "a spontaneous constructive intellect cannot be a trustworthy instrument": "We were released from all dogma and reinstated in the primordial assurance that we were all there was, but without understanding what we were, and without any means of controlling our destiny, though cheered by the magnificent feeling that that destiny was great." In Santayana's view, the spirit that "knows" the vanity of constructed knowledge is itself, as Hegel also charged, essentially vain. Thus he observes, in Hegelian fashion:

> [A] spirit that finds its only exercise in gloating on the consciousness that it is a spirit, one that has so little skill in expression that it feels all its embodiments to be betrayals and all its symbols to be misrepresentations, is a spirit evidently impotent and confused. It is self-inhibited, and cannot fulfil its essential vocation by reaching an embodiment at once definitive and ideal, philosophical and true.[5]

For Hegel too, the occasion of philosophy is the need to enable the spirit to "fulfil its essential vocation" by dispelling the apparent obstacles to that vocation which have been raised by the critique of reason. His account of how this vocation came to be challenged and how it is that philosophy emerged with new force because of challenge is tersely summarized in the following paragraphs from the introduction to the *Science of Logic,* which speak of "errors the refutation of which throughout every part of the spiritual and natural universe is *philosophy*":

> Ancient metaphysics had . . . a higher conception of thinking than is current today. For it based itself on the fact that the knowledge of things obtained through thinking is alone what is really true in them, that is, things not in their immediacy but as first raised into the form of thought, as things *thought*. Thus this metaphysics believed that thinking (and its determinations) is not anything alien to the object, but rather is its essential nature, or that things and the thinking of them—our language too expresses their kinship—are explicitly in full agreement, thinking in its

immanent determinations and the true nature of things forming one and the same content.

But *reflective* understanding took possession of philosophy. We must know exactly what is meant by this expression which moreover is often used as a slogan; in general it stands for the understanding as abstracting, and hence as separating and remaining fixed in its separations. Directed against reason, it behaves as ordinary common sense and imposes its view that truth rests on sensuous reality, that thoughts are *only* thoughts, meaning that it is sense perception that first gives them filling and reality and that reason left to its own resources engenders only figments of the brain. In this self-renunciation on the part of reason, the Notion of truth is lost; it is limited to knowing only subjective truth, only phenomena, appearances, only something to which the nature of the object itself does not correspond: knowing has lapsed into opinion.

However, this turn taken by cognition, which appears as a loss and a retrograde step is based on something more profound on which rests the elevation of reason into the loftier spirit of modern philosophy. The basis of that universally held conception is, namely, to be sought in the insight into the necessary conflict of the determinations of the understanding with themselves. The reflection already referred to is this, to transcend the concrete immediate object, and to determine it and separate it. But *equally* it must transcend these its *separating* determinations and straightway *connect* them. It is at the stage of this connecting of the determinations that their conflict emerges. This connecting activity of reflection belongs in itself to reason and the rising above those determinations which attains to an insight into their conflict is the great negative step towards the true Notion of reason. But the insight, when not thorough-going, commits the mistake of thinking that it is reason which is in contradiction with itself; it does not recognize that the contradiction is precisely the rising of reason above the limitations of the understanding and the resolving of them. Cognition, instead of taking from this stage the final step into the heights, has fled from the unsatisfactoriness of the categories of the understanding to sensuous existence, imagining that in this it possesses what is solid and self-consistent. But on the other hand, since this knowledge is self-confessedly knowledge only of appearances, the unsatisfactoriness of the latter is admitted, but at the same time presupposed: as much as to say that admittedly, we have no proper knowledge of things-in-themselves but we do have a proper knowledge of them within the sphere of appearances, as if, so to speak, only the *kind of objects* were different, and one kind, namely things-in-themselves, did not fall within the scope of our knowledge but the other kind, phenomena, did. This is like attributing to someone a correct perception, with the rider that nevertheless he is incapable of perceiving what is true but only what is false.

Absurd as this would be, it would not be more so than a true knowledge which did not know the object as it is in itself.[6]

When Santayana likewise observed that modern thought was collapsing into multiple, discontinuous systems of interpretation, each governed, as was supposed, by its own "historically contingent final vocabulary" and thus preoccupied with its own unique set of appearances which was not to be reconciled with other sets of appearances appearing to other systems, he noted, just as Hegel did, that it was only by *connecting* these systems speculatively (i.e., philosophically) that their conflicts emerged. In the 1920s, when many intellectuals had been excited by what they imagined were the negative or skeptical implications of Einstein's theory of relativity, Santayana remarked, in a letter, that "if 'relative' systems have no connexion, and no common object, each is absolute: and if they have a common object, or form a connected group of perspectives, then they are only relative views, like optical illusions, and the universe is not ambiguous in its true form."[7]

In short, we may say that both Hegel and Santayana are concerned to validate the constructive work of reason, in opposition to modern skepticism, and that both are concerned to show that philosophy is the legitimate outcome of this work, being a speculative comprehension not only of its positive aspects but also of the skepticism reason itself has spawned along the way. The effect of situating the critique of reason in relation to reason's other activities and productions is to demonstrate that philosophy cannot be thwarted in its ambition to comprehend the whole of what thought has thus far accomplished. In order to show the extent to which Hegel and Santayana present similar vindications of philosophy, I should now like to compare the view of philosophy that Hegel propounds in *The Encyclopedia Logic* with the view propounded by Santayana in two of his earliest books, *The Sense of Beauty* and *Interpretations of Poetry and Religion.*

In the opening pages of *The Encyclopedia Logic,* Hegel makes it clear that philosophy does not arise ex nihilo, out of a vacuum, but is preceded by other forms of consciousness which constitute the content of prephilosophical thinking. He says, for example, that "the human import of consciousness," although it is based on thinking, "*does not appear in the form of thought* straightaway, but as feeling, intuition, representation."[8] Thus, "in the order of time consciousness produces *representations* of ob-jects before it produces concepts of them."[9] And, since philosophy is only "a peculiar mode of thinking," to be distinguished from other modes, it follows that "philosophical thinking will also be diverse from the thinking that is active in everything human and brings about the very humanity of what is human."[10] This latter, prephilosophical thinking, *"thinking* in its broad sense," has already been at work when philosophy arrives on the scene. It has already produced a sense of "the world, the outer and inner world of consciousness."[11] Furthermore, through its "judicious consideration of the world," it "already distinguishes that which is only *appearance . . .* from that which truly and in itself merits the name of *actuality"*: "Since philosophy is distinguished only in form from other ways of becoming conscious of this same identical import, its accord with actuality and experience is necessary."[12] Feelings, beliefs, and representations pertaining to such matters as "religion, right, and ethical life" are already in place prior to the advent of philosophy as such. Philosophy creates none of these things ex nihilo; it generates none of them by the sheer power of thinking them into existence. Rather it takes what "thinking in its broad sense" has already developed, and reflects upon it. For, as Hegel puts it,

> [I]t is one thing to have feelings and representations that are *determined* and *permeated* by *thinking* [in the broad sense], and another to have *thoughts about them*. The thoughts *about* these modes of consciousness— generated by *thinking them over*—are what reflection, argumentation, and the like, as well as philosophy, are comprehended under.[13]

The task of philosophy is primarily a logical one, logic being, for Hegel, simply thinking about thinking, or "the thinking of thinking."[14] It is, as it were, an after-the-fact meditation on the world of human experience, a world that, after all, does not take its cue from philosophy. Just as Auden remarked, in his elegy on Yeats, that poetry makes nothing happen, so Hegel might say of philosophy that it makes nothing happen. To suppose that philosophy is the cause of the thinking it digests would be like supposing—to use Hegel's own analogy—"that we can only eat after we have become acquainted with the chemical, botanical, or zoological determinations of our food, and that we should delay our digestion until we have completed the study of anatomy and physiology."[15] Knowledge is simply not the cause of that with respect to which it is knowledge. Just as knowledge of the body and its processes does not cause the body and those processes to exist, so philosophy cannot be charged with the presumption of imagining that its own kind of thinking has summoned the world into existence. If this is a charge that is often made against philosophical forms of idealism, it is certainly not applicable to Hegel's philosophy.

On the other hand, the whole point of philosophy, as Hegel understands it, is to grasp and assess the import of what consciousness has already accomplished, and to do this it must think over this import. Philosophy is speculative, not in the sense that it embarks on wild flights of fancy, but in the sense that it reflects upon or reviews "the thinking that is active in everything human" and "that is originally produced and produces itself in the domain of the living spirit."[16] Philosophy takes under consideration "the *determinacy* of our feelings, intuitions, images, and representations"; it takes into account the productions of "ordinary consciousness," together with the "material with which we are familiar," wherein "we *mix* feelings, intuitions, and representations with thoughts"; and finally, it looks at the developed sciences, in which various schemes of organization have been worked out in relation to these already existing determinations.[17] Thus, "speculative science," in Hegel's understanding of it,

> does not leave the empirical content of the other sciences aside, but recognises and uses it, and in the same way recognises and employs what is universal in these sciences, [i.e.,] the laws, the classifications, etc., for its own content; but also it introduces other categories into these universals and gives them currency.[18]

It would seem, then, that thinking has a relatively easy time of it when it comes to sorting out the multitudinous elements of experience and building from these elements conceptions of the world. Philosophy is not required to instigate the process. On at least two occasions, Hegel appeals to common sense as though it constituted a sort of preliminary justification of the reliability of thinking, prior to the suspicions of sophisticated thinkers. In one place, he speaks approvingly of the "old prejudice" or "prejudgment" which holds that, "when we want to experience what is true in ob-jects and occurrences, as well as in feelings, intuitions, opinions, notions, etc., then we must *think them over*."[19] Elsewhere he observes, "it has been the conviction of every age that what is substantial is only reached through the reworking of the immediate by our thinking about it": "It has most notably been only in modern times . . . that doubts have been raised and the distinction between the products of our thinking and what things are in themselves has been insisted on."²⁰ For its own part, although it takes modern skepticism into account, philosophy as Hegel conceives it has the deepest affinity with the older confidence in the efficacy of thinking. "The business of philosophy," says Hegel, "consists only in bringing into consciousness explicitly what people have held to be valid about thought from time immemorial. Thus, philosophy establishes nothing new; what we have brought forth by our reflection here [in *The Encyclopedia Logic*] is what everyone already takes for granted without reflection."²¹

All of this sounds reassuring, and it would be, were it not for the fact that thinking things over has produced such a variety of incompatible results. Immediate sensuous experience may be at odds with what is called common sense, and the various methodical developments of sense that have taken the form of the natural sciences seem to be a third sort of thing. The interests of religion and ethical life are often difficult to reconcile with the objects of empirical investigations, and philosophy itself has appeared in numerous shapes or guises, in opposition not only to religion or common sense but also to each other. Thinking things over appears to have produced a mishmash of results. Or, to use Hegel's terms, "when it goes about its business in this way, what happens is that thinking gets entangled in contradictions; that is to say, it loses itself in the fixed nonidentity between thoughts, and therefore it does not reach itself, but rather stays stuck in its counterpart [in the world of ob-jects]."²² The various determinations associated with the various forms of thinking "join themselves," as Hegel says, "onto the content, with the result that each of these forms seems to give rise to a particular ob-ject, and that what is in-itself the same can look like a diverse content."²³ And yet the impulse of reason is such "that thinking will not give up, but remains faithful to itself even in this conscious loss of being at home with itself, *'so that it may overcome,'* and may accomplish in thinking itself the resolution of its own contradictions."²⁴ But how can it do this? Why is philosophy not embarrassed by the variety of the results spread out before it? Why does it not "degenerate into misology" or feel the need "to conduct itself polemically against itself"?²⁵

Hegel knew perfectly well that he was living in a time when thinking had begun to despair "of being able to bring about, *from its own resources,* the resolution of the contradiction in which it has put itself."²⁶ In response to the work of Hume and Kant, many philosophers seemed ready to turn philosophy back upon itself in hopes of wresting from it a confession of impotence. Why does Hegel resist this conclusion? He does so, I think, because he knows that the examination of reason is itself a rational activity, since "the investigation of cognition cannot take place in any other way than *cognitively*."[27] It is literally unthinkable to turn away from thinking, since the effort to do so is itself governed by thoughtful considerations. To be aware of the contradictions generated by the different forms of thinking is already to be on another level of thinking, beyond the contradictions and therefore beyond despair. There was never really any question of getting outside of thought in order to perform a thought-free inspection of it. All thinking, including the thinking that offers to make an inspection, involves an implementation of the forms of thinking. The critical philosophy associated with Kant was right, says Hegel, to demand that these forms be investigated, but it was naïve to imagine that an investigation of them might hold itself aloof from them or not be dependent upon them in carrying out its own operations:

> Certainly, the forms of thinking should not be used without investigation; but this process of investigation is itself a process of cognition. So the activity of the forms of thinking, and the critique of them, must be united within the process of cognition. The forms of thinking must be considered in and for themselves; they are the ob-ject and the activity of the object itself; they investigate themselves, [and] they must determine their own limits and point out their own defects. This [activity of thinking] . . . is not brought to bear on the thought-determinations from outside; on the contrary, it must be considered as dwelling within them.[28]

Since all thinking is determined by the forms of thinking, which are themselves determined by the concepts or categories therein deployed, why not investigate the scope and limits of the forms by considering how it is that the categories require or exclude each other according to their own internal relations or in terms of their own dialectical movement into and out of each other? This, of course, is what Hegel undertakes to determine in his own review of logic. His object is to situate the various concepts of logic in relation to each other so that the various thought-projects that depend upon them may likewise be situated according to the position they occupy in the dialectic that binds all of them together through logical implication or logical connection.

The effect of watching the concepts of logic pass into and out of each other is, quite simply, that it becomes impossible henceforth to regard any particular concept as a freestanding, self-subsisting determination apart from the dialectical process. To the extent that philosophy actually succeeds in reviewing the whole process from beginning to end, it cannot be said to be in the grip of any of the concepts that appear in the review, whereas it *can* be said that any view of things that is in the grip of one of these concepts is precisely a view that philosophy itself may legitimately claim to comprehend. From the standpoint of what Hegel refers to as the understanding, the concepts have the appearance of being independent or absolute, being fixed in a perpetual opposition, one to another, so that scientific investigations conducted on the basis of different concepts would result in seemingly incompatible or irreconcilable pronouncements. From the standpoint of what Hegel calls reason, the concepts are connected dialectically in a system, the knowledge of which enables us to plot the relative positions associated with sense experience, common sense, the empirical sciences, and religion, not to mention the previous shapes that philosophy has assumed in the past.

Thus it is that Hegel arrives at his conception of philosophy as the knowledge of knowledge. He certainly never makes knowledge, at any level, a *cause* of the things that it knows. Philosophy does not cause either the world or thinking about the world to spring into being. Nor does Hegel make mere ideas, in the subjective sense of the term, a creative power in relation to what are typically regarded as physical or material objects, according to common sense. Conversely, he explicitly repudiates the attempt to account for thinking by appealing to principles or substances supposedly inaccessible to thinking, for the simple reason that all such appeals are inherently self-contradictory. The relation of thinking to that which is beyond all conception is itself impossible to conceive, not because thinking as such is limited in its scope or power, but because the thing-in-itself *is itself a concept.* Those who wish to may imagine what lies outside experience or knowledge, but all imaginings on this subject will ultimately be an expression of the experience and knowledge of those who embark on such an exercise. In Hegel's system, there is no irreconcilable opposition, within the field of thinking, between knowledge and the objects of knowledge, but, by the same token, there is no prospect of jumping outside the entire field in order to see how the field as a whole may compare with a hypothesized unthinkable objectivity. Once this is understood, the feeling that thinking is narrowly circumscribed or that it consists only or merely of subjective ideas, having no access to reality, simply disappears.

If we turn now to Santayana, we shall find a curiously similar conception of philosophy, despite the fact that Santayana is known to have suspected that Hegel *did* regard the concepts of logic as causal in relation to the phenomena they comprehend, that Hegel *did* regard "the most verbal and subjective accidents to which the names of things are subject in human discourse . . . to be the groundwork of the things and their inmost being."[29] Indeed, it was Santayana's opinion that Hegel would finally have to be included with the transcendental philosophers for mistakenly believing that "discourse [is] the key to reality."[30] But, in fact, Santayana's misapprehension of Hegel as an idealist who is supposed to have believed that mere thinking (in the ordinary sense of the term) is capable of generating existences (in the sense of material or physical objects) does not prevent Santayana himself from arriving at his own version of Hegel's chief objections to transcendentalism. The will to reject everything associated with German idealism was strong when Santayana announced, with respect to his first philosophical book, *The Sense of Beauty,* that it had been written "under the inspiration of a naturalistic psychology."[31] This is usually taken to mean that, for Santayana, not only the sense of beauty but also every other form of awareness or judgment or determination is traceable back to the physical nature of man and, ultimately, back to matter itself, thus reversing idealism's error of explaining physical things in terms of ideas. Stephen C. Pepper observes, in this connection, that "Santayana started out as a convinced materialist," who "rather paraded this belief in the face of the idealists who were dominating philosophy during his youth."[32] "In *The Sense of Beauty,*" says Pepper, "existence covered the whole of being, both the physical and the mental categories."[33]

In fact, Santayana takes some pains to show in his book that, while nature is the physical basis of the actions of thinking organisms, nevertheless the discovery of nature per se is an achievement of what Hegel calls "thinking in its broad sense," i.e., thinking in which feelings, beliefs, images, and representations are in the process of being sorted out. Thus, the concept of "nature," as refined and employed by a naturalistic psychology, depends on the validity of thinking and cannot serve to rebuke this validity or to make it appear shaky and unreliable. Indeed, *The Sense of Beauty* is more than just an account of what constitutes an awareness of "the beautiful." It is an account of how all the conceptual categories arise, including those pertaining to common sense, the natural sciences, and philosophy. While it may be true that the inspiration of it was naturalistic psychology, it is equally true that, in the course of his demonstration, Santayana takes naturalistic psychology to be an event in the history of thinking or consciousness. Furthermore, it is clear that he regards thinking or consciousness as something that is ultimately not capable of being corroborated by, or correlated with, any foundation or context not determined by itself. Thus, the problem of having to account for a disparity between things as we think of them and things as they really are in themselves is not a theme in Santayana's meditations, although it might have been expected to loom large for a naturalistic philosopher. As Santayana informs us, his principal theme concerns the absolute or unconditioned activity that constitutes what he here calls "the life of intelligence" and will later call "the life of reason," which activity transcends the biological dramas at work in thinking organisms. In Santayana's own words:

> From the beginning to the end of our perceptive and imaginative activity, we are synthesising the material of experience into unities the independent reality of which is beyond proof, nay, beyond the possibility of a shadow of evidence. And yet the life of intelligence, like the joy of contemplation, lies entirely in the formation and inter-relation of these unities. This activity yields us all the objects with which we can deal. . . .[34]

If *The Sense of Beauty* refuses to explain our apprehension of beauty by appealing to the objective reality of beauty, it likewise refuses to explain our apprehension of matter by appealing to the objective reality of matter, as to something apart from our notions of it. And yet Santayana obviously endorses the "perceptive and imaginative activity" from which both of these apprehensions have arisen. If this seems to shift the emphasis of the discussion in the direction of idealism and away from naturalism, still it is clear that idealism as a particular result of the activity Santayana is talking about (like naturalism, which is similarly such a result) is really being presented, not as something that is capable of authorizing "perceptive and imaginative activity," but as something that emerges in the course of it. Such activity remains, in Santayana's view, not well-founded or well-grounded, but, in fact, inexplicable, except on its own terms or by means of its own operations. Thus, as he will later say in *Reason in Science,* "to sanction reason there is only reason, and to corroborate sense there is nothing but sense."[35]

Another designation for what Santayana means by "a naturalistic psychology" might very well be "the organization already inherent in our mental life" or "how thought really works." At the beginning of his inquiry in *The Sense of Beauty,* he says that he wants to avoid imposing an external explanation on the fruits and processes of thinking. "Speculation," he declares, "is an evil if it imposes a foreign organisation on our mental life; it is a good if it only brings to light, and makes more perfect by training, the organisation already inherent in it."[36] Thus, his true subject is revealed at the outset: the organization already inherent in, or exhibited by, "our mental life," taken in terms of what Hegel calls its "absolute import." Theories and explanations cannot be imagined as standing appropriately outside this organization, passing judgment upon it by showing how it relates to, or misrepresents, some independent principle or substance, like the Platonic forms or the sphere of material existence. Instead, all such theories and explanations, together with the principles and substances to which they appeal, must be regarded as expressions of our mental life, which are necessarily reflective of its actual or inherent organization. If Santayana were, in fact, able to bring this organization "to light" and make it "more perfect by training," he would be doing something very much like what Hegel does. He would be engaged in an after-the-fact meditation, whose object would be precisely "thinking in its broad sense." There would be no reference to what is *given* to thought or what forms the *basis* for thought. Rather, all the emphasis would go to what is formed *by* thought, to the forms that thought itself has actually taken.

Santayana does not attempt in his early work to demonstrate the dialectical organization of the concepts employed by thought, in the manner of Hegel's science of logic, although later, in *The Realms of Being,* he does make an effort, for the purposes of what he calls "organized reflection," to distinguish from each other the concepts of essence, matter, truth, and spirit, maintaining all the while that these terms are not to be thought of as denoting "separate cosmological regions, separately substantial" but instead as denoting "summary categories of logic, meant to describe a single natural dynamic process," the elucidation of which *is* "organized reflection."[37] This indeed is Santayana's principal effort to bring the structure of our mental life to light, and to make it more perfect by training, by giving it a "systematic" form that is "frankly ontological, and not humanistic like my earlier writings," but, at the same time also, not "metaphysical" in that it refuses to turn "logical, moral, or psychological figments" into "substances or powers" which are then "placed beneath or behind the material world, to create, govern, or explain it."[38]

In *The Sense of Beauty,* the project is much less ambitious, and Santayana is content to observe simply that the world as it appears to the understanding is a construction not to be despised by later reflection. He speaks approvingly of "the artifice of thought by which we separate the concept from its materials, the thing from our experiences,"[39] distinguishing each of these determinations from its original condition, wherein it was "at first compacted of all the data of the impressions, feelings, and memories, which offer themselves for association and fall within the vortex of the amalgamating imagination."[40] From this it follows, for Santayana, that "the scientific idea of a thing is a great abstraction"[41] and "the discovery of an eternal idea, like that of the external object, is seen to be an achievement of human intelligence, a symbol of experience, and an instrument of thought."[42] Within the world thus achieved by the understanding, and by using the categories of the understanding, it is perfectly possible to distinguish theory from fact, or subjective idea from objective entity. Indeed, it is a triumph of the understanding to arrive at these distinctions. What is impossible or inconsequential is to compare what the understanding has achieved with "facts" or "existences" beyond its scope or apart from its operations. And that is because an inquiry of this sort is an exercise devised by the understanding itself, and any result that might occur, whether positive or not, would immediately have to be classed together with its other achievements. If it were maintained that all thinking is merely theoretical in relation to something not theoretical, this "something not theoretical" would immediately be recognizable as a theoretical concept. That is why the forms of thought cannot be arraigned or exonerated by appealing to what is outside them. In fact, questions concerning the appropriateness or validity of thought arise by means of the forms of thought or in terms of the projects already devised by thought. Thus there is no alternative but to study the *logic* of the forms and/or the *history* of the projects wherein the forms are displayed. It is on the *history* of thought's projects that the early Santayana primarily focuses his attention, attempting thereby to show the stages wherein "our mental life" brought itself "to light" and made itself "more perfect by training," which development he calls "the life of reason."

And yet it proves impossible, finally, to trace the history of thought apart from or prior to an awareness of the inherent organization of thought, which has emerged as a fruit of that history. In his next philosophical book, *Interpretations of Poetry and Religion,* Santayana studies this organization, first abstractly, and then in terms of certain key episodes in the cultural history of the West. The standpoint he adopts is precisely the standpoint of speculative philosophy, on the basis of which he notes, at the outset, the fundamental fact he intends to explore: the fact "that we find incoherence and instability in human systems of ideas."[43] Thought seems to have taken a variety of different paths, with different outcomes characterized by antinomies and mutual animosities. The positive or natural sciences appear to be engaged in a sort of conflict with religion, while the relation of either science or religion to the content of imaginative literature is similarly vexed. Meanwhile, competing philosophies have also appeared on the scene, in conflict as much with common sense as with each other. Because it has assumed such a variety of distinctive shapes, knowledge has become problematic. And, by the same token, because he takes this problematic situation as his given, Santayana's own philosophy becomes an after-the-fact meditation on the difficulties generated by already existing knowledge.

At first, it seems that he explains these difficulties by attributing them to the unsatisfactory character of human knowledge or, in other words, by referring to the volatile and generally unreliable character of the knowing process itself. He breaks this process down, in the very first chapter, by distinguishing its component phases or elements, as these might be hypothesized by a psychology of mental faculties. Thus, he finds that our knowing is already severely limited by the fact that we are dependent on sense-data for our conceptions of the world. Sense-experience cannot by itself accomplish very much, however, since "a long labour of analysis and correction is needed before satisfactory conceptions can be extracted from it."[44] To explain this labor, Santayana invokes the faculty of the understanding. But long before it has finished its task, the understanding is assisted spontaneously by another faculty, the imagination, which imposes its own fanciful constructions on all materials whatsoever. This means that the understanding is in the position not only of having to develop satisfactory conceptions but also of ruling out conceptions that are more than satisfactory. Not only do we have an inadequate supply of sense-data, we have too much of "an irregular, passionate fancy," active from the very beginning, ever to arrive without much confusion and eddying at acceptable ideas of things. If, as Santayana claims, the ambition of the mind is "nothing less than to construct a picture of all reality, to comprehend its own origin and that of the universe, to discover the laws of both and prophesy their destiny,"[45] then it would seem, on the basis of this analysis, that "the resources of the mind are not commensurate with its ambition."[46]

To make matters worse, there apparently is no way of readily detaching pure sense-data from the imaginative activity they occasion. Even the understanding itself is imaginative in its initial operations, so much so that Santayana feels prompted to say that "imagination and intelligence do not differ in their origin, but only in their validity." As he puts it, "Those conceptions which, after they have spontaneously arisen, prove serviceable in practice, and capable of verification in sense, we call ideas of the understanding. The others remain ideas of the imagination."[47] Thus, "understanding is an applicable fiction, a kind of wit with a practical use":

> Common sense and science live in a world of expurgated mythology, such as Plato wished his poets to compose, a world where the objects are imaginative in their origin and essence, but useful, abstract, and beneficent in their suggestions. The sphere of common sense and science is concentric with the sphere of fancy; both move in virtue of the same imaginative impulses. The eventual distinction between intelligence and imagination is ideal; it arises when we discriminate various functions in a life that is dynamically one.[48]

Here we have a most curious situation. The limitations of knowing are established by the limits and confusions associated with the various faculties brought into play during the knowing process. But the discrimination of the faculties is itself a fruit of knowledge, which becomes more and more problematic, or less and less seemingly absolute, the further it is probed. To the extent that Santayana's critique of knowledge is rooted in an analysis of the knowing process that understands itself to be a product or an achievement of that process, rather than an objective basis for passing judgment on it, it cannot be employed to effect a repudiation of knowledge, nor does Santayana intend that it should. Instead of pursuing a skeptical argument based on the absolute validity of the categories of a quaint but outmoded faculty psychology (which is what the reader is expecting him to do), he turns suddenly around in order to criticize those who affect to despise knowledge from considerations that are evidently knowledge-dependent. He calls such persons "mystics," and he chides them for not grasping the extent to which their belief in the unknowability of reality must incorporate a degree of relied-upon knowledge. The "mystic," he says, who insists on the unknowable character of an "alleged external reality," which we can never have access to apart from our notions of it, forgets that "the notion of an external reality is a human notion," which is itself dependent on a whole train of observations and inferences.[49] In fact, Santayana's chief criticism of what he calls "mysticism" is not that it turns away (or tries to turn away) from the labor of thinking but that it hopes to effect a radical reorientation of thinking by privileging certain favored concepts at the expense of others. "The art of mysticism," he explains,

> is to be mystical in spots and to aim the heavy guns of your transcendental philosophy against those realities or those ideas which you find particularly galling. Planted on your dearest dogma, on your most precious postulate, you may then transcend everything else to your heart's content.[50]

Thus, in our own day, we have seen a mysticism concerning language (not unknown in some of its forms to Santayana himself), whereby all that passes for knowledge of the world or knowledge of history can be regarded skeptically as a sort of illusion produced by linguistic phenomena or textual phenomena. A special knowledge focused on these phenomena may then be substituted for what formerly passed as knowledge with respect to other kinds of phenomena. We have also seen a sort of psychological mysticism, according to which the content of what passes for knowledge in other spheres may be suspended in favor of a deeper consideration of the psychic forces responsible for the generation of knowledge, forces presumably known to certain kinds of psychologists but, in fact, no less problematic than the entities involved in the old faculty psychology of yesterday. The politics of power constitutes yet another form of contemporary mysticism, capturing all accounts of things, all descriptions of what is the case, and making them into the effects of power movements or power struggles, gestures, finally, of opposition or solidarity, rightly grasped only by the student of power dynamics. In each case, an esoteric analysis of the underlying conditions of knowledge (or such knowledge as one finds "particularly galling") aims at reorienting knowledge by translating it into its own preferred categories, which are either posited arbitrarily or else comprehensible only in terms of the knowledge it seeks to discredit. By holding fast to the ideal distinctions associated with these categories, by employing them in such a way as to render them absolute, the critic of knowledge, in effect, makes a bit of established knowledge the basis for the disestablishment of knowledge.

But, if this is unsatisfactory, what is the alternative? The alternative, for Santayana as for Hegel, is to abandon the view that knowledge can be, or ought to be, either validated or disallowed on the basis of a right apprehension of its relation to cognitive processes, on the one hand, or the objects of knowledge, on the other hand, there being no access either to the processes or to the objects except through knowledge itself—knowledge *not* construed to be incorrigibly problematic. As soon as it is perceived that all accounts of the foundations of knowledge, whether positive or negative, must necessarily beg the question they propose to examine, it becomes clear that the problem of knowledge, conceived as a fundamental problem, is simply a red herring, or, more accurately, *the* red herring of modern philosophy, as both Hegel and Santayana tirelessly insisted. As Hegel puts it, "the *factum* of philosophy is cognition already elaborated."[51] In Santayana's view, as represented by *Interpretations of Poetry and Religion,* the factum of philosophy is the already elaborated cognitions of the sciences, of philosophy, of poetry, of religion, and of common sense. The goal is to coordinate these cognitions, or to situate them in relation to each other; it is not to outflank them or to make an end run around them in order to establish the extent to which they correspond or fail to correspond to that which is outside cognition.

The possibility of coordinating the cognitions through a speculative grasp of the connections as well as the differences between science, philosophy, poetry, religion, and common sense, has everything to do with the fact that the divisions between the different kinds of cognitions are impossible to maintain absolutely. Hegel makes it the task of logic to show that the concepts used by every sort of cognition are dynamically connected, so that all thinking may be regarded as a unity when viewed speculatively.

He remarks crucially, at the very beginning of *The Encyclopedia Logic,* that, although "philosophy is a peculiar mode of thinking" and therefore to be distinguished from "the thinking that is active in everything human and brings about the very humanity of what is human," it is also identical with thinking in the latter sense, "and *in-itself* there is only *One* thinking."[52] As regards his excursion into faculty psychology, Santayana, as we have seen, admits openly that the distinctions between sensation, imagination, and understanding are not absolute but, in fact, arise "when we discriminate various functions in a life that is dynamically one." There is no beginning in pure sensation and no conclusion in pure understanding; rather there is, in every instance of thinking, an amalgamation of all the faculties, including imagination, making every amalgamation comparable and, as regards its psychological components, identical. As a result, speculative philosophy becomes, for Santayana, "the patient art of rationalising the various sides of life, the observational as well as the moral, without confusing them."[53] The chief differences that separate the forms of thinking surveyed by speculative philosophy are not essential differences so much as they are differences in scope and function. Santayana thus finds that all the forms involve what he calls poetry, being constructions with a greater or lesser degree of comprehensiveness consisting of greater or lesser amounts of expurgated (or unexpurgated) imagination. The senses themselves are poets, if it is true, as Santayana believes, that "among the ancients it was not an abstract observation of Nature, with conscious allegory supervening, that was the origin of mythology," but rather "the interpretation was spontaneous, the illusion was radical, a consciousness of the god's presence was the first impression produced by the phenomenon."[54] "The great function of poetry," says Santayana, "is precisely this: to repair to the material of experience, seizing hold of the reality of sensation and fancy beneath the surface of conventional ideas, and then out of that living but indefinite material to build new structures, richer, finer, fitter to the primary tendencies of our nature, truer to the ultimate possibilities of the soul."[55] This is not to be regarded merely as a subjective adventure, either, since the ambition of the mind remains "nothing less than to construct a picture of all reality, to comprehend its own origin and that of the universe, to discover the laws of both and prophesy their destiny."[56] Since we cannot coherently divest ourselves of this ambition ("because whatever picture of things we may carry about in our heads we are bound to regard as a map of reality"), "all we can do is, without abandoning the aspiration to knowledge which is the inalienable birthright of reason, to control as best we may the formation of our conceptions; to arrange them according to their derivation and measure them by their applicability to life . . . prudently watching over their growth."[57] To the speculative eye, "science and common sense are themselves poets of no mean order, since they take the material of experience and make out of it a clear, symmetrical, and beautiful world."[58] By the same token, "metaphysical theories" are no less poetical than "spontaneous superstitions," being equally imaginative in character and comparably addressed to the problem of comprehending reality: "did their promulgator understand the character of their justification he would give himself out for a simple poet."[59] And, lastly, "that the intuitions of religion are poetical, and that in such intuitions poetry has its ultimate function, are," for Santayana, "truths of which both religion and poetry become more conscious the more they advance in refinement and profundity."[60]

By making poetry, in this sense or in this fashion, the common aspiration or the common tendency in the thought-forms under review, Santayana makes it possible, not to dismiss any of them, but to grade all of them, or to arrange all of them, in terms of their scope and depth of comprehension. The conflicts between the thought-forms, which are real enough on one level and insoluble in terms of the particular categories and perspectives employed by each form in its turn, simply disappear when the entire spectacle is conceived in which the forms are but moments or phases or aspects. To the eye of speculation, each form is both distinctive and relatable to the others through a synthesis that holds them all in place and, apart from which, each becomes an abstraction. As an abstraction, each form is like a perspective or a point of view, inviolable in its own integrity, distinct in the nature of its own particular kind or degree of information, but also, at the same time, having relations or connections with other perspectives which are the essential means whereby it comes to be known as such, that is, *as a perspective*. To know that the world has been experienced differently by different people is precisely to assume the comparability of different subjectivities or, what amounts to the same thing, the continuity of subjectivity per se. Similarly, in order to know that I am seeing an object according to a particular aspect, I must have access to, or be able to hypothesize, other aspects of the *same* object. In either case, the plurality of subjective orientations, no less than the plurality of objective aspects, is readily amenable to synthesis and, in fact, is already the product of a synthesis. Thus one may speak plausibly of the evolution of consciousness or the progress of civilization, along the lines of Hegel's phenomenology of spirit or Santayana's life of reason. (This accounts, I think, for Hegel's reference to the fact that "there is only *One* thinking," and for Santayana's reference to "the various sides of life" or the "various functions in a life that is dynamically one.") On the other hand, one may speak just as plausibly of an increasing complexity in the concept of reality, which is associated with multiple and increasingly sophisticated notations of a common object. In short, the thought-forms surveyed by Hegel and by Santayana are intelligible only as *relatively* discrete expressions of (in Hegel's terms) a "thinking that is active in everything human and brings about the very humanity of what is human," just as the content of these thought-forms consists only of *relatively* discrete portions of what might be construed objectively as the truth of things.

It was the genius of post-rational criticism to eliminate, through what it took to be a rigorous and thorough skepticism, both the object of knowledge, conceived as truth or realty, and the subject of knowledge, conceived as mind or spirit. Accordingly, it was argued that the concept of mind or spirit was not so much the consequence or the fruit of speculation as it was the presupposition of speculation, just as the concept of truth or reality was not something attained to by science so much as it was something assumed by science. With these two concepts eliminated, speculative philosophy became an impossibility and science became a miscellany of various and sundry pragmatic operations. The thought-forms, to the extent that they could be distinguished from one another, came to be regarded as absolute and nonrectifiable, their differences being insurmountable. Objects were construed as the products of interpretation, interpretations as the products of language games or of historically contingent final vocabularies, which were themselves rooted in the forms of life practiced by different interpretive communities. By reducing all questions back to the level of the assumptions and practices of these communities, one reached, it was assumed, the bedrock, the ground, of interpretation itself. It was simply a fact that there were certain groups of people with certain ideas in their heads, which were foundational with respect to all possible interpretations. One could either gaze at this "fact" in wonderment, hoping for the best and forgetting that it too ought to be reducible to the outlook of some group, or, alternatively, one could admit to the arbitrariness of this "fact," together with everybody else's "facts," and thus permit one's insight into the conditioned nature of views to float serenely, as though in a vacuum, over the whole array of views thus conditioned.

Perversely, the concept of objective reality refused to disappear but instead was reinstated as the *nature* of language-game activity, or the *nature* of the discursive practices attributable to actual communities. The objective character of social processes and interpretive behaviors simply replaced the objective character of natural processes, about which it became fashionable to say that they had been "socially constructed." The old objective world that had been written of in books was now known to be infinitely problematic, having been made up by interpreters. The new objective world, in which interpreters busied themselves with various complex strategies and purposes while jockeying for power and influence, was appealed to without a qualm, as though *it* gave no trouble at all. Claims with respect to *this* world seemed relatively unproblematic, despite the fact that access to the events therein, i.e., books, had become a house of mirrors.

The concept of the subject of knowledge, conceived as mind or spirit, also refused to disappear, despite an immense effort to be post-humanistic or post-anthropological. As I indicated in the first chapter of this book, the function of mind or spirit was simply taken away from authors and handed over to the social or the psychological super-subject, or the questionable subject-in-process, or the infinite subjectivity that scorns embodiment in finite expressions or actual institutions. In opposition to the concept of Reason as a "thinking that is active in everything human and brings about the very humanity of what is human," in opposition to the concept of "man thinking" (to use Emerson's phrase), spirit became, for many post-rationalists, a force or a process "thinking man" and man's knowledge, but always in such a way as to be beyond the scope of knowledge, like a thing-in-itself on the side of subjectivity, or like Hardy's Immanent Will "that stirs and urges everything," albeit inscrutably.

The truth was that speculative philosophy had presupposed nothing concerning man or humanity, prior to its own investigations. It took for its occasion the problems already posed with respect to cognitions "already elaborated," as Hegel puts it. It offered to inspect these cognitions in order to assess their connections and disconnections, and in order to assess the crisis that skepticism had precipitated concerning their status. The necessity governing the concepts involved in cognition was not simply assumed. It was made the burden of demonstration in Hegel's exposition of logic, whose avowed aim was "to contribute to the insight that the questions about the nature of *cognition*, about *faith* and so on, that confront us in the [realm of] representation, and which we take to be fully *concrete*, are in point of fact reducible to simple determinations in thought, which only get their genuine treatment in the Logic."[61] Santayana's procedure was, in some ways, less strenuous. Instead of resolving the questions by establishing the logic of cognition, he contented himself with showing that the questions themselves were driven (and therefore resolvable) only by cognition, which formed its own continuum as it elaborated itself. Whatever might be said concerning the psychology of thinking or the history of man must, he observed, be a fruit of knowledge, not its condition or its foundation.

Viewed speculatively, post-rational criticism was infinitely less secure than the knowledge it opposed, and so, wisely, it proclaimed its victory over philosophy to be a fait accompli, beyond all haggling. The post-rationalists were essentially disrupters or underminers of the work of the understanding, but since their own work was rooted in bits and pieces of what the understanding had achieved, their criticism could not be fundamental. Instead of examining the concepts of the understanding in terms of their conceptual contexts (which is to say, in terms of what concepts actually imply or in terms of what they take for granted), the post-rationalist critics tried to account for the whole of knowledge by reducing knowledge to a few privileged concepts, such as those pertaining to language or psychology or the social process. The phenomena associated with these parts or aspects of knowledge were then taken to be metaphysically absolute, unknowable in themselves exactly to the extent that they were regarded as the ground or condition of that which could be known.

On its metaphysical side, post-rationalism, by embracing the rejection of authorial intention (which was, in effect, a rejection of all rational agency), committed itself to the task of finding ultimate substances or ultimate processes that might better explain what formerly had been taken to be the products of intention or agency. In this way, it hoped to explain subjectivity in terms of a primary objective principle, as the ancient philosophers had done. On its antimetaphysical or pragmatic side, it committed itself in just the opposite way to the task of explaining all objectivity in terms of the subjective machinations of persons and groups, understood to be in themselves irreducible and primary. Thus, the moral will became the absolute foundation, as it had been for the Romantics, of anything that might be proposed as objective or substantial. The much-vaunted claim that Cartesian dualism had been surpassed was true only in the sense that the overtly metaphysical post-rationalists appealed to objectivity in order to denounce subjectivity as an illusion, whereas the pragmatic post-rationalists appealed to subjectivity in order to denounce objectivity as an illusion. If the former might be said to have reverted to the philosophy of the pre-Socratics, the latter might be said to have revived the skepticism associated with the Sophists. As Santayana points out in *The Realm of Truth,* the skepticism of the Sophists was primarily aimed at philosophy itself, not at the dogmatisms of conventional thinking. "The Greek Sophists," he writes,

> were great men of the world addressing little men of the world: they could not be expected to push scepticism into the sphere of common sense; its use was merely to discredit speculation and authority. The Greeks in general were given to speech-making before the crowd. They might cast ridicule on all reported knowledge, and raise a laugh: they could hardly expect to carry their audience with them, if they denied the existence of that audience, or the intimate shrewd ratiocinations of each man in the crowd, hugging his own thoughts and his own interests. Therefore the unchallenged and unexpressed presuppositions of all criticism in this school must be the existence of conventional human society and the intelligent egoism of each of its members. All else in heaven and earth might be challenged with applause, if reduced to these comfortable and convincing terms.[62]

This was the same point Russell would later make concerning the tendency of ordinary language philosophy to permit actual linguistic practices to become normative with respect to philosophic inquiry. As Russell put it, the belief "that ordinary language is adequate, and that puzzles arise from philosophic solecism" tends to ignore "the fact that ordinary language is shot through with the fading hues of past philosophic theories."[63] Thus, as soon as one ascribes any content to the thinking that characterizes persons or groups, the old questions concerning the validity or propriety of this thinking rearise, because truth-claims of one sort or another are embedded in the content.

The upshot was that post-philosophy kept turning back into philosophy, producing, as it were, caricatures or parodies of speculation, in spite of its own strictures against speculation. The issues it raised, as I suggested at the beginning of this book, were not so much obstacles *to* consideration as they were matters *for* it. The more the issues were cogitated, the stronger became the case for speculative thinking. Predictions of the demise of philosophy were themselves, as much as anything else, productive of speculation, as Santayana demonstrated in *The Life of Reason* when he mused on the prospect of living in a post-rational society. "Life," he remarked,

> is older and more persistent than reason and the failure of a first [or even a second] experiment in rationality does not deprive mankind of that mental and moral vegetation which they possessed for ages in a wild state before the advent of civilisation. They merely revert to their uncivil condition and espouse whatever imaginative ideal comes to hand, by which some semblance of meaning and beauty may be given to existence without the labour of building this meaning and beauty systematically out of its positive elements.[64]

Whether they lived civilly on the basis of a shared intellectual framework or uncivilly on the basis of disparate clan mentalities, it was simply impossible to conceive of human beings at all without imagining them as existing in some sort of relation to each other, and this imagination was always essentially speculative because it always implied a common space for any or all possible relations, even negative ones. Every account of the ignorant armies clashing by night, every attempt to do justice to difference and otherness, every call for the peaceful coexistence of incompatible or irreconcilable projects (whether moral or intellectual) immediately assumed a common moral space, however much it might officially espouse relativism. It assumed also a common intellectual space, wherein differences could be made intelligible *as differences*. Always, indeed, the world came rushing back *as world* in opposition to the skeptical monadologies that sought to replace it but were themselves instead immediately cancelled by it. Thus, while it was always possible to look at prespeculative thinking with fascination or with pity or with anthropological condescension, it was impossible to retract the speculative grasp that was the very condition of each of these orientations. Genuine uncivility, as on a darkling plain, would require that this grasp be completely shattered or lost to mind—a possibility that, at the end of the twentieth century, still seemed relatively unlikely.

THESES FOR THE CRITIQUE OF THE POST-RATIONAL CRITIQUE OF REASON

1. The proof that all my experiences of reality are subjective (or conditioned) *interpretations* goes like this:

   (a) I see something, and I say, "That is A."

   (b) Further experience, or communication with others, leads me to believe, for a variety of reasons, that I was seeing this thing *as* A. Either I myself start seeing the thing differently or else I learn that others see it differently, and I then conclude I did not *see* A directly but instead *interpreted* an object *as* A, since it might be interpreted as A' or B.

   (c) Many such experiences occur, and I become convinced that all my seeing is really seeing-as. All my perceiving now looks like interpreting. It occurs to me that all we have to work with are interpretations, grounded in individual acts of meaning-making or else in communal acts of meaning-making.

But notice that, while the so-called objects of perception are now said never to be directly seen, the acts of perception in their similarities and differences *are* seen. How is it that I can't know the nature of things but I can know the nature of interpretations of things? How is that I can't see how reality is constituted but I can see how it is that various interpreters are engaged in various acts of interpreting reality? If reality is an inference with a problematic status, who can fail to see that "the social construction of reality" by communities of interpreters is also an inferred reality with exactly the same status? If there is anything problematic about the description of reality, then any description of "the social construction of reality" is equally problematic for precisely the same reasons.

2. How can the finite mind know that it is finite? How can my consciousness know that it is limited? By knowing that other consciousnesses exist with different contents? But to know this, I have to be conscious of these other consciousnesses. I have to include them, as it were, among the contents of my consciousness. If I do that, I can't be said to have gone outside my consciousness at all. The proof that my consciousness is limited seems to depend on my grasp that there are minds outside my own, but I find that, according to one theory of subjectivity, I can't get outside my own to be aware of them. Something must be wrong with this theory. If I *can* be aware of other minds (whose independent existence lets me know that my mind is not absolute but only relative), then I have escaped the supposed limits or constraints that keep me within my point of view. If I can see the limits of my mind as limits, I have to be aware in some sense of that which limits it, and that is to be aware of what a completely subjective view of things cannot be aware of. To believe in the existence of what is beyond the confines of my point of view is to believe in objectivity. To be aware of the problems posed by the existence of multiple points of view—a favorite postmodernist theme—is to affirm, paradoxically, the existence of an objective reality.

3. To believe that there are many different points of view, each confined within its own boundaries and impervious to the others, is to believe in a reality that is independent of any of the points of view that are being contemplated or imagined. To survey, with equanimity or alarm, the prospect of pluralism is to see an objective situation. If one is not seeing an objective situation, then one must be engaged in a solipsistic inventory of the contents of one's own consciousness, and the thought of different viewpoints is a mere fantasy. If the array of different viewpoints is posited in all seriousness, objective reality is simultaneously posited.

4. If I use reason to demonstrate that all reasoning is limited or hampered by factors that reason itself cannot account for, I shall have to deny the validity of my own demonstration or else revise its conclusion. A rational critique of reason—one that proposes to establish the limits of reason—by establishing the limits transcends the limits. If I can't transcend my own point of view, I can't be made aware that I even have a point of view.

5. But can't I think about the conditions of my own thinking? Certainly. I can describe those conditions and I can do so accurately, so long as my description of them is such that it does not rule out, or declare to be impossible, what the description itself is clearly capable of doing, which is to say, so long as what I claim about my thinking is not contradicted by the thinking that produces my claim. A statement about the principles of my thinking is possible because I can be conscious of my previous states of consciousness by inspecting their products. Even if I should find that all (or most) of these products are irrational, my power to know that this is the case affirms implicitly the validity of reason. As soon as I recognize *this,* I realize that all of my states of consciousness can't be irrational because the consciousness that performs the inspection is itself accepted as rational. Thus, I can believe that much of my thinking is irrational, but I can never believe that all of it is so. Philosophy is the building up of as much unflawed thinking as possible by separating the unflawed from the flawed, or the rational from the irrational. The possibility of doing philosophy is established by the possibility of making this separation, or rather by the impossibility of not making it.

6. None of the empirical accounts of the ways in which thought is limited or hampered—including the accounts given by Deconstruction, the New Pragmatism, and the New Historicism—can succeed in undermining this separation. Instead, they all presuppose it. As thought-projects, whatever power they possess depends absolutely on maintaining it. The same is true of Marxism, Feminism, and Psychoanalysis, which offer empirical accounts of the origins or conditions of seemingly rational thought in an effort to show that such thought is always impaired by misconceptions or a false consciousness of things. To the extent that these accounts of the origins of thought are accurate, they cannot invalidate thinking. All they can do is to supply information about the empirical circumstances of thinking. Such information relates to the validity of thinking in the same way that the observation that Husserl, Einstein, and Freud were Jews relates to the validity of phenomenology, relativity physics, and psychoanalysis. The attempt to undermine reason by giving an exposé of the empirical circumstances of thinking is, in effect, a type of *ad hominem* argument which has recently become extremely popular. The *ad hominem* argument looks past the content of thinking. It is interested above all in

demonstrating that the content of thinking is impaired by what may be inferred concerning the personal situations of the thinkers themselves.

7. The chief problem with all these post-rational exposés of reason (aside from the fact that they represent versions of the *ad hominem* argument) is that each of them either undermines, or else is contradicted by, its own implicit rationality. None of the post-rational schools of thought can suppose that its own insights are seriously impaired by the factors that impair everybody else's insights. Thus, a psychoanalyst could not plausibly argue that psychoanalysis as such would be invalidated if it could be shown that Freud was in the grip of a delusive anal retentiveness when he fantasized the concept of the unconscious mind. Nor could a Marxist convincingly demonstrate that Marx's insight into the dynamics of class conflict would be rendered nugatory if it were discovered that its true origin was Marx's need to rationalize his own personal inability to succeed as a bourgeois moneymaker. Nor could a feminist take pleasure in showing that feminist analyses of gender bias are best explained as *examples* of gender bias, so that Feminism itself may be understood as a sort of flanking movement in the battle of the sexes or as an expression of Nietzschean slave-resentment, rather than as an accurate description of the relations that have existed between men and women. In fact, the empirical circumstances of particular thinkers have nothing to do with the validity of thought per se. The truth of Psychoanalysis or Marxism or Feminism (or any of the other post-rational schools) does not stand or fall depending on whether or not their major proponents can be shown to have been afflicted by neurosis, class hatred, or sex bias. If the thinking that has gone into these projects can be said to hold up, the circumstances of their proponents are simply irrelevant. The same is true of the thinking that has gone into other projects.

8. All thinking has origins, but not all thinking is flawed. The origin of a thought in and of itself can neither validate nor invalidate the content of a thought.

9. The *ad hominem* argument favored by many recent thinkers leads to an infinite regress of refutations. Writer A's views are thought to be compromised by their empirical origins as revealed by Writer B. But Writer B's views on Writer A are themselves compromised by their own empirical origins as revealed by Writer C. And so on. In actual practice, the regress is not infinite because it is not permitted to unfold. We stop somewhere with some writer's views about one thing or another. These views are simply accepted on the basis of their validity or truth according to criteria that have nothing to do with the criticism of their empirical origins. Obviously, it is wrong to think that Writer B is less mystified than Writer A or that Writer C is less mystified than Writer B or that the further one goes with this kind of analysis the more enlightened one necessarily becomes.

10. The contemporary thinker's search for the empirical origins or the shaping circumstances of thinking represents a not unreasonable belief in the operations of causality. The search for causes is a large part, but only a part, of the project of Western thought. None of the post-rationalists is able to offer a fundamental criticism of the project as a whole, because none is outside the project, looking down at it or back on it. All of them are inside the project, inside Reason. The demonstration that this is so is the critique of post-rational criticism.

Notes

Introduction: What is Post-Rational Criticism?

1. George Santayana, *Reason in Science* (New York: Collier Books, 1962), p. 190. The term "post-rational" is used by Santayana in *The Life of Reason* in order to designate a kind of critical or skeptical thinking that imagines itself to be in a position to understand the futility of science and philosophy as a result of having become aware of the limitations of reason. Such thinking imagines itself to be beyond reason and, in a sense, beyond knowledge. "Knowingly," it repudiates both. The term "post-rational" gets to the heart of the matter in a way that the more familiar terms "postmodern" and "poststructuralist" do not, and therefore it is more precise, for my purposes, than either of the latter terms, which are more nearly time-bound in relation to periods or fashions.

2. *Hegel's Science of Logic,* trans. A. V. Miller (New York: Humanities Press, 1976), p. 46.

3. G. F. W. Hegel, "Relationship of Skepticism to Philosophy, Exposition of Its Different Modifications and Comparison to the Latest Form with the Ancient One," in *Between Kant and Hegel: Texts in the Development of Post-Kantian Idealism,* trans. George di Giovanni and H. S. Harris (Albany: State University of New York Press, 1985), pp. 336–37.

4. The rationalizations driving modern artistic practice are well displayed in Herschel B. Chipp's *Theories of Modern Art: A Source Book by Artists and Critics* (Berkeley: University of California Press, 1968).

5. The two collections are: *The New Historicism,* ed. H. Aram Veeser (New York and London: Routledge, 1989), and *New Historicism and Renaissance Drama,* ed. Richard Wilson and Richard Dutton (London and New York: Longman, 1992).

6. For an excellent account of the intellectual context of Hegel's philosophy, see Tom Rockmore, *Before and After Hegel: A Historical Introduction to Hegel's Thought* (Berkeley: University of California Press, 1993). As Rockmore states, "it is indispensable to understand Hegel's theory as a reaction to earlier and contemporary theories, which he knew intimately, and to which he responded" (p. x). In the classic work by Karl Löwith, *From Hegel to Nietzsche: The Revolution in Nineteenth-Century Thought* (New York: Columbia University Press, 1991), the point is made, from time to time, that Hegel himself wrestled with positions later taken to be advanced in relation to his own

275

but which he regarded as inadequate by comparison to his own. Thus, Löwith observes at one point: "The criticism of the Young Hegelians repeated the crisis which Hegel had gone through himself before overcoming it in his system" (pp. 163–64). And, in connection with Marx, we are told: "[T]he antitheses which Marx believed he discovered in Hegel's mediations are just those which Hegel reconciled. The mediating analyses of the philosophy of right proceeded from a criticism of the existing order which itself discovered the antitheses to be mediated" (p. 163). To a surprising extent, it might be argued, what comes after Hegel is the product of an effort to reinstate just those "earlier and contemporary theories" that Rockmore speaks of, those which Hegel "knew intimately, and to which he responded."

7. *The Encyclopedia Logic (Part I of the Encyclopedia of the Philosophical Sciences, with the Zusätze),* trans. T. F. Geraets, W. A. Suchting, and H. S. Harris (Indianapolis: Hackett Publishing Co., 1991), pp. 105–6.

8. For recent claims to the effect that speculative philosophy continues to offer a way out of, or a way beyond, our own contemporary forms of antiphilosophy, see Richard Dien Winfield, *Overcoming Foundations: Studies in Systematic Philosophy* (New York: Columbia University Press, 1989), and William Maker, *Philosophy Without Foundations: Rethinking Hegel* (Albany: State University of New York Press, 1994). The Hegelian alternative is indicated clearly and forcefully in these two books.

9. See the "Short Preface" written by Santayana in a copy of *Reason in Common Sense,* dated Cambridge, April 18, 1907, and published for the first time in *Journal of Philosophy, Psychology, and Scientific Methods* 15, no. 1 (January 1918): 82–83. Santayana was under the impression, and apparently remained convinced, that Hegel was guilty of hypostasizing reason as a metaphysical power or force, existing beyond the world and, therefore, capable of producing the world and reflecting upon it in the fashion of a god. In contrast, it often appears that Santayana himself was guilty of hypostasizing matter as a metaphysical power, producing finite, apprehensible existences and reflecting upon those existences by assuming the form of thoughts about itself in the heads of empirical inquirers. The truth is that Hegel did not think of reason (nor did Santayana think of matter) as a metaphysical entity, existing prior to the world and having causal or temporal relations with it. Rather it may be said that, for Hegel, reason is the ultimate form of the world, when the world is not taken, by thought, to be distinguishable from the thought determinations whereof our knowledge of the world is comprised. Similarly, for Santayana matter is the ultimate form of the world when the world *is* taken, by thought, as an opposed other to thought, i.e., as a set of physical existences in theory distinguishable from any ideas that might be had concerning them. Reason and matter may thus be regarded as the vanishing points of the world, so that the world may be resolved into one or the other, depending on the kind of analysis that is made of it. Reason *is* a hypostasis (or, as Hegel would say, an abstraction) when it is thought of all by itself, as it were, in a vacuum, just as matter also is a hypostasis or an abstraction when it is so considered. In the final analysis, the question is whether it is desirable or possible to distinguish our thoughts about the world from the world itself, and the answer (given, I think, by both Hegel *and* Santayana, and despite Santayana's suspicion of Hegel) is that, on one level, it is quite possible to do this while, on another level, it is

perfectly impossible to do it. Hegel's distinction between the relative merits and functions of the understanding, on the one hand, and reason, on the other, is an effort to do justice to both levels of analysis. In the same way, I think, in Santayana's philosophy the claims of philosophy are not permitted to obliterate the claims of (natural) science, and vice versa—philosophy being based on the discovery that it is impossible to distinguish clearly between thought and the objects of thought, and science being based on the hypothetical necessity of making just this distinction.

10. *Hegel's Science of Logic,* p. 46.

11. *The Encyclopedia Logic,* p. 35.

Chapter 1. The Transcendentalist Impulse in the Projects of Contemporary Criticism

1. See Williams's letter (25 June 1919) to Alva N. Turner in *The Selected Letters of William Carlos Williams,* ed. John C. Thirlwall (New York: New Directions, 1984), p. 44.

2. *The Dialogues of Plato,* trans. B. Jowett (New York: Random House, 1937), I, 865 (*Republic* 607B–C).

3. Ibid., II, 701 (*Laws* 967C).

4. Ibid., I, 45 (*Apology* 22B)

5. G. W. F. Hegel, *Aesthetics: Lectures on Fine Art,* trans. T. M. Knox (Oxford: Oxford University Press, 1975), I, 103.

6. *The Poetics,* trans. S. H. Butcher, in *Aristotle's Theory of Poetry and Fine Art* (New York: Dover Publications, 1951), p. 35,

7. In *Criticism: The Major Texts,* ed. Walter Jackson Bate (New York: Harcourt, Brace, 1952), p. 85.

8. Ibid., p. 100.

9. Ibid., p. 89.

10. "The Oldest Systematic Program of German Idealism," in *Philosophy of German Idealism,* ed. Ernst Behler (New York: Continuum, 1987), p. 162. The author of this text is not known. The manuscript edited by Franz Rosenzweig in 1917 was in Hegel's handwriting, although it has been suggested that the actual author of the sentiments was Schelling or even Hölderlin. The problem of attribution is described briefly in Behler's "Introduction," pp. xvi–xvii.

11. Walter Pater, "Conclusion," in *The Renaissance: Studies in Art and Poetry* (New York: New American Library, 1959), p. 159.

12. T. S. Eliot, "*Ulysses,* Order, and Myth," in *Selected Prose of T. S. Eliot,* ed. Frank Kermode (New York: Harcourt, Brace, 1975), p. 177.

13. Paul Valéry, "A Foreword," in *The Art of Poetry,* trans. Denise Folliot (New York: Vintage Books, 1961), pp. 43–44.

14. Letter to Charles Henri Ford entitled "Surrealism and the Moment," *View* 2, no. 2 (May 1942): [19] .

15. Letter to James Laughlin (Sept. 18, 1942), *The Literary Review* 1, no. 1 (Autumn 1957): 16.

16. George Santayana, *Reason in Common Sense* (New York: Collier Books, 1962), pp. 75, 76–77.

17. C. G. Jung, *Analytical Psychology: Its Theory and Practice* (The Tavistock Lectures) (New York: Vintage Books, 1970), p. 46.

18. Ibid., p. 46.

19. Ibid., pp. 39–40.

20. Ibid., p. 183.

21. Claude Lévi-Strauss, *Structural Anthropology,* trans. Claire Jacobson and Brooke Grundfest Schoepf (Garden City, N.Y.: Anchor Books, 1967), pp. 57–58.

22. Claude Lévi-Strauss, *Myth and Meaning* (New York: Schocken Books, 1979), p. 19.

23. Lévi-Strauss, *Structural Anthropology,* p. 117.

24. Lévi-Strauss, *Myth and Meaning,* pp. 3–4.

25. Ibid., p. 19; my italics.

26. Ibid., p. 20.

27. Lévi-Strauss, *Structural Anthropology,* p. 64.

28. Lévi-Strauss,, Myth and Meaning, p. 24.

29. Julia Kristeva, "From One Identity to an Other," in *Desire in Language: A Semiotic Approach to Literature and Art,* ed. Leon S. Roudiez, trans. Thomas Gora, Alice Jardine, and Leon S. Roudiez (New York: Columbia University Press, 1980), pp. 124–47. In this and the succeeding paragraph, the words in quotation marks have been taken from the English translation of this widely influential essay by Kristeva.

30. Michel Foucault, *Remarks on Marx: Conversations with Duccio Trombadori,* trans. R. James Goldstein and James Cascaito (New York: Semiotext(e), 1991), pp. 32–33.

31. Ibid., pp. 123–24.

32. Ibid., pp. 27, 29.

33. Ibid., pp. 31–32.

34. See J. Hillis Miller's reference, in "The Critic as Host" (*Deconstruction and Criticism* [New York: The Seabury Press, 1979], p. 224), to "the law that language is not an instrument or tool in man's hands, a submissive means of thinking" but that "language rather thinks man and his 'world,' including poems, if he will allow it to do so."

35. Kristeva, *Desire in Language,* p. 133.

36. By identifying "poetry" as the inherent texture or substance of *all* cultural materials, these transcendentalists were, in fact, expressing, as they had been from the beginning, a philosophical impulse to unify the entire field of cultural materials by arriving at a single, coherent explanation of them. As we shall see in chapter 11, the philosopher Santayana, in his book *Interpretations of Poetry and Religion,* makes a similar claim to the effect that science, philosophy, religion, and common sense are all forms of "poetry." But, in Santayana's hands, the term "poetry" does not denote an irrational component, such as the volatility of language, nor is it the expression of a metaphysical supermind, underneath or within the productions of thetic consciousness. It is clearly not an incorrigible "other" in relation to the ambitions of philosophy. Rather, in Santayana's hands, the term "poetry" is used to designate the formative or constructive power of the human mind to organize the materials of experience. According to this definition, any

organization of experience with a perceptible pattern or structure deserves to be called a "poem." The "best" organizations are those that comprehend, or take into account, the most materials, according to some rational principle. From beginning to end, "poetry" is a perceptible rationalization of its component elements. The divided line disappears, and the quarrel between philosophy and poetry is resolved, not by declaring a victor, but by conceiving a scale of organizations whereby poems reflective of immediate, sensuous experience are gradually succeeded by poems presenting larger, more complex organizations of experience. At the top of the scale would be a poem that made manifest a truly comprehensive understanding of experience which would dwarf by comparison the particularities of the verbal medium employed to convey it. From one point of view, everything on the scale is poetical to the extent that it exhibits a perceptible organization of experience, but also, from another point of view, everything on the scale is philosophical to the extent that it is, implicitly or explicitly, a rationalization or comprehension of experience. In a sense, then, the transcendentalists were trying to reduce philosophy to the level of mere poetry, whereas Santayana worked in the opposite direction to show that even mere poetry was philosophical by virtue of its organizational or pattern-producing tendencies.

37. Richard Rorty, *Consequences of Pragmatism (Essays: 1972–1980)* (Minneapolis: University of Minnesota Press, 1982), p. 155.

38. Ibid., p. 96.

Chapter 2. Hegel's Concept of the Dissolution of Art

1. Hegel, *Aesthetics*, I, 103.

2. Martin Heidegger, *Poetry, Language, Thought,* trans. Albert Hofstadter (New York: Harper and Row, 1971), p. 80.

3. Hegel, *Aesthetics*, I, 80.

4. Ibid., 103.

5. Ibid .

6. Ibid.

7. Ibid., 607.

8. Ibid., 605.

9. Ibid., 606.

10. Ibid., 594.

11. Ibid., 81.

12. Ibid., 599.

13. Ezra Pound, *Gaudier-Brzeska: A Memoir* (New York: New Directions, 1970), p. 98.

14. Hegel, *Aesthetics,* I, 600–601.

15. Ibid., 601–2.

16. "The Oldest Systematic Program of German Idealism," p. 162.

17. Hegel, *Aesthetics,* I, 64.

18. Ibid., 64–65. Hegel's characterization of the irony celebrated by Schlegel is, for

the most part, substantiated by Schlegel's own aphorisms in the *Lyceum* and *Athenaeum Fragments,* which Schlegel published between 1797 and 1800. For example, in *Lyceum Fragment* 42, Schlegel describes the ironic spirit in poetry as a "mood that surveys everything and rises infinitely above all limitations, even above its own art, virtue, or genius." In *Lyceum Fragment* 55, he writes: "A really free and cultivated person ought to be able to attune himself at will to being philosophical or philological, critical or poetical, historical or rhetorical, ancient or modern: quite arbitrarily, just as one tunes an instrument, at any time and to any degree." According to *Athenaeum Fragment* 116, the proper sphere for such a person is "romantic poetry," since "it alone is infinite, just as it alone is free; and it recognizes as its first commandment that the will of the poet can tolerate no law above itself." That Schlegel was celebrating absolute egotism seemed unmistakably clear in view of the following passage from *Athenaeum Fragment* 121: "But to transport oneself arbitrarily now into this, now into that sphere, as if into another world, not merely with one's reason and imagination, but with one's whole soul; to freely relinquish first one and then another part of one's being, and confine oneself entirely to a third; to seek and find now in this, now in that individual the be-all and the end-all of existence, and intentionally forget everyone else: of this only a mind is capable that contains within itself simultaneously a plurality of minds and a whole system of persons, and in whose inner being the universe which, as they say, should germinate in every monad, has grown to fullness and maturity." For these and other key texts by Schlegel, see *Friedrich Schlegel's "Lucinde" and the Fragments,* trans. Peter Firchow (Minneapolis: University of Minnesota Press, 1971).

19. Hegel, *Aesthetics,* I, 66.

20. Ibid., 66–67.

21. G. W. F. Hegel, *Lectures on the History of Philosophy,* trans. E. S. Haldane and Frances H. Simson (Atlantic Highlands, N.J.: Humanities Press, 1983), III, 510.

22. Ibid., 507–8.

23. G. W. F. Hegel, *Phenomenology of Spirit,* trans. A. V. Miller (Oxford: Oxford University Press, 1979), p. 400.

24. Wallace Stevens, *Collected Poems* (New York: Knopf, 1968), p. 534.

25. Wallace Stevens, *Opus Posthumous,* ed. Milton J. Bates (New York: Random House, 1990), p. 183.

26. Ibid., p. 197.

27. Ibid., p. 202.

28. Ibid., p. 197.

29. Ibid., p. 262.

30. Ibid., p. 189.

31. Ibid., p. 135.

32. Ibid., p. 200.

33. Stevens, *Collected Poems,* pp. 27, 29.

34. Stevens, *Opus Posthumous,* p. 191.

35. Ibid.

36. Ibid., p. 141.

37. Stevens, *Collected Poems,* p. 10.

38. Richard Rorty, "Nineteenth-Century Idealism and Twentieth-Century Textualism," in *Consequences of Pragmatism,* pp. 139–59.

39. Harold Bloom, "Prophets of Sensibility: Precursors of Modern Cultural Thought," an unpaginated, three-page preface used to introduce numerous volumes of reprints of "the most influential classics of nineteenth-century literary thought," published as a series in the 1980s by Chelsea House Publishers under the general editorship of Bloom. All quotations from Bloom are taken from this general preface to the series.

40. Richard Rorty, *Contingency, Irony, and Solidarity* (Cambridge: Cambridge University Press, 1989), p. 73.

41. Ibid., pp. 73–74.

42. Hegel, *Aesthetics,* I, 65.

43. Rorty, *Contingency, Irony, and Solidarity,* pp. xiv–xv.

44. Ibid., p. xvi.

45. Ibid., p. xv.

46. Jacques Derrida, *Writing and Difference,* trans. Alan Bass (Chicago: University of Chicago Press, 1978), p. 10.

47. Ibid., p. 11.

48. Ibid .

49. Ibid.

50. Ibid., pp. 12–13.

51. Ibid., p. 14.

52. Ibid.

53. Ibid., p. 292.

54. Ibid., p. 293.

55. Ibid., p. 292.

56. Ibid., p. 305.

57. Michel Foucault, *Foucault Live (Interviews, 1961-1984),* ed. Sylvère Lotringer (New York: Semiotext(e), 1996), p. 306.

58. Ibid., pp. 435, 433.

59. Foucault, *Remarks on Marx,* pp. 123–24.

60. Ibid., p. 48.

61. Foucault, *Foucault Live,* pp. 306–7.

62. Ibid., p. 225.

63. Hegel, *Aesthetics,* I, 67.

64. Ibid .

65. Rorty, *Contingency, Irony, and Solidarity,* pp. 175–76.

66. Ibid., p. 178.

67. Foucault, *Remarks on Marx,* p. 52.

Chapter 3. William Carlos Williams and the Art of Infinite Spirituality

1. See especially Bram Dijkstra's groundbreaking study *The Hieroglyphics of a New Speech: Cubism, Stieglitz, and the Early Poetry of William Carlos Williams*

(Princeton: Princeton University Press, 1969); Dickran Tashjian's *William Carlos Williams and the American Scene, 1920–1940* (Berkeley: University of California Press, 1978); William Marling's *William Carlos Williams and the Painters, 1909–1923* (Athens: Ohio University Press, 1982); Henry M. Sayre's *The Visual Text of William Carlos Williams* (Urbana: University of Illinois Press, 1983); and Peter Schmidt's *William Carlos Williams, the Arts, and Literary Tradition* (Baton Rouse: Louisiana State University Press, 1988).

2. Dijkstra, *Hieroglyphics of a New Speech,* p. 64.

3. Sayre, *Visual Text,* p. 13.

4. See especially Schmidt's account of Williams's efforts "to reconcile the contrasting working principles of his art" (*William Carlos Williams,* p. 172), first in the epic poem *Paterson* and subsequently in Williams's poems of the 1950s.

5. Hegel, *Aesthetics,* I, 80.

6. Sayre, *Visual Text,* p. 4.

7. Ibid., p. 124.

8. Ibid., p. 10.

9. Ibid., pp. 11, 12.

10. Wassily Kandinsky, "On the Problem of Form," in Chipp, ed., *Theories of Modern Art,* p. 161.

11. Ibid., p. 162.

12. Ibid., pp. 164–65.

13. Ibid., p. 159.

14. Hegel, *Aesthetics,* I, 594.

15. Ibid., p. 81.

16. Kandinsky, "On the Problem of Form," p. 164.

17. "The Portrait: Emanuel Romano," in *A Recognizable Image: William Carlos Williams on Art and Artists,* ed. Bram Dijkstra (New York: New Directions, 1978), p. 197.

18. "Four Foreigners," *The Little Review* 6, no. 5 (1919): 38.

19. Sayre, *Visual Text,* pp. 131–32.

20. Ibid .

21. "The Work of Gertrude Stein," in *Selected Essays of William Carlos Williams* (New York: New Directions, 1969), pp. 117-18.

22. "Prologue to *Kora in Hell,*" in *Imaginations,* ed. Webster Schott (New York: New Directions, 1970), p. 14.

23. Ibid.

24. *The Embodiment of Knowledge,* ed. Ron Loewinsohn (New York: New Directions, 1974), pp. 62–63.

25. Cited in Mike Weaver, *William Carlos Williams: The American Background* (Cambridge: Cambridge University Press, 1971), p. 164.

26. Hegel, *Aesthetics,* I, 576.

27. *Selected Letters of William Carlos Williams,* pp. 330–31.

Chapter 4. The Metaphysics of Deconstruction

1. J. Hillis Miller, "Stevens' Rock and Criticism as Cure," in *Aesthetics Today,* ed. Morris Philipson and Paul J. Gudel (New York: New American Library, 1980), p. 521.

2. I shall refer to this essay as it appears in *Aesthetics Today,* cited above.

3. See Miller, *Deconstruction and Criticism.*

4. Miller, "Stevens' Rock and Criticism as Cure," p. 522.

5. Ibid., p. 501.

6. Ibid., p. 502.

7. Ibid., p. 518.

8. Ibid., p. 517.

9. Ibid., p. 520.

10. Ibid., p. 499.

11. Ibid., p. 523.

12. Ibid., p. 531.

13. Ibid., p. 518.

14. Miller, "The Critic as Host," p. 220.

15. Ibid., p. 221.

16. Ibid., 231–32.

17. Ibid., p. 223.

18. Miller, "Stevens' Rock and Criticism as Cure," p. 523.

19. Miller, "The Critic as Host, p. 224.

20. Miller, "Stevens' Rock and Criticism as Cure," p. 530.

21. Ludwig Wittgenstein, *The Blue and Brown Books* (New York: Harper and Row, 1965), pp. 45–46.

22. Ludwig Wittgenstein, *Philosophical Investigations* (New York: Macmillan, 1958)p. 110e.

23. Miller, "Stevens' Rock and Criticism as Cure," p. 523.

24. Ibid., p. 522.

25. Martin Luther, *The Bondage of the Will,* trans. Henry Cole (Grand Rapids, Mich.: Baker Book House, 1976), p. 263. Luther's point about the dangers of focusing too intently on particular, isolated words may be compared with the following remark made by Wittgenstein: "We pay attention to the expressions we use concerning . . . things; we do not understand them, however, but misinterpret them. When we do philosophy we are like savages, primitive people, who hear the expressions of civilized men, put a false interpretation on them, and then draw queer conclusions from it. Imagine someone not understanding our past tense: 'he has had it'. — He says: "'he *has*' — that's present, so the proposition says that in some sense the past is present" (*Remarks on the Foundations of Mathematics* (Cambridge: M.I.T. Press, 1967), p. 39e).

26. Luther, *Bondage of the Will,* p. 209.

27. Ibid., p. 231.

28. Miller, "Stevens' Rock and Criticism as Cure," p. 536.

29. Hegel, *Aesthetics,* I, 64. The idea that one needs to "produce" or "reproduce" the texts one reads through an exercise of one's own interpretive authority is well illustrated by Derrida in his essay "From Restricted to General Economy: A Hegelianism without Reserve." There, Derrida asserts the view that interpretation is not a function of knowledge or under the governance of logic ("no logic governs the meaning of interpretation"). "Discourse, meaning, history, etc." are not to be thought of as determinative with respect to interpretation; rather, they are to be regarded as constraints that may be accepted or rejected according to the will of the interpreter. For example, "each proposition" in the text of Hegel "is an interpretation submitted to an interpretive decision." Hegel could have decided in favor of play or chance; instead, he "bet against play, against chance," not realizing, apparently, that "the conscientious suspension of play . . . was itself a phase of play," not realizing that "play includes the work of meaning" so that meaning is only "a function of play." Because Hegel "blinded himself to the possibility of his own bet," he imagined falsely that his own project was bound by "the necessity of logical continuity" or held in check by the constraints of discourse, meaning, history, etc. But since, in fact, "interpretive decision" rises up over all these things and governs them arbitrarily (knowing them to occupy only "a certain place in the configuration of a meaningless play"), a new decision can be made in opposition to the old one ("Hegel's own interpretation can be reinterpreted against him") (Derrida, *Writing and Difference,* p. 260). In this way, the pure joy or Nietzschean affirmation of the completely self-conscious will of the interpreter makes everything subordinate to its own "interpretive milieu" and itself subordinate to nothing.

Chapter 5. Ideology and the New Pragmatism

1. Rorty, *Consequences of Pragmatism,* p. 160.
2. Ibid., p. xviii.
3. The whole debate (including the original paper, the nine responses, and two replies by Knapp and Michaels) was published in 1985 by the University of Chicago Press under the title *Against Theory: Literary Studies and the New Pragmatism,* ed. W. J. T. Mitchell.
4. See, for example, Charles Morris's *The Pragmatic Movement in American Philosophy* (New York: George Braziller, 1970), in which Morris, a self-declared pragmatist, makes the following claim (p. 81): "The American pragmatists have all been value-oriented philosophers. At the center of their attention has been man's intelligence-guided goal-seeking activity. Activity has never been regarded by them as mere motion, nor has mere movement ever been extolled by them. They have envisaged life in terms of actions directed to ends or goals, with human life being regarded as distinctive in the degree to which reflective intelligence can guide such actions." This observation seems to me to be true with respect to an "old" pragmatist like William James, but, as I argue below, I do not see how it is applicable to the New Pragmatists, as represented by Rorty and Fish.
5. Rorty, *Consequences of Pragmatism,* p. xiv.

6. Ibid., p. xl.
7. Ibid., p. xxx.
8. Ibid., pp. xxix–xxx.
9. Ibid., pp. xxxvi–xxxvii.
10. Ibid., p. xxxvii.
11. Ibid., p. xxxv.
12. Ibid., p. xxxvii.
13. Ibid., p. xxxviii.
14. B. F. Skinner, *Beyond Freedom and Dignity* (New York: Bantam Books, 1972),
p. 122.
15. Rorty, *Consequences of Pragmatism,* p. xxi.
16. Ibid., pp. xxxviii–xxxix.
17. Ibid., p. xxxviii .
18. Stanley Fish, "Consequences," *Critical Inquiry* 11, no. 3 (March 1985): 437.
19. Ibid., 438–39.
20. Ibid., 446.
21. Ibid., 454.
22. Ibid.
23. Ibid., 450.
24. Ibid.
25. Jonathan Culler, "A Critic Against the Christians," *Times Literary Supplement,*
23 November 1984, 1327–28.
26. Ibid., 1328.
27. Ibid.
28. Rorty, *Consequences of Pragmatism,* p. xli.
29. G. W. F. Hegel, *The Difference between the Fichtean and Schellingian Systems
of Philosophy,* trans. Jere Paul Surber (Atascadero, Calif.: Ridgeview Publishing Co.,
1978), pp. 6–7.

Chapter 6. The Self-Contradictions of Pragmatism

1. Stanley Fish, *Is There a Text in This Class?: The Authority of Interpretive Communities* (Cambridge and London: Harvard University Press, 1980), pp. 16–17.
2. Ibid., p. 1.
3. Ibid., pp. 10–11.
4. Ibid., p. 11.
5. Ibid., p. 14.
6. Ibid.
7. Ibid., p. 15.
8. Ibid., p. 16.
9. Ibid., p. 15.
10. Ibid., p. 11.
11. Stanley Fish, *Doing What Comes Naturally: Change, Rhetoric, and the Practice*

of Theory in Literary and Legal Studies (Durham and London: Duke University Press, 1989), p. [ix].

    12. Ibid., p. 342.

    13. Ibid., p. 349. In the passage Fish quotes from Bruffee's essay "Liberal Education and the Social Justification of Belief," Bruffee gives some examples of the kinds of communities that might become both self-aware and aware of each other, such as "Protestant students from Kansas City, Jewish students from Atlanta, Catholic students from Boston, Vietnamese from Michigan, Polish-Americans from Toledo, Chicanos, . . . blacks and whites, . . . middle class and poor, rock fans, bridge players, hockey addicts," and so on. Refusing to question the *theory* of antifoundationalism, which must be preserved at all cost as "the true picture" or "the correct picture of the human situation" (p. 346), Fish puts himself in the position of having to recommend that these groups acknowledge (to themselves? to each other? to pragmatist umpires?) their own incapacity to understand either themselves or each other. Such an acknowledgment would require a correct perception or a correct interpretation of the monadic isolation that is supposed to rule out such things as correct perceptions or correct interpretations. Even if it were only Fish's group of antifoundationalists who had the savvy to make the requisite acknowledgment, the acknowledgment itself would be incompatible with the *theory* of monadic groups, which *theory*, incidentally, is never more than just accepted as *the given* in Fish's essays, where it functions as an absolute *foundation* for all possible inferences.

    14. Ibid., p. 350.

    15. Ibid., p. 353. Because "we can never be at any distance from the knowledge we need," inquiry into the nature of this knowledge (which implies a certain measure of distance) is strictly impossible. On the other hand, for exactly the same reason, knowledge beyond that which we already have may be disregarded as needless or useless, being not pertinent to us. This is Fish's version of what John Burnet refers to (in *Aristotle on Education* [Cambridge: Cambridge University Press, 1967]) as the *ignava ratio* or the "argument of indolence" (pp. 138–39), according to which inquiry into both that which we know *and* that which we do not know is either pleonastic or impossible. Recognizing it as a specimen of sophistry, Plato satirizes this argument in the *Euthydemus* and outflanks it in the *Meno*.

    16. Fish, *Doing What Comes Naturally*, p. 352.

    17. Ibid.

    18. Ibid., p. 157. In tracing knowledge back to its supposed origins in knowledge-situations whose very volatility makes them unknowable or indeterminate, Fish arrives at the same conclusion Socrates reaches when he warns Cratylus that knowledge itself must disappear "if everything is in a state of transition and there is nothing abiding": "But if the very nature of knowledge changes [says Socrates], at the time when the change occurs there will be no knowledge; and if the transition is always going on, there will always be no knowledge, and, according to this view, there will be no one to know and nothing to be known." Hence no valid propositions can be made concerning the processes that are supposed to determine the propriety of propositions. See *The Dialogues of Plato*, I, 229 (*Cratylus* 440 A–D).

    19. In the world of monadlike "practices" or "situations" envisioned by Fish, dis-

tinctions between different types or kinds of knowledge are absolute. Literary history is one kind of thing, literary criticism is a second kind of thing, philosophy is a third kind of thing, and so on. Thus, in opposition to Cleanth Brooks's assertion that "the literary historian and the critic need to work together" and that "the ideal case is that in which both functions are united in one and the same man," Fish observes: "The composite historian-critic Brooks imagines would not be a single man but two men, or one (physically defined) man who took on alternate tasks and was, as he moved from one to another, alternate persons." (See Fish's *Professional Correctness: Literary Studies and Political Change* [Oxford: Clarendon Press, 1995], 135-41.) Similarly, "objects including texts, come into view *within* the vocabularies of specific enterprises (law, literature, economics, history, etc.) and in relation to the *purposes* of which that enterprise is the instantiation." It follows from this, I think, that persons and objects are what they are only in relation to the disciplines that define them, whereas the disciplines themselves are free-standing and independent, one from another. And yet it is not clear how the different disciplines can be anything other than pure abstractions, if the knowledge situations they reflect are always "on the wing" and if all attempts to capture such situations can only succeed in fixing them in shapes they no longer have. To know, in fact, that the various enterprises of knowledge *are* distinct in character, one cannot be confined to the vocabulary or purposes of just one or another of them. One must have a speculative knowledge of them that is different from the particular knowledges they themselves are capable of generating.

20. Richard Rorty, *Essays on Heidegger and Others: Philosophical Papers*, vol. 2 (Cambridge: Cambridge University Press, 1991), p. 4.

21. Ibid., p. 9.

22. Ibid., p. 4.

23. Ibid.

24. Ibid., p. 11.

25. Ibid., p. 9.

26. It should be remembered in this context that one of the great defenders of the principle of the priority of practice in relation to theory is Joseph de Maistre, a vigorous opponent of the French Revolution, who scorned the notion that actual social practices can, or should, be affected by theoretical considerations According to de Maistre, the Revolution established unequivocally the folly of attempting to reconstruct social practices in the light of philosophy-based theory: "Everything brings us back to the general rule. *Man cannot create a constitution, and no legitimate constitution can be written.* The collection of fundamental laws which necessarily constitute a civil or religious society never has been or will be written *a priori.* Only when society discovers itself already constituted, not knowing how, can certain particular articles be made known or explained in writing. But almost invariably, these declarations are the effect or the cause of very great evils, and they always cost the people more than they are worth" (de Maistre, *On God and Society: Essay on the Generative Principle of Political Constitutions and other Human Institutions,* ed. Elisha Greifer [South Bend, Ind.: Gateway Editions, 1959], pp. 40-41). Hard though it may be to accept, the case against theory made by Fish and Rorty is not all that different from the case made against it by de Maistre, nor is it

all that different from Pope's acceptance of the status quo in the remark, "Whatever is, is right."

27. Rorty, *Essays on Heidegger and Others*, p. 149.

28. Ibid., pp. 152, 153.

29. Ibid., p. 155.

30. Ibid., p. 181.

31. Ibid., p. 186.

32. Ibid., p. 190.

33. Ibid., p. 191.

34. Ibid. This might be described as a sort of political version of the ontological argument, in which the reader is asked to imagine a perfect society or a perfect state, one of whose perfections is that it actually exists or actually works. Objections to such an imagination can then be waived on the grounds that they must be irrelevant to the concept of an *actually existing* utopia. That is, an actually existing utopia cannot be dismissed as unachievable or nonexistent, because it is only the prospect of an *achieved* utopia that one has been asked to consider. Objectors to the concept of such might thus be said not yet to have grasped the full content of the concept, according to which *existing* utopias cannot be properly imagined as *not* existing.

35. Ibid., p. 195.

36. Ibid., p. 75

Chapter 7. Postmodern Fantasies of Pluralism

1. Fredric Jameson, "The Politics of Theory: Ideological Positions in the Postmodernism Debate," *New German Critique,* no. 33 (Fall 1984): 53.

2. Rorty, *Consequences of Pragmatism,* pp. xxxviii–xxxix..

3. Andreas Huyssen, "Mapping the Postmodern," *New German Critique,* no. 33 (Fall 1984): 50.

4. Christopher Norris, *The Contest of Faculties* (London and New York: Methuen, 1985), pp. 156–57.

5. Hal Foster, "Postmodernism: A Preface," in *The Anti-Aesthetic: Essays on Postmodern Culture,* ed. Hal Foster (Port Townsend, Wash.: Bay Press, 1983), p. xii.

6. Norris, *Contest of Faculties,* p. 8.

7. Ibid.

8. Miller, "The Critic as Host," pp. 252–53.

9. Norris, *Contest of Faculties,* p. 42.

10. Ibid., p. 43.

11. Matei Calinescu, "From the One to the Many: Pluralism in Today's Thought," in *Innovation/Renovation,* ed. Ihab Hassan and Sally Hassan (Madison: University of Wisconsin Press, 1983), p. 285.

12. Christopher Butler, *Interpretation, Deconstruction, and Ideology* (Oxford: Clarendon Press, 1984), p. 22.

13. William James, "What Pragmatism Means," in *Pragmatism and The Meaning of Truth* (Cambridge: Harvard University Press, 1975). p. 32.

14. Norris, *Contest of Faculties,* p. 34.

15. Calinescu, "From the One to the Many," p. 269.

16. G. W. F. Hegel, *Lectures on the Philosophy of Religion,* ed. Peter C. Hodgson (Berkeley: University of California Press, 1984), I, 138–39. See also *The Encyclopedia Logic,* § 10.

17. *Hegel's Lectures on the History of Philosophy,* trans. E. S. Haldane and Frances H. Simson (Atlantic Highlands, N.J.: Humanities Press, 1983), III, 429.

Chapter 8. The Crisis of Reason in Contemporary Thought

1. Jean-François Lyotard, *The Postmodern Condition: A Report on Knowledge,* trans. Geoff Bennington and Brian Massumi (Minneapolis: University of Minnesota Press, 1984), hereafter cited throughout this chapter as *PC.*

2. Anthony J. Cascardi, ed., *Literature and the Question of Philosophy* (Baltimore and London: The Johns Hopkins University Press, 1987), hereafter cited throughout this chapter as *LQP.*

3. Thomas Hobbes, *Leviathan,* ed. C. B. Macpherson (Baltimore: Penguin Books, 1968), p. 626.

4. Hegel, *Lectures on the History of Philosophy,* p. xv.

5. Hegel, *Encyclopedia Logic,* p. 82.

6. Ibid., p. 68.

7. Ibid., p. 70.

8. Ibid., 77–78.

9. Ibid., p. 82

10. Ibid., p. 87.

11. Ibid., p. 123.

12. J. Hillis Miller, *The Ethics of Reading: Kant, de Man, Eliot, Trollope, James, and Benjamin* (New York: Columbia University Press, 1987), p. 5.

13. Barbara Johnson, "Teaching Deconstructively," in *Writing and Reading Differently: Deconstruction and the Teaching of Composition and Literature,* ed. G. Douglas Atkins and Michael L. Johnson (Lawrence: University Press of Kansas, 1985), p. 140.

14. Pater, *The Renaissance,* p. 158.

15. Daniel S. Robinson, ed., *Royce's Logical Essays: Collected Logical Essays of Josiah Royce* (Dubuque, Iowa:: Wm. C. Brown Company, 1951), pp. 364–65.

Chapter 9. Concrete History or Mere Hologram?: Hegel versus the New Historicism

1. Wilson, "Introduction: Historicizing New Historicism," in *New Historicism and Renaissance Drama,* p. 6.

2. Veeser, *New Historicism,* p. xiii.

3. Stephen Greenblatt, "Towards a Poetics of Culture," in Veeser, ed., *New Historicism,* p. 12.

4. Wilson and Dutton, eds., *New Historicism and Renaissance Drama,* p. 1.

5. Louis A. Montrose, "Professing the Renaissance: The Poetics and Politics of Culture," in Veeser, ed. *New Historicism,* pp. 29–30.

6. Hegel, *Aesthetics,* I, 64–65.

7. Veeser, ed., *New Historicism,* p. 30.

8. Hegel, "Foreword to the Third Edition," in *Encyclopedia Logic,* p. 21.

9. Cited in Wilson and Dutton, eds., *New Historicism and Renaissance Drama,* p. 7.

10. Veeser, ed., *New Historicism,* p. 30. Consider, for a moment, the difficulties involved in attempting to grasp what is meant by a "partial," "unstable" knowledge consisting of the ability "to experience facets of our own subjection" through reading, "as in a refracted light, one fragment of our ideological inscription by means of another." One has to imagine a series of intellectuals, each empowered by a particular ideology whose virtue is that it can blow the whistle on some other ideology. Thus, Intellectual A knows that Intellectual B is befuddled by an ideology, Intellectual B knows that Intellectual C is similarly befuddled, and Intellectual C has made the same determination with respect to Intellectual A. We are not asked to believe that some sort of truth can be constructed by considering all three positions. Rather we are asked to believe that each intellectual has correctly determined that some other intellectual is incapable of making correct determinations, so that, by accepting the insights of each, we find ourselves empowered to reject the insights of all, thereby experiencing facets of our own subjection "at shifting internal distances." This is like having a right knowledge of the fact that we can't have a right knowledge of things, a conclusion that is obliged to revise itself upward or downward as soon as it is drawn. If we suppose that we have correctly discerned whatever it is these intellectuals are doing, we shall have to revise upward. If we suppose, on the other hand, that our own insight into the befuddlement of thinking is no less befuddled than any other thinking, we shall have to revise downward, simultaneously positing and cancelling our own insights as we do so. The tendency of the New Historicism, in general, is to revise downward, although Montrose in this passage appears to be resisting this tendency as much as possible without quite being able to bring himself to reverse it.

11. Veeser, ed., *New Historicism,* p. 41

12. Ibid., p. 28.

13. Hegel, "Preface to the First Edition (1817)," in *Encyclopedia Logic,* p. 2.

14. Ibid.

15. Ibid., pp. 2, 3.

16. Hegel, *Encyclopedia Logic,* p. 22.

17. *Hegel's Philosophy of Right,* trans. T. M. Knox (Oxford: Oxford University Press, 1967), p. 3.

18. *Encyclopedia Logic,* p. 5.

19. Ibid., p. 14.

20. G. W. F. Hegel, *Lectures on the Philosophy of World History (Introduction: Reason in History),* trans. H. B. Nisbet (Cambridge: Cambridge University Press, 1975), pp. 137–38.

21. Ibid., p. 30.
22. Cited in Wilson and Dutton, eds., *New Historicism and Renaissance Drama,* p. 15.
23. Hegel, *Lectures on the Philosophy of World History,* p. 21.
24. Ibid., p. 171.
25. G. W. F. Hegel, "Solger's Posthumous Writings and Correspondence," in *Encyclopedia of the Philosophical Sciences in Outline and Critical Writings,* ed. Ernst Behler (New York: Continuum, 1990), p. 288.

Chapter 10. Santayana's Critique of Transcendentalism

1. Lyotard, *Postmodern Condition,* p. 41.
2. George Santayana, *The Realm of Truth: Book Third of Realms of Being* (New York: Scribner's, 1938), p. 125.
3. George Santayana, *The Realm of Essence: Book First of Realms of Being* (New York: Scribner's, 1927), pp. 168~69.
4. George Santayana, *The Sense of Beauty: Being the Outlines of Aesthetic Theory,* ed. William G. Holzberger and Herman J. Saatkamp Jr. (Cambridge and London: MIT Press, 1988), p. 88.
5. Ibid., p. 119.
6. Ibid.
7. Santayana, *Interpretations of Poetry and Religion,* p. 17.
8. Santayana, *Reason in Science,* pp. 28–29.
9. George Santayana, *The German Mind: A Philosophical Diagnosis* (New York: Thomas Y. Crowell Company, 1968), p. 42.
10. Ibid .
11. George Santayana, *Winds of Doctrine* (New York: Harper and Brothers, 1957), p. 197.
12. Ibid., p. 192.
13. Ibid .
14. George Santayana, *Scepticism and Animal Faith: Introduction to a System of Philosophy* (New York: Dover Publications, 1955), p. 291. Santayana's remark here concerning the credulity involved in positing the existence of discourse may be usefully compared with the criticism made of Saussure by Ogden and Richards in *The Meaning of Meaning.* According to Ogden and Richards, Saussure's entire system of linguistics was vitiated from the start by the fact that it began by positing the existence of *la langue:* "This author [Saussure] begins by inquiring, 'What is the object at once integral and concrete of linguistic?' He does not ask whether it has one, he obeys blindly the primitive impulse to infer from a word some object for which it stands, and sets out determined to find it. . . . De Saussure does not pause at this point to ask himself what he is looking for, or whether there is any reason why there should be such a thing. He proceeds instead in a fashion familiar in the beginnings of all sciences, and concocts a suitable object—'*la langue,*' the language, as opposed to speech" (*The Meaning of Meaning: A*

Study of the Influence of Language upon Thought and of the Science of Symbolism [New York: Harcourt, Brace, 1944], p. 4).

15. Santayana, *Winds of Doctrine*, pp. 130–31.

16. George Santayana, *Character and Opinion in the United States* (Garden City, N.Y.: Doubleday Anchor, n.d.), pp. 82–83.

17. Santayana, *Scepticism and Animal Faith*, pp. 291–92.

18. Santayana, *Reason in Science*, p. 220.

19. George Santayana, *Persons and Places: Fragments of Autobiography*, ed. William G. Holzberger and Herman J. Saatkamp Jr. (Cambridge and London: MIT Press, 1987), p. 443.

20. Santayana, *Scepticism and Animal Faith*, pp. 295–97.

Chapter 11. Hegel and Santayana on the Nature of Philosophy

1. Santayana, *Reason in Science*, p. 190.

2. Ibid., p. 223.

3. Hegel, *Encyclopedia Logic*, p. 48.

4. Hegel, "Preface to the Second Edition (1827)," in ibid., pp. 4–5.

5. Santayana, *Reason in Science*, pp. 218–19.

6. *Hegel's Science of Logic*, trans. A. V. Miller (New York: Humanities Press, 1976), pp. 45–46.

7. *The Letters of George Santayana*, ed. Daniel Cory (New York: Charles Scribner's Sons, 1955), p. 202.

8. Hegel, *Encyclopedia Logic*, p. 25.

9. Ibid., p. 24.

10. Ibid., p. 25.

11. Ibid., pp. 28–29.

12. Ibid., p. 29.

13. Ibid., p. 25.

14. Ibid., p. 46.

15. Ibid ., p. 26.

16. Ibid., pp. 28–29.

17. Ibid., pp. 26–27.

18. Ibid., p. 33.

19. Ibid., p. 28.

20. Ibid., p. 54.

21. Ibid., p. 55.

22. Ibid., p. 35.

23. Ibid., p. 26.

24. Ibid., p. 35.

25. Ibid.

26. Ibid.

27. Ibid., p. 34.

28. Ibid., p. 82.

29. Santayana, *German Mind,* p. 90. Santayana's suspicion that Hegel regarded concepts or categories as causal in relation to actually existing objects was the primary reason why he lumped him together with other thinkers whom he considered to be "transcendentalists" or "idealists." In fact, Hegel explicitly repudiated this accusation when it was made by his own contemporaries. See especially his review of G. E. Schulze's *Critique of Theoretical Philosophy* (Hegel, "Relationship of Skepticism to Philosophy," pp. 313–62). There, Hegel states plainly: "But this assumption about speculative philosophy, that the causality-relationship is peculiarly dominant in it, is once again radically false; for on the contrary, the causal relation is wholly banned from speculative thought . . . [P]hilosophy is not at all concerned with plucking a thing out of concepts . . . and it does not infer causes from effects" (pp. 345–46).

30. Santayana, *German Mind,* p. 84. In fact, Hegel did not regard discourse, with its customary notions and usages, as the "key" to reality in the sense of having the power to impose qualities or characteristics on an independently existing material, or in the sense of determining, by divination if not by imposition, such qualities from somewhere outside reality. He did, however, maintain that a philosophical apprehension of reality depended, finally, on a right apprehension of the categories inherent in our various cognitions of reality, and he denied that reality could be conceived apart from conceptions of it. For Hegel, as for Santayana himself, there was no royal road to reality around thinking.

31. Santayana, *Sense of Beauty,* p. [3].

32. Stephen C. Pepper, "Santayana's Retreat from Existence," *Southern Journal of Philosophy* 10, no. 2 (Summer 1972): 187.

33. Ibid., p. 193.

34. Santayana, *Sense of Beauty,* p. 119.

35. Santayana, *Reason in Science,* p. 217.

36. Santayana, *Sense of Beauty,* p. 8.

37. George Santayana, *The Realm of Spirit: Book Fourth of Realms of Being* (New York: Scribner's, 1940), p. 277.

38. Ibid., p. 274.

39. Santayana, *Sense of Beauty,* p. 32.

40. Ibid., p. 31.

41. Ibid., p. 32.

42. Ibid., p. 75.

43. Santayana, *Interpretations of Poetry and Religion,* p. [7].

44. Ibid.

45. Ibid., p. 8.

46. Ibid., p. [7].

47. Ibid., p. 9.

48. Ibid.

49. Ibid., p. 13.

50. Ibid., p. 15.

51. Hegel, *Encyclopedia Logic,* p. 6.

52. Ibid., p. 25.

53. Santayana, *Interpretations of Poetry and Religion,* p. 15.
54. Ibid., pp. 67–68.
55. Ibid., p. 161.
56. Ibid., p. 8.
57. Ibid.
58. Ibid., p. 161.
59. Ibid., p. 67.
60. Ibid., p. 169.
61. Hegel, *Encyclopedia Logic,* pp. 64–65.
62. Santayana, *Realm of Truth,* p. 126.
63. Bertrand Russell, *Wisdom of the West,* ed. Paul Foulkes (New York: Crescent Books, 1989), p. 309.
64. Santayana, *Reason in Science,* p. 188.

Index